THE ART OF PUBLIC WRITING

THE ART OF
PUBLIC WRITING

Zachary Michael Jack

Parlor Press
Anderson, South Carolina
www.parlorpress.com

Parlor Press LLC, Anderson, South Carolina, USA
© 2021 by Parlor Press
Printed in the United States of America on acid-free paper.

S A N : 2 5 4 - 8 8 7 9

Library of Congress Cataloging-in-Publication Data

Names: Jack, Zachary Michael, 1973- author.
Title: The art of public writing / Zachary Michael Jack.
Description: Anderson, South Carolina : Parlor Press, [2021] | Includes
    bibliographical references. | Summary: "Offers invaluable advice and
    examples for researchers, scholars, and professionals determined to share
    field-specific debates, address complex issues, and engage readers"-- Pro-
    vided by publisher.
Identifiers: LCCN 2021026629 (print) | LCCN 2021026630 (ebok) | ISBN
    9781643172170 (paperback ; acid-free paper) | ISBN 9781643172187
    (pdf) | ISBN 9781643172194 (epub)
Subjects: LCSH: Rhetoric. | Written communication. | Authorship.
Classification: LCC P301 .J26 2021 (print) | LCC P301 (ebook) | DDC
    808--dc23
LC record available at https://lccn.loc.gov/2021026629
LC ebook record available at https://lccn.loc.gov/2021026630

978-1-64317-217-0 (paperback)
978-1-64317-218-7 (PDF)
978-1-64317-219-4 (ePub)

1 2 3 4 5

Cover image: Photo by Mark Boss on Unsplash. Bates Hall, Boston Pub-
    lic Library
Copyeditor: Jared Jameson.
Cover design: David Blakesley

Parlor Press, LLC is an independent publisher of scholarly and trade titles in
print and multimedia formats. This book is available in paper, cloth and eBook
formats from Parlor Press on the World Wide Web at https://parlorpress.com
or through online and brick-and-mortar bookstores. For submission information or to find out about Parlor Press publications, write to Parlor Press,
3015 Brackenberry Drive, Anderson, South Carolina, 29621, or email edi-
tor@parlorpress.com.

Contents

To my teachers,

fellow disciples

of this difficult

and necessary art

Jim,

Chris,

Diane,

Bill,

Janie

& Tom

Preface: Calling All Public Writers

The advent of the COVID-19 crisis in 2020 reminded the world of the urgent need for clear communication with the public. In the initial stages of the pandemic, global citizens looked to their governments for best practices. Sometimes they found useful guidance from national health institutes, centers for disease control, and world health organizations. At other times they encountered a litany of mixed messages, political grandstanding, alleged data manipulation, and even mock advice delivered with sarcasm.

The unsparing round-the-clock nature of the pandemic quickly led to the identification of public officials who connected well with concerned citizens, including the likes of NIAID director Dr. Anthony Fauci and US Special Representative for Global Health Diplomacy Dr. Deborah L. Birx. Lacking Fauci's and Birx's medical training, however, chief executives on both sides of the partisan divide found themselves faced with exigencies that relied not on the charismatic rhetoric that had helped them win elections but on the need for cogent communication about math and science, in particular. The national emergency left the nation's elected leaders with little choice; though most had been trained as lawyers, circumstances now required that they become skilled translators of epidemiology and immunology.

Coronavirus wasn't about picking political winners and losers among hard-pressed public officials tasked with disseminating its difficult data sets. Still, the crisis ultimately exposed those who lacked the requisite communication skills or the willingness to engage. In a global pandemic, clear, concise communication on technical and scientific matters mattered more than ever. "Messages aimed at a mass audience during an emergency should be clear, as concise as possible, consistent with other messages, and suitable for repetition or multiple exposures over time," warned James Kimble, Professor of Communication at Seton Hall and an expert in government messaging. "If a message is confusing, contradicts other messages, or receives limited exposure, it is unlikely to have the intended effect."[1]

And it wasn't just scientific and mathematical literacy that the emerging crisis required of public servants but also the ability to put into words the ineffable fears and hopes of a people yearning to feel safe.

Long before the outbreak of COVID-19, corporate America clamored for better communication skills. According to an influential study conducted by Hart Research Associates, nearly ninety-three percent of employers surveyed agreed that a candidate's capacity for the kind of critical thinking and clear communication that helps solve complex problems is more important than their undergraduate major. Meanwhile, eighty percent of those same employers flagged broader writing and communications skills as needing much greater emphasis. Research labs across the country reported the need for better writing among their new employees and recent graduates. On the political front, public writing gained crucial momentum with the passage of the Plain Writing Act in 2010. On January 18, 2011, President Barack Obama doubled down, issuing Executive Order 13563 mandating that government regulations be "accessible, consistent, written in plain language, and easy to understand."

Meanwhile, a generation of visionary public intellectuals and scholars have made public writing the currency of the realm. Many, like Steven Levitt, Professor of Economics at the University of Chicago, have become household names and best-selling authors. *Freakonomics*, Levitt's book of public writing, spent more than two years on *The New York Times* Best Seller list, selling more than four million copies worldwide. Other public intellectuals, such as physician and New York University professor of neurology Oliver Sacks, have had their far-reaching scholarship used as fodder for major motion pictures. Indeed, Sacks has been called the "Poet Laureate of Medicine" by the *New York Times*. Similarly, Daniel J. Levitin, James McGill Professor of Psychology and Behavioral Neuroscience at McGill University in Montreal, effectively translates the often mysterious world of his home discipline to the layperson. Levitin's book *This Is Your Brain on Music* achieved best-seller status, propelled in large part by public writing's trademark balance of rigorous scholarship and accessible writing. And trained journalists-cum-public intellectuals

---

1. James Kimble and Michael Ricciardelli, "The Role of Government Messaging in the Covid-19 Battle," Seton Hall University, April 28, 2020, https://www.shu.edu/communication-arts/news/the-role-of-government-messaging-in-the-covid-19-battle.cfm

such as Malcolm Gladwell and Michael Pollan help interpret field-specific debates for wider audiences while articulating complex issues in the public sphere.

While high-profile practitioners like these demonstrate public writing's ability to shape popular debate and discourse (concepts like *the tipping point* and *freakonomics* have entered the popular vernacular), few textbooks exist to help others achieve similarly powerful effects. As a generation of educators, scientists, business leaders, and communication specialists seek to elevate the art of writing beyond argument-driven pedantry and pontification, apprenticing writers determined to expand and update their skill set need an accessible manual suitable for students and professionals writing in academic, corporate, scientific, and other professional settings.

The Art of Public Writing aims to serve would-be public writers working within the public and private sectors as well as graduate and undergraduate students determined not to perpetuate the exclusionary and sometimes elitist practices baked into academic writing. The need for better more accessible language is felt acutely in business, finance, advertising, marketing, public relations, science, law, and government, all of which experience a pressing need to reach the people they serve with language they can understand.

THE ART OF PUBLIC WRITING

1 Going Rogue, Staying Grounded

Why shouldn't we want more for our writing? We've worked hard on it—considered it deeply, researched it thoroughly, drafted it diligently, revised it endlessly. To what end? To be skimmed by our superiors and tucked away in a folder? For many writers, obscurity registers as indignity when the same work-related opus that made us strangers to our friends and families for weeks or months languishes in a corner office filing cabinet or the proverbial "circular file" better known as the workplace recycle bin. In the end, desiring the widest possible audience is as natural as wanting to be heard.

I've written *The Art of Public Writing* for those who long to share their professional writing with a readership larger than a supervisor, spouse, coworker, or friend. Each year I lead workshops for public writers across the country. My pitch is that informed writing about pressing public issues needn't be stilted, stuffy, hyper-specialized, or holier than thou. In fact, the kind of public writing we'll discuss in the pages that follow dominates the nonfiction bestsellers list, and the public intellectuals who have popularized the genre have become household names via techniques it's possible for the rest of us to learn. Writers like Malcolm Gladwell and Michael Pollan have blazed trails, blending the best of serious nonfiction with rigorous research in academic journals. Journalists at heart and by training, these public writers have taken their original journalistic beat or niche and made the leap to popular nonfiction valued by scholars.

I recommend their work wholeheartedly, and discuss it thoroughly in the pages that follow, but my special interest lies in fascinating thinkers and public intellectuals with a propensity for projecting their highly specialized knowledge into the public sphere. Such writers do what Carl Sagan (PhD in astrophysics from the University of Chicago) did for our knowledge of the cosmos. If Carl Sagan is too old-school an example, consider how much Stephen Hawking (PhD at Cambridge in Cosmology) did to expand our understanding of space-time, extraterrestrial life, and artificial intelligence. More recently, writer and public television host Neil deGrasse Tyson (PhD in astrophysics from Columbia University) has taken up Sagan's mantle, sharing with the masses the wonders, mysteries, and challenges of his field in his aptly titled book *Astrophysics for People in a Hurry.*

While writers like these carry impressive academic credentials, the ambitions of public writers have often been at odds with those in the Ivory Tower. Indeed, the most gifted public intellectuals inevitably possess a maverick streak. Some, like economist Steven Levitt, author of *Freakonomics*, or sociologist Sudhir Venkatesh, author of *Gang Leader for a Day*, describe their place within academe as "rogue." Meanwhile, Tyson spent, by his own admission, as much energy on the wrestling, dancing, and rowing teams at the University of Texas at Austin as he did hitting the books—so much so that his professors encouraged him to pursue alternate careers and dissolved his dissertation committee altogether.

Talk about rejection.

Sagan suffered similar rebuke in 1968 when he was denied tenure at Harvard. The reasons cited since have ranged from the off-putting breadth of his intellect to the need Sagan felt to serve as an advocate for science more generally, a stance which struck some of his more hidebound professors as perilously close to self-promotion. More recently, Susan Cain, author of the best-selling *Quiet: The Power of Introverts in a World That Can't Stop Talking,* details her own process of going rogue. After graduating Harvard Law this self-described introvert began practicing as expected. But even as she did, she wondered how someone with her retiring nature could find success in a field known for captivating juries with charismatic verbal arguments. Cain's difference from her colleagues ultimately led her to quit the field, finding work as a negotiations consultant, and, years later, to write a book-length recitation of the virtues inherent in introversion and inwardness. Meanwhile, Cain's one-time colleague at Harvard University, social psychologist Daniel Gilbert, didn't jettison his field, challenge its definitions, or subvert its assumptions, but he did subvert ours. Publishing his bestselling book *Stumbling on Happiness* after a long line of find-your-happiness self-help books and memoirs topped the publishing charts, Gilbert played the role of professor-contrarian, using social psychology to show us why so many previous attempts at finding happiness have been misguided.

If you sometimes feel like an outcast, outlier, or outright alien among the people you work with and write for, and if you sometimes refuse to drink the Kool-Aid they pour around the conference table, take heart: you exist firmly within the tradition of public writers past and present who have embraced their difference. Critical thinking, resistance to conventional analyses, and impatience with "things as they are" are hallmarks of serious-minded public intellectuals past and present.

My aim is to share with you what I've learned in a twenty-year career of teaching students, teachers, and working professionals how to reach the widest possible audience. As a first-generation college student who later became a professor, I still sometimes cringe at the uppity presumptuousness of the term *public intellectual*, though I wholeheartedly embrace the thoughtfulness at the heart of that job description. The public intellectual's inclination to ask tough questions and to think outside-the-box promises to put them at odds with play-it-safe conventional thinkers. That's a very good thing if you're a public writer wanting to be heard. Anthropologists and sociologists call those who refuse to drink the Kool-Aid *liminal* figures, liminal from the Latin *limen*, meaning "threshold." For sociologists, liminality describes an ambiguity experienced by someone betwixt and between a recognized stage, status, or ritual. Teenagers are classically liminal characters, and given their ability to move between cliques, interest groups, and cultures, so too are public writers. Metaphorically, liminal characters speak multiple languages and enjoy quasi membership in multiple worlds, without completely or exclusively belonging to any one of them. For example, if you're a theoretical scientist with a love of hands-on lab work, you're liminal. If you're a dollars-and-cents number-cruncher who prefers to hang out with Creatives, you're liminal, too.

Very often, what initially feels to the public writer like an existential curse becomes a professional blessing. As a result, many have found themselves thrust circumstantially into the role of translator or emissary between parties who do not speak the same language, whether those opposing parties are parents ("Mom, I think what Dad's trying to say is . . .") or fellow professionals at work ("My take on what the marketing team is trying to communicate is . . ."). Public writers aren't necessarily diplomats, peacemakers, or negotiators, though they draw from the skill sets of all three to distill pertinent information, locate areas of common cause, and broach fair-minded solutions among those who don't always agree on the facts. So, if you're the sort who was routinely conscripted in the past to be a go-between for mom and dad, teacher and students, or boss and coworkers, life may have been giving you a crash course in public writing.

In an interview with *The Atlantic*, best-selling public writer Malcom Gladwell says this about the go-between role he relishes:

> I see my role as a writer to act as a kind of translator between the academic and non-academic worlds. There's just all sorts of fantastic stuff out there, but there's not nearly enough time and attention paid to that act of translation. Most people leave college in their early twenties, and that ends their exposure to the academic world. To me that's a tragedy. So what I'm trying to do . . . is to package a lot of the wonderful work that has gone on in the worlds of psychology and sociology and epidemiology, and to present it to people who would otherwise never encounter it.[1]

As Gladwell suggests, the thing that makes us liminal is also what draws us to the art of public writing. It's what caused astrophysicists Sagan and Tyson to eschew parochial academic accolades in favor of TV audiences in the millions; it's what caused economics professor Levitt to go rogue and create *Freakonomics*, applying the tools of his discipline to subjects as diverse as cheating teachers and self-serving realtors. Liminality is the force that caused Cain to shelve her prestigious Harvard Law degree in favor of starting up an independent negotiations business, and what in turn caused her to evolve from that identity into her new role as a best-selling public writer.

Public science writer Randall Munroe makes the case perfectly. After studying physics at Christopher Newport University, Munroe landed a job building robots at NASA Langley Research Center. By 2005 this restless, intellectually curious savant began channeling his funny, witty, sometimes sardonic thoughts on scientific culture into a personal website entitled *xkcd*, whose tagline described it as "a webcomic of romance, sarcasm, math, and language."

The public loved Munroe's comical stick-figure representations of difficult concepts and his trademark blend of scientific clarity and hi-

---

1. Malcom Gladwell. "Epidemic Proportions," interview by Toby Lester, *Atlantic Unbound*, March 29, 2000, https://www.theatlantic.com/past/docs/unbound/interviews/ba2000-03-29.htm.

larity. A year later, this young entrepreneur left his NASA gig to draw comics on the Internet full-time, supporting himself through the sale of *xkcd* t-shirts, prints, posters, and books. By 2014 he went further rogue, seeking a still larger audience than the millions who visited xkcd.com each week by publishing the book *What If? Serious Scientific Answers to Absurd Hypothetical Questions*. The liminal space he carved for himself was perfect for this outside-the-box thinker and self-professed devotee of geek culture. In *What If?* Munroe begins each section with a question received from one of his readers and proceeds to answer it scientifically. In some cases his undergraduate education in physics speaks fairly directly to the question ("What if everyone on earth aimed a laser pointer at the moon at the same time?), but at other times the imponderable ("How many Lego bricks would it take to build a bridge capable of carrying traffic from London to New York?") compels him to reach outside his academic training for an explanation. In this case the answer (350 million Legos) requires the author to take a liminal, lateral step into the language of engineering and architecture, translating notions as complex as tensile strength.

Liminality is what will cause you to push back on the forces telling you to be content with family, friends, and coworkers as the sole audience for the ideas and theories about which you care deeply. Once you've embraced your liminality you'll stop assuming that attracting a wider audience means downplaying or deemphasizing your originality or unconventionality for the sake of professional expediency. You'll pursue greater outreach and better exposure for the good work you and others do in office, lab, and classroom.

This book is about cultivating the proven writing techniques and habits of mind that have the power to make that wider audience possible for you. If you're aiming high, you'll find countless examples in the following chapters of the best public writing published in the best periodicals, from venerable magazines such as *The New Yorker, Harper's, The Atlantic, Newsweek, National Geographic*, and *Scientific American* to upstart online outlets such as *Vox, The Conversation, Live Science*, and *Fast Company*. If you're a public servant or government employee looking for a primer on how to write more clearly and concisely, you'll find plenty of passages in these pages sourced from government documents ranging from revamped FDA guidelines to revised OSHA regulations to guidance from the CDC. If you work in business or finance, you'll find exemplary nuggets from *Fast Company* to *Forbes*. If you're a scientist, take heart: you won't be slighted, as *The Art of Public Writing* cites examples from the National Institutes of Health to *Scientific American*, from exoplanets to astrophysics. Law, medicine, and the social sciences—we've got you covered, too.

If you've come to these pages simply to rekindle your love of language or to seek a refresher on prose style, you'll find practical suggestions sprinkled throughout. If you're searching between these covers for tips on how to write a particular genre of public writing—popular scholarship, popular science, business, history, public statements, institutional or government messaging, grant narratives, evidence-based news analysis, explanatory reporting, blog posts, editorials and op-eds, open letters, first-person journalism, narrative nonfiction, and more— you'll find meaningful coverage devoted to each.

If your goal is to be next Malcolm Gladwell, or, better yet, the next incarnation of you (only with a bigger audience) read on. P.S.: If you do become the next Gladwell, remember me when your first royalty check rolls in.

Down from the Ivory Tower

Most professionals go their entire working lives without once being assigned to write to the world outside their industry. Meanwhile, for many journalists and technical writers, hardly a day goes by when they're not thinking about how best to reach a wider audience with need-to-know information. Many of the rest of us—educators, researchers, scientists, policy experts, businesspeople, entrepreneurs, marketers, advertisers, leaders of not-for-profits—occupy a position somewhere in the middle. For weeks and sometimes months at a time we attend to our current project with obsessive focus. Blinders blissfully on, we worry little about what John or Jane Q. Public thinks, as we hermetically perfect our scholarly article, white paper, case study, or report. During those fits of insular overwork, we sometimes feel as if we can survive on air alone, pounding the work out, keeping our would-be critics on mute.

Eventually, however, even the most lofty or self-assured among us must come down from their towers, down to the watering hole to get a drink. When I picture the watering hole I see the deep clear pool in *The Jungle Book* where animals of every size and shape go to quench their thirst. If we've grown accustomed to hearing only our own voice, as if in an echo chamber, the cacophony of the public watering hole—of a broader audience—can make us feel displaced and disoriented, and yet the whole point is to join the crowd, to rub shoulders.

Nowhere is the watering hole metaphor more apropos than the grant writing on which an increasing number of scholarly and scientific fields depend. Here the self-serving or self-reliant scholar can no longer only talk to those inside their field; they must speak to those of all kinds, including the fortunate few who have dominion over the water. Often the watering-hole transformation is remarkable! Now it's our job to convince others of our need for water, of our place at the deep pool. Now we have an audience and an urgency. Now we must find a way to ask not with the language we might prefer (specialized, painstaking, obtuse) but with the language spoken by those with the ability to let the water flow.

A sentence like the one that follows, cited by Michael Alley in his book *The Craft of Scientific Writing*, is not very likely to win us water, claims Robert Porter, a program development manager in the research division at Virginia Tech University:

> The objective of this study is to develop an effective commercialization strategy for solar energy systems by analyzing the factors that are impeding commercial projects and by prioritizing the potential government and industry actions that can facilitate the viability of the projects.[2]

"A sentence like this could kill a grant proposal on the first page," Porter argues, suggesting that public writers seeking resources "cannot afford to lose even one reviewer in a barrage of obtuse phrasing." Translation: language like this is more likely to get us bounced from the watering hole than to earn us a generous drink. Now we must learn to communicate with a more diverse group, since we're not sure whom, exactly, will hear our appeal, and whether they will be sympathetic. Some may come from a background similar to ours, and be simpatico. But others will be different from us, and be predisposed to refuse our request if only for lack of familiarity with our background and methods.

---

2. Robert Porter, "Why Academics Have a Hard Time Writing Good Grant Proposals," (paper presented at Symposium at the Society of Research Administrators International, Quebec City, Canada, October 2006), https://www.tamiu.edu/gradschool/grant/documents/WritingGoodGrantProposals.pdf.

So we try again:

> This study will consider why current solar energy systems
> have not yet reached the commercial stage and will evalu-
> ate the steps that industry and government can take to make
> these systems commercial.[3]

It's not poetry, but it's clear enough. It's simpler and more refreshing.
It's water.

PUBLIC WRITING IS A FLUID CONCEPT

Public writing is such a slippery concept that it's often defined by its
antithesis: academic writing. Porter defines academic writing as "that
style commonly adopted for scholarly papers, essays, and journal articles," and he obliges us with a telltale example taken from the *Journal
of Applied Psychology*:

> Taken together with the findings from the present study that
> (a) workplace aggression in the primary job was more closely
> associated with negative work experiences and (b) both situ-
> ational and individual characteristics played a role in aggres-
> sion in the secondary job, future research might benefit from
> a greater focus on the subjective salience of the job as a mod-
> erator of the relationship between workplace experiences and
> supervisor-targeted aggression. Indeed, despite the differential
> effects of situational and individual difference factors on ag-
> gression, it is notable that the individual difference factors ex-
> erted a consistent but relatively low-level effect on aggression
> across contexts, whereas the more salient situational experi-
> ences exerted context-specific effects.

We recognize the warning signs here, surely: polysyllabic jargon (a.k.a.
big words often derived from Latin or Greek), passive (a.k.a. "static")
verbs, and a particular kind of noncommittal, cautious language that
seems to hedge. For example, the line "both situational and individual
characteristics played a role in aggression in the secondary job" feels
needlessly vague. Porter puts a fine point on the question most public
scholars and intellectuals must ask eventually: "How can one consis-

---

3. Michael Alley, *The Craft of Scientific Writing*, 3rd ed. (New York: Springer
1996), 85.

tently strike a balance between scholarly precision and meaning that is clear to a mixed audience?"[4] He suggests that writers looking for examples of effective public writing refer to a respected publication in their field for examples. Scientists eager to court larger and more diverse readerships might consult the magazine *Scientific American* as a place where "world-class scientists use accessible language to teach a general readership about complex subjects while simultaneously informing them of cutting-edge developments."

Jargon = Tone-Deafness

Jargon is the bane of a public writer's existence because public writers, by definition, translate discipline-specific language and concepts to broader publics. Jargon—field-specific language—offers no ready cognate. It's a finely-honed tool made for a very specific purpose, the kind a jack-of-all-trades handyman or handywoman would pick out of a toolbox, scratch his or her head, and say, "Now what would I do with *this*?"

Jargon is a bit like the inside jokes we share with family and friends. My father, for example, was overly fond of obscure acronyms. Our weekly Sunday night supper at my grandparents' house quickly morphed into the abbreviation "SNS" in Dad Vernacular; paper towels turned into "PTs." I understood his hermetic meanings, but anyone outside our little club would surely have been mystified when Dad asked me what hot-dish I would be bringing to the SNS that week while wondering aloud whether we had enough PTs to clean up the mess.

Perfectly awful examples of jargon-laden academic language abound in the erstwhile "Bad Writing" contest sponsored by the journal *Philosophy and Literature* and its Internet discussion group PHIL-LIT. In its heyday the Bad Writing Contest attempted to locate what competition judges called "the ugliest, most stylistically awful passage found in a scholarly book or article published in the last few years." Journalism, fiction, poetry, and parodies were ineligible. Entries had to be non-ironic and taken from serious academic journals or books. As the selection committee cheekily put it, "In a field where unintended self-parody is so widespread, deliberate send-ups are hardly necessary." The third annual competition selected the work of scholar Fredric

4. Robert Porter, "Why Academics," 5.

Jameson, a man who, the sponsors rather snarkily noted, "finds it difficult to write intelligibly and impossible to write well. Whether this is because of the deep complexity of Professor Jameson's ideas or their patent absurdity is something readers must decide for themselves."[5]

Here is a sample of Jameson's prizewinning jargon-heavy entry from his book: *Signatures of the Visible*:

> The visual is essentially pornographic, which is to say that it has its end in rapt, mindless fascination; thinking about its attributes becomes an adjunct to that, if it is unwilling to betray its object; while the most austere films necessarily draw their energy from the attempt to repress their own excess (rather than from the more thankless effort to discipline the viewer).

When we read the passage aloud in workshop, I challenge participants to explain Jameson's meaning line by line. Usually a current or former humanities major gives it a college try but ends up bogging down midway through the first sentence, their attempt ending in a round of cathartic laughter. It's then that I admit that I likewise have no idea what exact meaning the passage intends, and, moreover, that the writer has provided me zero incentive to figure it out. It's not that Jameson deserves ridicule for crafting such exacting, finely hewn prose but that any good thing taken too far begins to look silly. I'm all for the avant-garde fashions of the New York and Paris runways, but a dress that looks like a giant isosceles triangle turned on its side is not very practical for running errands. Academic pontifications like Jameson's are to academe what haute couture is to fashion, or what experimental cars are to the annual Detroit Auto Show; a fascinating concept that's not yet consumer-friendly.

To illustrate, suppose we invented something called the jargon meter, where a score of zero signified a passage that contained no jargon at all while a score of one hundred meant pure unadulterated jargon. Of course, no single sample text would score zero or one hundred, though Jameson's sample would surely score in the nineties while the famously monosyllabic utterances of Donald J. Trump might land somewhere closer to twenty. A president needs to be understood by all,

5. Linda Vavra, "Bad Academic Writing," H-Net Discussion Network, May 23, 1997, accessed October 14, 2019, https://lists.h-net.org/cgi-bin/log-browse.pl?trx=vx&list=h-rhetor&month=9705&week=d&msg=68qVT42iCFU5qFosrFclWQ&user=&pw=.

while Jameson wants to be understood, we can infer, by those relative few who share his academic subspecialty.

It isn't that jargon is intrinsically bad, but that it's carefully coded insider's language that leaves most of us on the outside looking in. If we care to be inclusive, we'll have to learn to write in a way that registers somewhere in the low-middle of the jargon meter—enough profession-specific language to get our point across efficiently to our colleagues and coworkers; but enough common, translative language to welcome in those who don't share our work or our years of training.

STRIKING A MIDDLE GROUND

In *Scientific American* we find Francesca Gino, an award-winning behavioral scientist and Tandon Family Professor of Business Administration at Harvard Business School. Gino successfully taps into our need for a better and more scientific understanding of workplace dynamics. In her article "How Dishonesty Drains You," she exemplifies a scholar writing from inside her field to interested readers on the outside, deploying jargon selectively and only as needed. And she writes about an issue—workplace integrity—with which many of us grapple every day:

> Have you ever told a friend a made-up story to entertain that person or spare his or her feelings? Do you know anyone who confessed to you he or she overreported the number of hours worked to pad a paycheck? Some may think of these "white lies," or small instances of dishonest behavior, as relatively harmless, a slight ethical lapse, when compared with full-scale corporate fraud. We may consider a white lie to be especially harmless if it is in service of protecting an important relationship. Researchers have studied the potential financial and legal consequences of such small instances of dishonesty as padding expense reports and pilfering pens. But are these consequences all that we should be concerned about? We examined the possibility that small instances of dishonest behavior have unintended consequences for our emotional intelligence—it seeps into our ability to read others' emotions. Our research indicates the harm is real—and lasting.
>
> In a series of studies, we concluded that an act of deceit can undermine a person's ability to interact with peers, even

those removed from the original lie. Specifically, we found that when people engage in dishonest behavior, they are less likely to see themselves as relational (for example, as a sister, friend, colleague or father) and are subsequently less accurate in judging the emotions of others. This investigation is a critical step in understanding the underlying interpersonal dynamics in organizations, specifically, because work relationships can be generative—a source of enrichment and vitality—or corrosive—a source of pain and dysfunction. The ability to accurately read and respond to others' emotional states enables supportive, prosocial and compassionate behaviors, so it is particularly important for building strong networks in professional settings. Because of an increase in relational distance and a decrease in empathetic accuracy, those who are dishonest at work may experience a vicious cycle of mutual misunderstandings and missed opportunities for building supporting relationships, which could be detrimental for individuals, as well as for the organizations in which they work.[6]

Do we find jargon in Gino's work—absolutely. Words like "prosocial behavior," "relational distance," and "empathetic accuracy" originate in behavioral psychology, though the words themselves are sufficiently descriptive that a general reader may easily infer their meaning. Other techniques—first-person and second-person pronouns, relatable examples, cultural touchstones, and idiomatic expressions (i.e., "white lies" to relay the more abstract concept of allegedly harmless acts of deceit) and strongly connotative language (i.e., "corrosive" to suggest dishonesty's ability to eat away at anything it touches)—all help convey the scientist's meaning to those outside her specialized field of knowledge. Gino's is public writing in practice.

While scientists seeking to mitigate their use of professional jargon are likely to find articles in *Scientific American* instructive, writers in business and the humanities look to publications such as *The Atlantic* for models of craft. A click on the publication's advertising link shows the magazine's synergy with the stated goals of the public writer, including its tagline—"We reach thinking people—and make

---

6. Julia Lee, Ashley Hardin, Bidhan Parmar, and Francesca Gino, "How Dishonesty Drains You," *Scientific American*, October 2, 2019, https://www.scientificamerican.com/article/how-dishonesty-drains-you/.

them think harder"—and this: "*The Atlantic*'s audience is influential, curious, and eager to leave a lasting mark on the world. Never ones to shy away from change, they seek out new ideas, challenge conventions—including their own—and ultimately aim to foster progress." Elsewhere the venerable magazine reminds its potential advertisers: "*The Atlantic* doesn't just report the news. For 161 years we've been questioning the status quo—and challenging readers to rethink the world they live in."

Asking questions, troubling the status quo, challenging readers to think—all these serve as fair and accurate descriptors for the good work public writers take on, as does the magazine's stated commitment to the "relentless pursuit of the ideas that matter" and the telling of "stories that captivate." The takeaway isn't that we only qualify as public writers if we're publishing in *Scientific American* or *The Atlantic*, but that public writers in science, business, and the humanities should take heart that publications like these have likewise staked their reputations on vital public outreach. They remind us that writing in service to the greater good is a task of abiding importance.

WRAPPING UP

In a world driven by specialized knowledge, the public writer is a throwback, a Renaissance man or woman who refuses to yield to the myopia endemic to so many Digital Age professions. Rather than submit to the straightjacketing or gag rule implicit in professional membership, some scholars and public intellectuals go rogue, bypassing the traditional gatekeepers in their field to write directly to, and for, the public. This choice can occasionally backfire, however, alienating insiders who feel that the renegade writer lacks decorum or respect for the sobriety of scholarly and professional traditions. By its very definition public writing is a risk-taking if not sometimes radical act.

But as writers like Sagan and Levitt show, the public writer's sometimes revolutionary, rock-the-boat M.O. is quintessentially American in its boldness, audacity, and egalitarian creed. In writing for readers from all walks of life, the public writer seeks clarity and in clarity, renewal. Neither above or below their reader, and thirsty for the sort of knowledge and understanding that feels like sustenance, the writer comes humbly to the watering hole.

2 Changing Your Lens

Though public writing is often produced by credentialed experts in their field, as a genre it differs from traditional academic writing and pure scholarship in a number of crucial ways. In conventional scholarship the writer-researcher writes mostly for colleagues within their field, while the public writer most often writes from their field or fields to readers largely on the outside looking in. It's a shift not so much in subject matter as in optics. When Darwin published *On the Origin of Species* in November of 1859, he wrote from his disciplinary expertise as a naturalist, geologist, and biologist. But because he dared to write to an audience of non-specialists, he created a text whose profound implications soon changed the way we see ourselves and our world.

In many of our professions, what we want (better pay, upward mobility, the chance to make meaningful contributions, a little R-E-S-P-E-C-T) is most likely earned by convincing the gatekeepers that we believe as they do. And to convince supervisors and other gatekeepers of our worthiness we're asked to apprentice ourselves, learning to wield the language they wield, "buying-in" such that we see the landscape as they do. Thus, for many of us, our most significant audience—the one which has the greatest impact on our perceived success or failure—sits as close as the corner office or the administrative suite. If our writing makes it beyond our hall, floor, or building, it often goes directly to those in similar halls, floors, and buildings somewhere else. Too often we talk only to others in our industry—others like ourselves—and in circles far too small for achieving our personal and professional goals.

Let's use my field as an example of why growing an audience is an idea worthy of our investment. Professors are a dime a dozen, right? At least that's what the superabundance of obscure academic journals would lead us to believe. Yet, according to the US Bureau of Labor and Statistics, there are about 1.3 million post-secondary teachers in America, which sounds like a lot until one recalculates the statistic as a percentage of the total American workforce of an estimated 160 million. As it turns out, professors make up far less than one percent of that figure. To get a better fix on the true number of colleagues occupying a similar position, the professor must divide 1.3 million by rank, status (tenured, tenure-track, or contingent), institution type, academic discipline, and other filters and factors to arrive at a more accurate estimate of the numbers of their professional peers. What initially seems as if it might be a huge potential audience of like minds (1.3 million!) quickly boils down to 10,000–20,000 kindred souls at best. Our professional world gets pretty small, pretty fast.

A similar winnowing happens in most industries, challenging us to find ways to avoid insularity. I think of my friend Leo who works in IT, a sector that employs approximately five million people in America, or about four times the number of postsecondary teachers. That's a lot of information technology! Yet, Leo's actual job description—Apple end-user support for faculty and staff on a college campus—is shared by a significantly smaller percentage of IT workers nationwide. Indeed, an online search for jobs similar to Leo's yields precious few results. If Leo has his heart set on communicating only to those who share his specialty, he would quickly exhaust an audience of comrades so small it would barely fill a conference hall. In reality, that's true for most of us when we consider our professional specialty in its most nuanced form. What once felt like a broad and fathomless sea now feels like a small and potentially insignificant puddle. It suggests what public writers understand intuitively: writing to those on the "outside" is as much a matter of survival as civic responsibility. Writing for an audience beyond our narrow specialty amounts to a wise diversification of our professional portfolio, a purposeful putting of our eggs in multiple baskets.

GROWING YOUR AUDIENCE

Not long after the online publication *The Conversation* commenced its US operations, I eagerly sought out information about the upstart venue whose tagline promised to combine "academic rigor" with "journalistic flair." The independent not-for-profit global network of newsrooms launched in Australia in 2011 and, once up and running Down Under, set its sights on North America. The website's language echoed many public writers' "deep-seated concerns for the fading quality of our public discourse" and a concurrent recognition "of the vital role that academic experts can play in the public arena."

I was skeptical at first. The website employed a different editorial process than many of the other outlets with whom I had published my scholarship and journalism. Each of *The Conversation's* content editors closely followed the news in their respective areas, keeping their finger on the pulse of what resonated in the nation's newsrooms and breakrooms. Once they had identified the most important issues, they reached out to top scholars working in academe, working with them to "unlock their knowledge for the broad public."

Browsing the site, I clicked on an article with an attention-getting headline, "Trophies made from human skulls hint at regional conflicts around the time of Mayan civilization's mysterious collapse," and read the opening paragraph with interest: "Two trophy skulls, recently discovered by archaeologists in the jungles of Belize, may help shed light on the little-understood collapse of the once powerful Classic Maya civilization."[1] The mention of "trophy skulls" piqued the archaeologist in me, the one who wanted to be Indiana Jones when he was in fifth grade. The article, written by Gabriel Wrobel, an associate professor of Anthropology at Michigan State University, pegged itself to the release several months earlier of an article in the journal *Latin American Antiquity (LAA)*, for which Wrobel had served as one of four chief authors. Now Wrobel and his colleagues wanted to connect with an audience far larger than the one they had reached when their scholarly article was published in *LAA*.

The publisher of *LAA*, Cambridge University Press, kept detailed metrics on each scholarly paper published online, assigning each article its own "Attention Score" (The score is derived from an automated algorithm and represents a weighted count of the amount of attention they've picked up for a research output.). The score of ninety-four earned by the article "Two Trophy Skulls . . ." was based largely on the article's mention in ten news outlets, including *The Conversation*, which had distributed the article to its publishing partners. On *The Conversation* site alone, the article on the collapse of the Mayan civilization had received over two thousand Facebook shares. By comparison, the journal article version of the same research published several

---

1. Gabriel D. Wrobel, "Trophies made from human skulls hint at regional conflicts around the time of Maya civilization's mysterious collapse," *The Conversation*, June 10, 2019, https://theconversation.com/trophies-made-from-human-skulls-hint-at-regional-conflicts-around-the-time-of-maya-civilizations-mysterious-collapse-115025.

months earlier in *LAA* had attracted only a modest number of readers. In total, the journal article had been downloaded less than one hundred times in full-text, including HTML full-text views across the world.

The staggering differences in readers/viewers reflect what public writers have long known: readerships of more obscure academic journals are tiny, often boiling down to less than a hundred active scholars working in the same field as the author. In short, Wrobel's willingness to re-write, re-cast, and re-package his article in a style and manner appropriate for readers of publications such as *Live Science, Discover Magazine,* and *Science Alert* as well as daily metro newspapers such as the *Seattle Post-Intelligencer* and *SFGate* resulted in readership at least twenty times larger than it might otherwise have achieved.

Growing Your Audience within Your Home Discipline

Another illustration may help demonstrate how the writer's bold decision to reach beyond immediate colleagues can yield big dividends. Over the years I've proudly served on the faculties of Leadership Studies, Environmental Studies, Urban and Suburban Studies, and Sports Studies programs, among others, but English is home. In English Studies, *PMLA*, the journal of the Modern Language Association (MLA), bills itself as the most widely circulated humanities journal in America, with just over 25,000 individual subscribers. By academic journal standards that's huge, and yet the scholar submitting their work for publication in *PMLA* guarantees themselves an audience made up almost exclusively of postsecondary teachers of English and foreign languages—in other words, people largely like themselves.

For many humanities scholars a publication in *PMLA* is a career milestone. But suppose the aspiring public intellectual wants a wider audience of fellow academics? What's beyond *PMLA* ? *The Paris Review?* Not so much. The venerable international literary journal that once routinely published such luminaries as Hemingway and Faulkner still puts out high-quality issues, yet only reaches about twenty-three thousand readers in total circulation. By contrast, pitching the *Chronicle of Higher Education*, with a circulation just under forty-five thousand, stands to double the scholar's potential audience while simultaneously introducing their work to colleagues across multiple

disciplines. Beyond the *Chronicle* are thoughtful general interest magazines, such as *The Atlantic* that cover higher education for audiences
of non-specialists. *The Atlantic's* total circulation tallies just under half
a million. The English Studies scholar resolved to pitch a piece there
stands to reach an exponentially larger audience.

Of course, there's a Catch 22: when we act as public writers in the
truest sense, we're emissaries and ambassadors to a world that doesn't
understand our work. Often the inside-out juggling act means we feel
as if we're damned if we do and damned if we don't, to borrow the old
saying. When we focus our writing on our industry-specific colleagues
we're sometimes accused of being insular, exclusionary, or even elitist.
If, on the other hand, we aim our specialized work at the broader public, we're sometimes accused of dumbing it down or considered traitors
to our home profession, as if aspiring to a large audience is somehow
an act of betrayal.

Malcolm Gladwell is the poster-boy for the perilous yet powerful
perch on which the public writer sits. More than any other popular
writer of serious nonfiction, Gladwell has reaped the benefits and paid
the cost of moving boldly into the public sphere, while simultaneously
becoming a lightning rod for hidebound scholars resentful of his success and troubled by what they see as his oversimplification of complex issues. Academics in psychology departments have accused him
of draping himself "in the garb of an expert"; they have cast aspersions
on his prodigious speaking fees, going so far as to accuse him of "deceit and fraud."[2] Others have claimed he foments a dangerous sense of
"intellectual rebellion."[3] Writing for the *Guardian* in the UK, Oliver
Burkeman opines that the iconic public intellectual may have become
a victim of his own success, observing, "We are now sufficiently far
into the Gladwell era that the Gladwell backlash is well underway. He
is routinely accused of oversimplifying his material, or attacking straw
men."[4] Indeed, Gladwell's influence as a public intellectual and prose

2. Jim Taylor, "So What Makes Malcolm Gladwell Such an Expert?" *Psychology Today*, June 17, 2014, https://www.psychologytoday.com/us/blog/the-
power-prime/201406/so-what-makes-malcolm-gladwell-such-expert.
3. Eric J. Hollenberg, "Why You Shouldn't Trust Malcolm Gladwell," *The
Harvard Crimson*, August 7, 2014, https://www.thecrimson.com/column/
behavioral-economist/article/2014/8/7/why-you-shouldnt-trust/.
4. Oliver Burkeman, "Malcolm Gladwell: 'If my books appear oversimplified,
then you shouldn't read them,'" *The Guardian*, September 29, 2013, https://
www.theguardian.com/books/2013/sep/29/malcolm-gladwell-david-and-

stylist has been so complete in recent years that it has spawned its own adjective: "Gladwellian."

In his defense, Gladwell points out that he serves individual readers rather than industries such as academia. "The reason I don't do things their way is because their way has a cost: it makes their writing inaccessible. If you are someone who has as their goal . . . to reach a lay audience . . . you can't do it their way," he maintains.[5] Elsewhere he says: "If you're in the business of translating ideas in the academic realm to a general audience, you have to simplify . . . .. If my books appear to a reader to be oversimplified, then you shouldn't read them: you're not the audience!"[6]

Other academics have come to Gladwell's defense, including William Dembski, a former senior fellow at Discovery Institute's Center for Science and Culture and a professor of philosophy. In his essay "Defending Malcolm Gladwell to Intellectuals," he remarks:

> An unfortunate characteristic of many intellectuals is that unless you have been properly educated and socialized in their discipline, especially by paying attention to its nuances and steering clear of its solecisms, they will dismiss you as having lost all credibility. To me, this seems unfair, for it suggests that the important thing in discoursing about a discipline is to be a card-carrying member of the discipline's guild, displaying all its proper accoutrements, rather than understanding the gist of what's at stake in the discipline. In my own view, Gladwell has a gift for cutting to the heart of a subject or discipline, understanding its gist, even if he lacks the nuance required to satisfy a Steven Pinker.[7]

"I'm just trying to get people to take human psychology seriously and to respect the complexity of human behavior and motivations," Gladwell told the *Guardian* in 2019.[8] Springboarding from an un-

---

goliath-interview.
5. Malcom Gladwell, "Malcom Gladwell on 'David and Goliath,'" interview by Brian Lehrer, *The Brian Lehrer Show*, WNYC, October 2, 2013, https://www.wnyc.org/story/malcolm-gladwell/.
6. Burkeman, Oliver, "Malcolm Gladwell."
7. William Dembski, "Defending Malcom Gladwell to Intellectuals," *The Best Schools*, accessed October 14, 2019, https://thebestschools.org/features/defending-malcolm-gladwell-intellectuals/.
8. Sean O, Hagan, "Malcolm Gladwell: 'I'm just trying to get people to take

dergraduate degree in the social sciences (history), he treats the social sciences—psychology and sociology in particular—as his go-to
disciplinary center and deep well. So successful has Gladwell been in
this larger project—applying social-science-based theories to everyday
problems faced by everyday readers—that the American Sociological Association awarded him for excellence in "disseminating sociological research" to wider audiences. Sean O'Hagan notes, "Part of
Gladwell's genius—and his success—is to render the complex theories
and dogged statistical research of academics palatable to a mass audience often by anecdotally illustrating their effectiveness. He is an unabashed popularizer."

CHALLENGING READERS TO THINK CRITICALLY

While much public-facing writing is produced to please, or at least
ping, a known demographic's pet interests, public intellectuals have
long made their reputations by challenging readers' ideological cer-
tainties, risking ad dollars and audience plaudits in the process. The
late David Foster Wallace was a master of this brand of contrarian
writing, as he showed in "Consider the Lobster," a think-piece originally published in *Gourmet* magazine.

The now defunct publication that billed itself as "the magazine
of good living," catered to readers who, on average, made well over
$80,000—a sizeable individual income and about twice the national
average in the early 2000s. *Gourmet* readers were, on balance, older
foodies and epicureans who celebrated the sensual pleasures of eating
and drinking. *Gourmet* initially commissioned Wallace to write one of
its trademark culinary travel pieces and, for the first half of the piece,
the author writes on spec. But as the article proceeds he increasingly
plays the public writer as provocateur, challenging the bedrock beliefs of the publication's target demographic as he makes the case that
readers reconsider live-boiling lobsters. Wallace is fair-minded in his
exploration, and often Socratic, until the very end, when he calls both
himself and his readers out:

---

psychology seriously'" *The Guardian*, September 1, 2019, https://www.the-
guardian.com/books/2019/sep/01/malcolm-gladwell-interview-talking-to-
strangers-apolitical.

Given this article's venue and my own lack of culinary sophisti-
cation, I'm curious about whether the reader can identify with
any of these reactions and acknowledgments and discomforts.
I am also concerned not to come off as shrill or preachy when
what I really am is confused. Given the (possible) moral status
and (very possible) physical suffering of the animals involved,
what ethical convictions do gourmets evolve that allow them
not just to eat but to savor and enjoy flesh-based viands (since
of course refined *enjoyment*, rather than just ingestion, is the
whole point of gastronomy)? And for those gourmets who'll
have no truck with convictions or rationales and who regard
stuff like the previous paragraph as just so much pointless
navel-gazing, what makes it feel okay, inside, to dismiss the
whole issue out of hand? That is, is their refusal to think about
any of this the product of actual thought, or is it just that they
don't want to think about it? Do they ever think about their
reluctance to think about it? After all, isn't being extra aware
and attentive and thoughtful about one's food and its overall
context part of what distinguishes a real gourmet? Or is all the
gourmet's extra attention and sensibility just supposed to be
aesthetic, gustatory?[9]

Setting aside for the moment the author's highly stylized writing—
the piece's invocation of meta-nonfiction and its antiquated direct address of the reader—his final question surely hits *Gourmet* readers in
a vulnerable place: their very identity as sensitive people distinguished
by a single-minded devotion to food's sensual and sensory pleasures.
Wallace gently suggests that sentience and conscience deserve at least
as much consideration as gustatory flavor. It's a brave and risky move,
and one that resonates in the annals of public writing nearly a generation after its first appearance in print.

THE PUBLIC WRITER HOLDS A MEGAPHONE

I envision the inside-out dynamic implicit in most public writing as a
kind of megaphone: narrow at the source and wide at the end, like an

---

9. David Foster Wallace, "Consider the Lobster," *Gourmet Magazine*, August 2004, http://www.gourmet.com.s3-website-us-east-1.amazonaws.com/
magazine/2000s/2004/08/consider_the_lobsterae09.html?currentPage=7.

old Victrola phonograph with its fluted speaker ready to broadcast to the world. The narrow end—the source—represents our home discipline, industry, business, or beat, while the wide end opens up like a flower. Like a phonograph the public writer interprets and amplifies. Inevitably some distortion occurs with amplification, but what may be lost in accuracy is often gained in projection. Mind you, writing from the inside-out doesn't mean distancing oneself from one's field in hopes of achieving some Oz-like degree of objectivity or omniscience; in fact, bolstering and bulwarking the inside—one's industry connections, one's professional knowledge and fluency—makes for higher fidelity at the source. That's why jack-of-all-trades journalists develop a beat even though they're routinely asked to cover stories of all sorts. Their beat becomes their de facto disciplinary center—acting as a Rosetta Stone that helps them translate fields less familiar into their own vernacular.

On a fundamental level, we as public writers attempt to explain our field or specialty to others who may not have a working knowledge of its methodologies and truths. If the writer's home discipline is really that—a home—public writers are akin to memoirists eager to explain their idiosyncratic inside (their individual and in many ways irreducible childhoods and young adulthoods) to audiences eager to understand despite growing up in very different settings. For the public writer, the equivalent of family is the home field or subfield they feel compelled to explain to others even as they draw on it for strength, purpose, and meaning.

Of course, the field the writer seeks to explicate and interpolate need not be a white-collar one. I think of my friend Robert Leonard, who spent many years teaching in the anthropology department at the University of New Mexico, while simultaneously moonlighting as a taxi driver in Albuquerque. A cabbie is accustomed to hearing their passengers talk about their respective professions, but in *Yellow Cab* Leonard turns the tables, explaining the art of cab driving to highly educated readers.

Not long ago, I received an object lesson in public writing that likewise involved calling for a ride. I wasn't hailing a cab, like Leonard's passengers in *Yellow Cab*, but calling for a tow when my key fob, submerged in water, stopped working sixty miles from home. I ended up taking an hour-plus drive in a tow truck. What do two strangers, thrown together by circumstance, talk about in the dead of the night on a deserted interstate? By the time the ride was over and the car safely deposited, I had emerged with an intimate understanding, rendered in layperson terms, of what Matthew did for a living, ranging from the cost of his new tow truck with its aluminum rust-free bed to his work schedule to the highly seasonal nature of his work. On the long tow home Matthew was quite literally in the driver's seat, setting the tone, subject matter, and pace of the discourse about his profession, much as the public writer does, translating as necessary when he sensed my comprehension suffering or my interest on the wane.

Public writing abounds with writers driven to explain their work to the wider world. No one does it better than Richard Selzer in his book *Mortal Lessons: Notes on the Art of Surgery*. As kids many of us play doctor, but precious few of us will ever experience firsthand what it feels like to wield the knife on which another's life depends. Selzer understands the need readers have to understand his ancient profession, and he crafts an explanation that is nothing short of high art:

> One holds the knife as one holds the bow of a cello or a tulip—by the stem. Not palmed nor gripped nor grasped, but lightly, with the tips of the fingers. The knife is not for pressing. It is for drawing across the field of skin. Like a slender fish, it waits, at the ready, then, go! It darts, followed by a fine wake of red. The flesh parts, falling away to yellow globules of fat. Even now, after so many times, I still marvel at its power—cold, gleaming, silent. More, I am still struck with a kind of dread that it is I in whose hand the blade travels, that my hand is its vehicle, that yet again this terrible steel-bellied thing and I have conspired for a most unnatural purpose, the laying open of the body of a human being.
>
> A stillness settles in my heart and is carried to my hand. It is the quietude of resolve layered over fear. And it is this resolve that lowers us, my knife and me, deeper and deeper into the person beneath. It is an entry into the body that is nothing like a caress; still, it is among the gentlest of acts. Then stroke and stroke again, and we are joined by other instruments, hemostats and forceps, until the wound blooms with strange flowers whose looped handles fall to the sides in steely array.[10]

---

10. Richard Selzer, *Mortal Lessons: Notes on the Art of Surgery* (New York: Simon and Schuster, 1976), 92.

Selzer first published his classic inside-out essay, "The Knife," in a 1974 edition of *Esquire*, a venue that allowed him to reach an audience much larger than what he might have attracted in a medical journal. More than twenty years after *Esquire* readers first thrilled to "The Knife," the author edited the essay for inclusion in *Mortal Lessons*. Curiously, the first paragraph of "The Knife" was missing when it appeared in book form. The AWOL opening paragraph went like this:

> Vivacious instrument! Hobbled steed in the surgeon's hand! Awful brilliance parting skin's deluded sleep! Brutish guest! Semaphore of dread! Quiet, gentlemen—the scalpel speaks!

Why axe such artful and exuberant writing? Selzer never says, but it's easy to see why the passage was cut. It's overly poetic and self-conscious. It's a strange sort of graft to a piece so intrinsically interesting that it doesn't need a self-dramatizing prologue ("Quiet, Gentlemen— the scalpel speaks!"). The excised opener is also sexist, exclusively addressing gentlemen. The takeaway: even the most sure-handed writer can slip up when their public writing strays too far from bedrock professional identity. Selzer is a surgeon after all, and while we understand that a surgeon can also be an artist, we may not be ready for him to sound like a big-top impresario or snake-oil salesman. In the excised paragraph he sounds a bit like both.

The author makes a similar point himself in the introduction to *Mortal Lessons*, wherein he addresses explicitly the stereotypes and tropes with which he must grapple:

> All through literature the doctor is portrayed as a figure of fun . . . . Moliere delighted in pricking his pompous medicine men, and they well-deserve it. The doctor is ripe for caricature. But I believe that the truly great writing about doctors has not yet been done. I think it must be done *by* a doctor, one who is through with the love affair with his technique . . . . Perhaps he will be a nonbeliever who, after a lifetime of grand gestures and mighty deeds, comes upon the knowledge that he has done no more than meddle in the lives of his fellows.[11]

Selzer is justifiably piqued at the way non-doctors have written medicine men and women throughout history, in much the same way that most of us feel the trade to which we have devoted our professional

---

11. Ibid. 18.

lives is not properly respected by the public at large. He's also sufficiently ambivalent to realize that surgeons can and do fall in love
with their own command over life and death, leading to narcissistic
self-aggrandizement. Selzer's perfectly ambivalent writing embodies
what the poet John Keats called Negative Capability, an elusive trait
he notes as belonging to writers who are "capable of being in uncer-
tainties, mysteries, and doubts, without any irritable reaching after fact
and reason." In showing us the inside of his own mortal professional,
Selzer refuses to perform as mere booster or confidence man. He's as
slippery as any liminal figure with a shamanic view of the big-picture
beyond himself.

THE IMPOSTER SYNDROME

At one time or another every public writer is stricken with the Imposter Syndrome, the notion that we haven't earned the right to speak au-
thoritatively. The best public intellectuals own the Imposter Syndrome
in their work, neither pretending to be the last word on a subject nor
issuing needless disclaimers to their reader by way of apology or mea
culpa. In her book *Welcome to the Writer's Life*, writing coach Paulette
Perhach reminds scribes struck with the Imposter Syndrome to "leverage the utility of your limitations."[12] From the introduction to *Mortal
Lessons,* it's clear that Selzer has overcome this particular malady, implying as he does that he has ceased to be unduly infatuated or enamored with his art. Rather than reduce himself to a has-been or present
himself with false modesty as a mediocre or indifferent surgeon, he
leverages his liminality, reminding readers of the crucial role played by
"non-believers" who have achieved a productive level of detachment
from the trade that once animated and consumed them. He reiterates
what contemporary practice makes abundantly clear: many of the best
practitioners of public writing are ex, emeritus, retired, or rejected, a
phenomenon we will explore in greater depth in future chapters. Perhach is cut from a similar cloth. Portraying herself as an auto-didact,
she refers to herself as "lifelong student" in her own "renegade education" via which she has turned self-doubt and initial professional
disadvantage into a sympathy for the underdog, a teacher's heart for

12. Paulette Perhach, *Welcome to the Writer's Life* (Seattle: Sasquatch Books,
2018), 7.

equality and equity, and a native empathy for those striving, and sometimes struggling, to learn.

When Your Inside-Out Is Too Much Inside

An art and pre-architecture student in my first year at university, I attended my fair share of gallery openings and art installations, wanting
badly to play the role of "artiste." Almost without exception, however,
I found my experience negatively impacted by the artist's own statement about their work, which often muddied already murky waters. In
a recent article Iris Jaffee agrees, opining:

> As an artist, they are almost always awkward and painful to
> write, and as a viewer they are similarly painful and uninfor-
> mative to read.
>
> I also don't know who decided that artists should be re-
> sponsible for writing their own "artist statement." Maybe it
> was an understaffed gallery in the 1980s, or a control freak
> think-inside-my-box-or-get-out MFA program director, but
> regardless of how this standardized practice came to be, the
> artist's statement as professional prerequisite (at least for art-
> ists who have yet to be validated by the established art world)
> has long overstayed its welcome. And I don't think a new one
> should be required in its place.[13]

If you haven't been to a gallery opening in a while, here's a sample
of the kind of opaque statement Jaffee laments:

> Comprising layer upon layer of stacked virgin cork coated in
> pure black pigment, the squatting sculpture dominates its set-
> ting. The work is impossible to understand in a single perspec-
> tive and the spectator is forced to negotiate its sides and edges,
> unable to access its top. Its natural undulations and inconsis-
> tencies echo the raw, worked, sculptural surfaces of Martin's
> pigments. The form of Behemoth, and its physical presence in
> the gallery space, echo the theatrical preoccupations of Min-
> imalist sculpture but the ancient and organic nature of the

---

13. Iris Jaffee, "The Anti-artist-statement Statement," *Hyperallergic*, March 29,
2013, https://hyperallergic.com/67670/the-anti-artist-statement-statement/.

material conversely alludes to an inherent human narrative that belies these conceptual concerns.[14]

In statements as confoundingly idiosyncratic as these, only the artist seems to matter. The nonsensical passage comes from the website Art Amiba, which mounts a yearly contest for "Top Bad Artist Statements" hosted by the artist Karen Ami. Ami's concerns about the impenetrability of her fellow artists' written statements echo Jaffee's, though she concedes, "Curators and the public like to hear what your intention is in your work and, perhaps your process. Less is more and the more one tries to impress with pretend art talk . . ., the more the Bullshit Meter goes off."

As artist statements demonstrate, too often we as practitioners struggle to name the ineffable thing behind our craft or trade. Jaffe and others argue that artists should simply abandon all hope of articulating the origin, meaning, inspiration, and intention behind their work and let the work speak for itself. But that's a bit like saying a meteorologist should simply let the weather maps do the talking. Ami takes a more reasonable stance, reminding that her industry, like so many others, demands that makers and sellers articulate value and meaning to buyers, aficionados, and critics; artist statements cannot simply be abandoned any more than furniture companies should jettison assembly instructions. If artists truly believe that art is essential to Everyman and Everywoman, then they owe John and Jane Doe a readable statement of their vision and intention. Rather than abandon the fraught genre altogether, it makes sense to apply the public writer's toolkit to redeem it.

Sadly, some art-speak has become sufficiently impenetrable to readers that websites like *Market-O-Matic* have been created to generate random artist statements at the push of a button. The website's deeply ironic invitation reads like meta-commentary on the inanity of the project itself:

> **The Market-O-Matic (1.0) Fine Arts Version** is here! Just fill in the blanks below, hit the "Crank Out the Crap" button, email the results to your nearest digital arts festival jury panel, then sit back and enjoy a well-earned coffee break!

---

14. Karen Ami, "Top Bad Artist Statement Winners," *Art Amiba*, July 7, 2015, http://www.artamiba.com/index.php/top-bad-artist-statement-winners/.

When I tried the Market-O-Matic, I received this as the opening to an artistic statement for my artistic alter ego, an individual I call Art Person:

> Art Person's work investigates the nuances of modulations through the use of jump-cut motion and close-ups which emphasize the mechanical nature of digital media. Person explores abstract and limpid scenery as motifs to describe the idea of infinite space. Using opaque loops, non-linear narratives, and slow-motion images as patterns, Person creates meditative environments which suggest the expansion of time.

Admittedly, random text generators like these are silly, and when I completed the required fields and hit "generate," the page appropriately read "garbage out." Still, such generators help dramatize an important point not only about the inanity of gratuitous jargon but also about the thought clichés and language clichés that populate much of our professional writing. For example, consider this artist's statement:

> Be that in the battles of the self or the overwhelming and confusing chaos that is our modern times, I seek to find the essence of what it means to be human today; be that the fragility of the resilience of the human animal in the face of endless and impossible questions of life itself.

When compared to other incomprehensible statements, this one seems almost palatable. Still, it perpetuates the professional cliché of the artist as wilting wallflower. Note that a statement as generic as this could be posted beside any work of art and make perfect sense—or no sense at all.

Professional Truths, Professional Assumptions

Early in my public writing workshops I group participants according to their chosen profession or academic discipline. Artists gather with artists, scientists with scientists, entrepreneurs with entrepreneurs until no individual practitioner is left without a vocational home. When they are all together, happily buzzing with the energy of those who share their particular professional bliss and pain, I ask, "What are the big mysteries that your profession attempts to fathom or better understand?"

My goal is to ask them to consider as a collective the underlying values of the work they have undertaken. Answering the question moves them toward greater consciousness of the intellectual mystery they embarked upon when they chose their life's work—or when it chose them. For many it's a true paradigm shift: instead of working professionals, scholars, researchers, or businesspeople, what if instead we are truth-seekers trying to solve a core mystery? If we are such detectives, what is the mystery we are pursuing? Who are its principle players? What is its primary setting?

Three exercise scientists enrolled in one of my recent workshops. The first insisted that the big question of their profession concerned the damage repetitive physical activity could do to the body. Another claimed the big mystery was how science itself might be enlisted to help exercisers become more efficient. The third took a more client-centered approach, arguing that the biggest mystery was how to help people feel good about themselves. Often there is spirited disagreement about the big questions our chosen trades aim to answer.

Next, I ask them to think about the claims to truth their profession makes. To what principle does their profession or academic discipline assign the greatest truth? To this query the mathematicians, statisticians, and actuaries in the room tend to reply with something like, "The truth exists in the numbers," though under questioning their initial certainty gives way to caveats: numbers behave erratically; statistics lie. Meanwhile, the business professionals, entrepreneurs, and economists are inclined to respond that their truth is the truth of profits, and yet that pronouncement leads to a vigorous debate about whether the profit motive underlies all of business and economics. Perhaps the core truth of business isn't profit, but satisfying the material and emotional needs of customers. Others counter that satisfying human needs is only a means to the end of realizing profit. Fair enough, but what then is the larger truth of profits? In their path-making book *Freakonomics*, Levitt and Dubner argue that economics is not fundamentally the study of profits but the study of incentives—how people get what they want, or need, especially when they must compete, in a condition of limited resources, to fulfill those needs. *Freakonomics* poses a particularly provocative question: If morality represents how we would like the world to work, perhaps economics represents how it actually functions in light of human nature.

Most of my workshop participants come to me already *disciplined*, which is to say that they've been sufficiently initiated into their field that they can recite its goals and outcomes. Often the most eye-opening part of the professional truths exercise is the debriefing that happens when we reassemble as a workshop and learn what each group of practitioners settled on as their core truth, method, and mystery. For example, a group of occupational therapists caught us all in the false assumption that their profession centers on rehabilitation after injury. Not so, said the OTs, who pointed to the statement of their professional association, which reads:

> Occupational therapy is the only profession that helps people across the lifespan to do the things they want and need to do through the therapeutic use of daily activities (occupations). Occupational therapy practitioners enable people of all ages to live life to its fullest by helping them promote health, and prevent—or live better with—injury, illness, or disability.

Their professional society's definition not only enlightens the lay reader prone to viewing the OT reductively or stereotypically, it also begets further questions for exploration. For example, if "daily activities" are synonymous with "occupations," as the definition implies, is it possible to imagine, for example, video gaming as an occupation that might fall under the occupational therapist's case load, since many avid gamers game daily. The answer to the question would make for a fascinating article on the unexpected or unorthodox "occupations" for which today's occupational therapists offer therapy.

The goal of the exercise is that we view our chosen fields with a fresh set of eyes, not so that we might love them less, but that we might love them more completely and circumspectly. It's also worth asking ourselves what we like least about our field, or what we would most like to change about it, for in dissatisfaction with the status quo often lies the key to future innovation. In offering an answer to the what-would-I-most-like-to-change question, we have simultaneously found an issue fit for further exploration by public intellectuals. For example, one imagines *Freakonomics* as Levitt's and Dubner's book-length answer to what they liked least about their field as conventionally practiced: its too infrequent application to everyday problems. As the *Freakonomics* blog makes clear, Levitt takes pride in applying his discipline to "the riddles of everyday life—from cheating and crime to sports and child-rearing—and whose conclusions turn the conventional wisdom on its head."[15]

The trouble with letting our profession's biases, assumptions, and claims go unexamined finds lyrical expression in Sherwood Anderson's collection of short stories *Winesburg, Ohio*, wherein Anderson introduces a notion he calls the "Theory of the Grotesque":

> The old man had listed hundreds of the truths in his book. I will not try to tell you of all of them. There was the truth of virginity and the truth of passion, the truth of wealth and of poverty, of thrift and of profligacy, of carelessness and abandon. Hundreds and hundreds were the truths and they were all beautiful.
>
> And then the people came along. Each as he appeared snatched up one of the truths and some who were quite strong snatched up a dozen of them.
>
> It was the truths that made the people grotesques. The old man had quite an elaborate theory concerning the matter. It was his notion that the moment one of the people took one of the truths to himself, called it his truth, and tried to live his life by it, he became a grotesque and the truth he embraced became a falsehood.[16]

Similarly, when a single, sanctioned professional truth becomes all-consuming, the writer who calls that profession home may be unable to entertain other truths worthy of equal consideration. Specialty becomes straitjacket, and the writer becomes a kind of grotesque.

FROM DIFFICULT TO CLEAR

Just as surgeons and concert pianists exercise their fingers to stay nimble, I encourage my public writing workshoppers to undertake smaller etudes meant to develop versatility and range. In one such exercise called "Difficult to Clear," I ask participants to take the most complicated or counterintuitive concept in their field and render it in a language readily understood by the lay reader. I can see the gears turning

---

15. G. Clemmons, "Freakonomics," January 2, 2016, http://freakonomics.com/book/freakonomics/.

16. Sherwood Anderson, *Winesburg, Ohio* (Oxford, MS: Oxford University Press, 1997), 9.

as they select their single most difficult concept to clarify, then begin to think about the words by which they might further illuminate it, making it easier for the rest of us to understand. They leave workshop that afternoon mulling it over before returning the next day ready to give the exercise the old college try.

Over the years they've generated many compelling transformations from difficult to clear. One of my art historians bravely landed on the Baroque style of Caravaggio as the most ineffable or inexplicable aspect of their profession, and dutifully set to work explaining it:

> Caravaggio was always something of a rebel. Orphaned at a young age, he drifted from place to place until finally he found himself in Rome. In those days there was only one way to become a great artist: land a good apprenticeship, join a good guild, and get good commissions. Caravaggio failed spectacularly at all of these; he drank too much, picked fights with anyone he could, gambled heavily, and was always in debt. However, there was one thing he could do—he painted like no one else. In a day when artists focused on perfection, painting perfect people, perfect perspective, and perfect shading, Caravaggio painted flaws. He used his neighbors and the poor people in the Roman slums as models for Greek Gods and Christian saints. He painted with heavy shadows and theatrical lighting. His paintings were windows to humanity when every other painter was striving to create windows to heaven . . . . Religious figures called it heretical. The leaders of the art world called it trashy and sensationalist. No matter what was said about it, though, it was infectiously popular, and people began to copy it. Caravaggio complained, he said it was copyright, he took people to court, but a trickle of copycat artists became a flood, and a flood eventually became a movement.

The writer successfully synthesizes several decades of art history into a single coherent treatment not just of a movement (the Baroque) but also of that movement's exemplar (Caravaggio). While the difficult concept the writer attempts to illustrate shifts somewhat in their overlong paragraph, we come away from the passage with greater clarity than confusion, and we have the public writer to thank for our increased understanding.

Meanwhile, a psychologist chose to tackle a concept that had long vexed them: the heuristic. Their translation begins:

> A Heuristic —A Her-WHAT?
>
> You ever wonder how ideas can just pop into our head when we are asked a question? How, almost like magic, images quickly appear whenever a teacher says, "Now class, please think of an example for . . ."
>
> Even now when you read the words *squirrel, prom dress, flower,* or *bed,* images appear in your head, giving your conscious mind a working example of whatever is being talked about. The process of your brain giving your conscious mind an example can be considered a mental shortcut. Think of it as a secret passageway, which allows for little to no effort for information to travel from a hidden compartment in your brain to the "center stage" of your memory. In psychology, this mental shortcut is called a **Heuristic**. Heuristics allows for our brains to make automatic connections about information with no conscious effort. The fascinating thing about heuristics is that everyone can experience different mental images from heuristics.
>
> Remember the words I gave you that "sent" images straight to your mind? *Prom dress,* for example? What was the color of the dress? Was it long or short? Was it covered in bright sparkles or made entirely of dark, silky material? While your image of the prom dress might be the dress you wore to prom or the dress your date wore, everyone can have different images pop into his or her mind. As you can see, heuristics are mostly controlled and created by our past experiences.

I was grateful that the author tackled such a big academic buzzword, as I too must have used the term *heuristic* dozens of times with only an intuitive sense of its most literal meaning.

In future chapters we'll examine by name the techniques the writer uses to make this difficult concept easier for readers to grasp, but we sense already the psychologist's keen desire to explain their hard-won knowledge in sentence-by-sentence translations from their professional language into a more common vernacular. It's not a perfect write-up (the opening heading a "Her-WHAT" and the breezy tone of that initial second-person "you" are reminiscent of the original opening paragraph Selzer wisely axed in "The Knife"), but in nearly every other way the writer hits their mark.

The discipline required to honor the difficult is one shared by many public intellectuals, who, rather than shy away from that which needs explaining, are often drawn to difficulty like moths to a flame. Like talented gymnasts jazzed by a high degree of difficulty in their chosen floor routine, audacious public writers meet the challenge head on. And what The Difficult reveals to them is very often the crux of the matter, the core conflict, complication, confusion, or contention that calls forth their most nimble and daring thinking. Sometimes the difficulty the public intellectual confronts is logistical or circumstantial or historical; at other times it is technical or technological, and at others it is spiritual, ontological, ethical, philosophical, or even epistemological. Whatever the singular difficulty may be, it calls for the skills the public writer uniquely possesses, in much the same way that a medical emergency calls for a doctor in the house.

WRITING THE OUTSIDE-OUT PERSPECTIVE

While expert public writing often comes when we write from inside our vocations to those outside of them, there is also much to recommend in what I call the "outside-out" perspective: the uninitiated observer writing to other observers in the general public, effectively saying, "oh, so you're new here, too?" For example, though writer Judith Herbst was not herself a trained scientist, she introduced a generation of young readers to the wonders of science via her Great Ideas of Science series. In titles such as *Bio Amazing* and *Animal Amazing*, Herbst, neither journalist nor scientist, investigates unexplained phenomena in the natural world. In one of her best-known articles, "The Body Shop," she takes a page from Selzer's playbook as she describes what it's like to make a surgical incision, not as a trained doctor, but as a mere student with a scalpel:

> It often comes as something of a shock to be told by your biology teacher to "gently make three horizontal slices" in the living, breathing animal waiting patiently on your lab tray. Even the toughest shrink back. For several minutes, the air in the classroom is heavy with 1) loathing for the teaching 2) self-disgust at the murderous act you are about to commit, and 3) cowardice in technicolor. Scalpels hang poised. Throats gulp.

And then almost in unison, the entire class gently makes three horizontal slices.[17]

In the scene above, Herbst and her fellow apprenticing scientists are cutting into a "cross-eyed flatworm called a planarian" rather than, thank goodness, a human being on an operating table. Herbst's initial abhorrence at the "murderous act" she's poised to undertake is a far cry from the way Selzer, a trained surgeon, would describe an incision, and yet Herbst's writing is no less informative or revealing. In many ways, it is more relatable, since readers are more likely to have been a squeamish biology student than an MD. Herbst writes from an outsider's perspective to readers likewise on the outside—exemplifying the outside-outside praxis. Later she will examine in scientifically accurate terms the regenerative power of particular species. In closing she predicts a "brave new world in which we are able to regenerate bits and pieces of ourselves as easily as starfish and the planarian. The artificial limbs and hearts, the hearing aids and implants will no longer have to be shipped in from the body shop." Instead she boldly declares, "The body shop will be us."

WRITING THE UPSIDE-DOWN PERSPECTIVE

I loved art class in elementary school, in part because I loved how art introduced me to a world where I could readily change my perspective, viewing the same object through a different lens. Terms like *worms-eye view* and *birds-eye view* spoke volumes about the particular voodoo a change of perspective could do. Art's allure charmed me into studying art and pre-architecture at university. Though I eventually chose English as my undergraduate major, I continued to pursue art history, regarding my "minor" field of study as an alternate lens by which I could achieve a compound vision.

Sometimes public writers choose to look through a lens adjacent to the one they know best. By analogy, it would be as if the politician looked at the world from their constituents' perspective. In this case, the categories are not mutually exclusive, for the politician is also presumably a voter, and yet the public servant who sees with the eyes of a voter is bravely doing some of the particular voodoo public writers do, this time adjacent to their own professional perspective. Michael Pol-

17. Judith Herbst, *Animal Amazing* (New York: Atheneum Books, 1991).

lan masters this move in his popular works of intellectual nonfiction such as *The Botany of Desire.* Pollan subtitles his book "A Plant's-Eye View of the World," and that is exactly what he offers. The author opens *Botany of Desire* with a vignette in which he lords, god-like, over his own backyard garden. A mere few pages into his account, however, Pollan flips the perspective from lord to vassal, writing:

> That May afternoon, the garden suddenly appeared before me in a whole new light. All these plants, which I'd always regarded as the objects of my desire, were also, I realized, sub-jects, acting on me, getting me to do things for them they couldn't do for themselves. Could it be that we are drawn in-stinctively to flowers? And that's when I had the idea:
>
> What would happen if we looked at the world beyond the garden this way, regarded our place in nature from the same upside-down perspective?
>
> This book attempts to do just that, by telling the story of four familiar plants—the apple, the tulip, cannabis, and the potato—and the human desires that link their destinies to our own.
>
> Its broader subject is the complex reciprocal relationship between the human and natural world, which I approach from a somewhat unconventional angle: I take seriously the plant's point of view.[18]

Pollan writes from an upside-down perspective, flipping the script as he reports from inside the buzzing, fertile world of his garden and, as an outgrowth of his beat in botany, to a broader public who likewise sees the bees and smells the flowers but perhaps fails to understand the evolutionary or ontological relationship between them. While Pol-lan is not a credentialed botanist, he had, prior to writing *The Botany of Desire*, established a solid beat in food writing and environmental journalism that his subsequent bestseller, *The Omnivore's Dilemma*, helped cement.

Public writer and literary journalist Tracy Kidder makes a similar inside-out, upside-down move in his nonfiction *Among Schoolchildren.* By the time he published the book in the early 1980s, Kidder had been a student much of his adult life, earning degrees first from Harvard

---

18. Michael Pollan, *The Botany of Desire: A Plant's-Eye View of the World* (New York: Random House, 2002), xv.

and later from the famed Writers' Workshop at the University of Iowa, as well as working as a visiting professor and writer-in-residence at colleges and universities nationwide. In *Among Schoolchildren*, he turns that academic pedigree on its head as he goes back to school as an adult, joining a fifth-grade class in a racially mixed school in a poor district of Holyoke, Massachusetts. Professor Kidder successfully switches the paradigm, adopting an upside-down perspective. In so choosing, he demonstrates the public writer's desire to see their subject completely and circumspectly, regarding it as a luminous object to be viewed top to bottom, and bottom to top, lest one miss a single telling refraction.

WRITING FROM THE OUTSIDE-IN

On rarer occasions, public writers will find themselves tasked with writing from the outside to those inside a devoted group or subculture who know it well. Social scientists sometimes call this cognitive device a "Martian perspective"—that is, imagining how a man or woman from Mars might view a particular object, tradition, or ritual. The Martian perspective is a metaphor for how the most open-minded, impartial observer might see things differently than those too emmeshed in a culture or ritual to see it clearly. Most works of cultural criticism employ the outside-in perspective to some degree, as when Wallace, a complete outsider to the world of gourmet eating, writes back to those in the inside (gourmands), challenging them to reevaluate the ethics of live-boiling lobsters in "Consider the Lobster." In "Lifelike," writer Susan Orlean productively employs the Martian lens to reveal to readers of *The New Yorker* the surreal world of taxidermists gathered together for their annual trade convention:

> I heard conversations analyzing such arcane subjects as exactly how much a javelina's snout wrinkles when it snarls and which molars deer use to chew acorns as opposed to which ones they use to chew leaves. This is important because the ultimate goal of a taxidermist is to make the animal look exactly as if it had never died, as if it were still in the middle of doing ordinary animal things like plucking berries off a bush or taking a nap. When I walked around with the judges one morning, I heard discussions that were practically Talmudic, about whether the eyelids on a bison mount were over-detailed, and whether the nostrils on a springbok were too wide,

and whether the placement of whiskers on an otter appeared too deliberate. "You do get compulsive," a taxidermist in the exhibit hall explained to me one afternoon. At the time, he was running a feather duster over his entry—a bobcat hanging off an icicle-covered rock—in the last moments before the judging would begin.[19]

Sometimes a public writer already enmeshed in an industry must cut ties, achieving outsider optics by first disavowing, divorcing, disclaiming, or otherwise divesting themselves of their particular subculture, enabling them to write back to those still inside of it with a bracing wake-up call. Famed sportswriter and cultural critic Paul Gallico offers a compelling example. Years ago I was asked to edit and introduce the Gallico classic *Farewell to Sport* for publication in a new edition. Gallico had been among the most famous celebrity sportswriters of the Roaring Twenties, but by the late 1930s he had grown utterly disaffected with the graft, greed, and corruption of sport, abandoning it completely. As its title implies, *Farewell to Sport* served simultaneously as his swan song and his shot across the bow of the foolish believers who had stayed behind, gamely cheering on the sordid affair. "We are, by dint of practice, the greatest nation of hypocrites on the globe," the disgruntled sportsman wrote, adding that there was nothing more he could do to wake up his former colleagues other than "have myself one more big yell and then slam the door."[20] Gallico's "big yell" lasted for well over two hundred pages of unsparing critique and close critical analysis of an arena in which he had reveled just ten years earlier.

Wrapping Up

Many of us have an "it's complicated" relationship with our chosen profession. Often our quibble isn't with our trade per se, but with the way it is practiced or preached. Regardless, our professional identity follows us everywhere: into airplanes, coffee shops, and conference centers, where questions like "What do you do?" or "What do you study?" are ubiquitous. At times, our profession is sufficiently sticky as

19. Susan Orlean, "Lifelike," *The New Yorker*, June 9, 2003, http://www.susanorlean.com/articles/lifelike.html
20. Paul Gallico, *Farewell to Sport* (New York: Open Road Media, 2015), https://www.google.com/books/edition/Farewell_to_Sport/e8eZBgAAQBAJ?hl=en&gbpv=1&bsq=Farewell%20to%20Sport.

to cling to us, so that each time we make a new acquaintance we find ourselves re-explaining what we do and why we do it.

Unlike many other duties in our lives, profession is a cross we choose to bear, and one that, if we're willing to look closely, reveals much about what we love, what we value, and where we find truth, beauty, and mystery. Writing from inside our profession to those on the outside helps introduce ourselves and our work to those eager to learn what we do and why, as well as to project our research and writing into new spheres of influence and synergy. A writer willing to look honestly at their profession and to think critically about it can meet with uncommon success when, by asking tough questions and posing new problems, they blaze new trails.

3 Finding Your Topic, Growing Your Audience

Public writing sometimes answers to the more high-falutin' handle *public scholarship*. *Scholar* nicely describes what public intellectuals are, *scholar* being defined alternately as "a specialist in a particular branch of study" and a "learned or erudite person, especially one who has profound knowledge of a particular subject."

Take heart, you're more of a scholar than you might think. If you hold an associate's degree you've specialized in a subject you've come to know well. If you matriculated in a four-year degree program, you graduated with a major field of study—a body of knowledge you mastered (or fooled your professors into thinking you mastered!). You may also have a minor certifying your expertise in an additional field that, while secondary to your major interest, nevertheless extends your interdisciplinary reach. That academic minor, certification, or extra endorsement signifies hundreds of additional hours of study and practice—far more than you might expect to acquire in months of continuing education courses. And if perchance you still doubt the meaningfulness of your expertise, remember private pilots only need forty hours of total flying time (only ten of which must be solo) to earn their wings.

Whether you hold an AA, BA, MA, or PhD (or an AS, BS, or MS) or are currently on your way to earning one, you're likely already researching and writing in your major area, or an area closely adjacent to it. If so, you're a scholar. I know a woman in her fifties who served in the Air Force in Japan who never earned an undergraduate degree, but who has nevertheless worked her way to a senior position at a research lab. Is she a scholar by virtue of over twenty years of experience and well over ten thousand hours in the lab? Absolutely! Is a student, still studying in the field that will become their craft and trade, a scholar of a sort? You bet. In fact, one definition of a scholar is to be a student— a role at which nearly all of us have at least twelve or thirteen years of experience.

While we'll favor the inclusivity of the term *public writer* and *public intellectual* throughout this book, the term *public scholar* is equally apropos. As a term *scholar* implies learning, erudition, and study, and the kind of writing we're talking about cannot happen without engaging in critical thinking and close reading. In fact, critical thinking and analysis distinguish the public writer's practice, differentiating us from imaginative writers, though we occasionally borrow from the creative writing toolkit to leaven our fact-based, idea-driven examinations. Our depth of expertise likewise distinguishes us from journalists who function as jacks-of-all-trade and masters of none.

We'll discuss the overlap between the public scholar and the journalist in future chapters, but for now a few key distinctions. First, the deadline journalist's material often has a short shelf life dictated by the round-the-clock news cycle, whereas the public writer's work does not typically depend for its relevance on what's in today's news. This is also true for public writing and journalism hybrids such as op-eds, personal commentaries, and explanatory reporting, which typically have a much longer shelf life than deadline news. Though the public writer's work is timely, it is not likely to be as time-bound or time-stamped as the journalist's. The public intellectual has the luxury of viewing events through a somewhat longer lens in a genre that benefits from retrospection and hindsight. The public writer and public scholar are typically called on to examine complex issues and questions at a much greater depth, often in long-form work that sometimes includes their original research, as opposed to the just-the-facts journalistic brief that distills what others have said recently about the topic at hand. Indeed, a public writer may write an entire book on their subject without once conducting an original interview, whereas a traditional news journalist could be fired for that same omission.

Once we've established that we as professionals have something valuable to say—lived subject matter, relevant training, and book learning—and that we qualify as scholars in the most inclusive sense, it's useful to make a list of things we're expert in, whether or not we're formally credentialed in them. Go on then: Inventory the subjects you follow closely, keep current in, and can honestly say you know well. We'll revisit your list in a moment after looking at how scientists locate the novelty-factor within their own current research.

PITCHING YOUR CURRENT RESEARCH AS PUBLIC WRITING

Let's begin with the premise that your current research is more likely to find its way into print than work you have done in the distant past. For most of us, past research and writing is difficult to reenter; we've changed, the work has changed, and the world has changed. The Greek philosopher Heraclitus, of the Heraclitan River fame, is associated with the philosophical notion, "No man [read: "no person"] ever steps in the same river twice," by which he means to suggest that we exist in a state of constant flux.

Scientists often work at a different pace than those in the humanities. Provisioning labs and hiring research assistants is time-consuming and expensive, and amassing the necessary amount of experimental data can take years if not decades. A biologist friend of mine, Tom, studied the tiger salamander his entire career. Whenever I would see him in the halls, I would call out good naturedly, "What's new in salamanders, Tom?" And he'd reply with a wry smile, and a tiger salamander headline for me.

If you, like Tom, are a researcher with a long-term commitment to studying what seems like a single, niche topic, you don't have to abandon your research to be a public writer; you just have to look for what's new or noteworthy within your existing study. It pays to carefully read the news. If you don't, you may miss out on an opportunity to submit a timely guest column or bit of expert analysis the next time salamanders make national headlines, and, trust me, it happens more than we might think. In fact, the *Smithsonian* magazine and other national venues recently covered the release of a study on the European olm salamander, a cave-dwelling species said to be capable of living nearly one hundred years. Citing a study in the *Journal of Zoology*, *Smithsonian* reports that one olm was found, unmoving, in the same spot for 2,569 days, or just over seven years.

And I thought professors were sedentary!

There's no reason to make like an olm and wait, though. It's practically in a public writer's job description to look for ways today's headlines intersect with their research area. For example, if you're a herpetologist, you know that salamanders are known to be the source of many active compounds, including potent neurotoxins. Setting your Google News alert to notify you of any headline news involving neurotoxins might provide you the news peg you need to contribute to the national discussion. For example, science publications across the world recently covered the release of new research that found that a peptide in the skin of salamanders could help promote wound-healing in humans. When headlines like these happen, your body of work is suddenly relevant again, and even if you don't decide to author a piece of public writing on the subject, you can offer yourself up for interviews, quotes for the press, and more. Of course a publicist can help do this work for you, but their assistance comes at a hefty price, and they will still depend on you to explain your research to them, so that they, in turn, can explain it to their media contacts. In the end, most middle-income professionals are money ahead to make their own arguments for relevance, arguments that will, in turn, sharpen their sense of where their work makes the greatest potential contribution to society.

Most of the time, it will fall to you to think creatively about what within your area is most relevant and timely to the lay reader. For example, not long ago my newsfeed lit up with the headline "Hundreds of Tiny Arachnids are Likely on your Face Right Now." Now there's a headline to make you stand up and take notice! Down the Google rabbit hole I went until I had several headlines on my screen, including NPR's "Meet the Mites that Live on Your Face."[1] The scientist behind the headline, Michelle Trautwein at the California Academy of Sciences, had been studying face mites for years, scraping a spoon across the greasy part of her nearly two thousand human subjects to collect genetic samples. Research like Trautwein's would typically languish in obscurity, doing well to make the pages of a respected science news publication. But in this case, Trautwein proved uniquely adept at representing the novelty of her research to the journalists who, beginning in 2019, began seeking her out for comment. Trautwein demonstrated herself to be so adept at the quintessential job of the public writer—finding the subject's relevance to a wider audience—that she made the reporters' jobs easier. In comments made to KQED journalist Josh Cassidy, Trautwein offers both a tagline ("No one is thrilled at the initial notion that they have arachnids on their face. But people are often curious—even in their revulsion") and a larger reflection about the big picture amd so-what factor in her otherwise innocuous research: "Face mites are definitely the species of animal that we have the closest

---

1. Josh Cassidy, "Meet the Mites that Live on Your Face," May 21, 2019, www.npr.org, accessed June 1, 2020.

connection with as humans, even though most of us don't know about them or ever see one in our lifetime."

Whether you're the expert writing your own piece of public writing, as you might for the publication *The Conversation*, or a freelancer translating the discoveries made by a scientist into language a broader audience can understand, it helps to hone in on the element of the story most likely to attract distractible readers' attention. Check out this unforgettable headline crafted by Brandon Specktor on the science news website *Live Science*:

> "Face Mites Live in Your Pores, Eat Your Grease and Mate on your Face While You Sleep."

If Trautwein and Specktor are able to make harmless microscopic mites the stuff of morning headlines, then surely no subject is too small, quite literally, to turn the heads (and stomachs) of readers.

Establishing Your "So-What" Factor

Nearly twenty years after James Raymond first introduced me to it as the cornerstone of his composition classes, the "so-what factor" sticks with me. In his book *The Moves Writers Make*, Raymond defines the so-what factor as the "surprise" that makes any piece of writing worth reading. It is, he insists, "always the result of a departure from the norm: the writer sees the data in a way most readers would not have seen it on their own."[2] The real subject of an essay or article, he maintains, isn't its surface topic or subject (i.e., euthanasia, performance-enhancing drugs, body-shaming), but the "element that makes it worthy of reader attention," which is to say the "writer's interpretation of the material."

Twenty-years later I present this enduring notion to students enrolled in my public writing workshops by comparing the so-what factor to a movie tagline or an "elevator pitch" (You have fifteen seconds to get the gist of your idea across in an elevator ride with an important influencer or gatekeeper in your field . . . go!). In both analogies there's a nod to existential urgency, to the clock ticking down on even the most merciful reader's attention span. For me the beauty of the so-what factor (SWF for short) is that it's a *quality* of good public writing perhaps more than a specific technique. Like the ineffable essence of

---

2. James Raymond, *Moves Writers Make* (Upper Saddle River, NJ: Prentice Hall, 1999), xviii.

prose style, our articles and reports either have it, or they don't. If we're in doubt about what the so-what factor is and how to manifest it in our own work, it's worth asking ourselves what's novel or different about our topic or our take.

To help locate the SWF in their own work, I invite workshoppers to think of a subtitle for their imagined book or manuscript that begins "The surprising truth about [blank]," or, alternately, "uncovering the hidden truth behind [blank]." While the exercise may seem melodramatic, it packs a powerful revelation for those willing to try it. If a writer's self-evident take is a poor fit when grafted to such an otherwise sexy subtitle, their piece may be lacking the requisite "surprising truth" altogether. For example, if Susan Cain's book *Quiet* fails to live up to the enticing so-what factor embedded in its subtitle: "The Power of Introverts in a World That Can't Stop Talking," we're likely to feel a bit cheated. Equally often today's popular works of nonfiction ditch the coy SWF-in-the-subtitle strategy, imbuing a muscular main title with a powerful so-what factor. For instance, the seven words of Stephen Covey's phenomenally successful *The 7 Habits of Highly Effective People* advertise the SWF right from the get-go.

RECALLING FIFTH-GRADE YOU

How'd you do at the expertise inventorying exercise I assigned you earlier in this chapter? We'll look at one public writer's inventory in a moment, but for now I want to suggest a couple of prompts that may help shake loose additional topics and overlooked areas of expertise.

If you would, please make a second list. This time recall the subjects you liked to read about most in fourth or fifth grade, back when you weren't stuck reading for someone else every waking hour. Be as specific as possible in your recollection; after all, pre-teens can be pretty particular in their tastes.

The exercise may seem self-evident at first, but for me it was anything but. The epiphany hit me when, as an early career writer, I came to the startling, humbling, frustrating discovery that what I was choosing to write about then, as an adult, was almost exactly synonymous with the topics I loved to read about as a kid (okay, minus saltwater fish). Why had it taken me twenty years to get back to writing about the things that fascinated me almost from the beginning? Lots of reasons, I suppose. One, my Rip Van Winkle twenty-year lapse happened during years spent acquiring a formal education and, later, a nascent career in journalism. Both were endeavors in which I was busy writing topics assigned me, rather than satisfying my own intellectual curiosities. Second, I was so focused on learning *how* to write (craft and technique) that I forgot almost entirely the wide world of *what* to write about (content and subject matter). I spent years learning the fine art of writing essays, reports, papers, and stories, without giving equal thought to *what* I was writing about within those genres. I remember one moment in workshop when a trusted friend and reader told me, "I think place is really important in your work," and the comment hit me like a ton of bricks. Why hadn't I noticed those themes myself?

So, how's that list of yours coming along? My list of what I loved to read about in fourth grade might include:

> Atlantis and Ancient Egypt
>
> Pro Football
>
> US Presidents

They're pretty specific items (aren't kids gloriously fussy in their fixations?). Granted, it's true that I'm not writing about these subjects, verbatim, now as a mid-career writer. But with just a little widening of the lens, the specifics broaden and the topical picture resolves to this:

> Ancient civilizations and mysteries
>
> Sports
>
> Politics

As it turns out, my fourth and fifth grade fixations strongly endure in my contemporary writing practice. With a little broadening of your own list, do you see a continuum from elementary school reader to you now, as an adult professional? I hope so. I like to think that kid curled up long ago in the school library bears some resemblance to you now in the office, lab, or cubicle.

Now I want you to traipse on over to your home bookshelf, whether real or virtual. Focus initially on the nonfiction you find there. More than likely, some of the titles you'll find were assigned as texts in your college major or minor. That's an important data point. Others among the tomes are likely related to your current work—those trade publications, reads, and references that allow you to do what you do a little bit better. Those are revealing as well. Still, I'm most interested in the nonfiction books (and fiction, too, if you can suss out the subject area behind the story) you've purchased for yourself, or that friends and loved ones purchased for you over the years. What is the most common subject among your books of nonfiction? Is their content area the same (or closely analogous to) the field you currently work in, or is it noticeably different, maybe even idiosyncratic, having little or nothing to do with your workaday nine-to-five?

Relationship experts and armchair psychologists tell us we can learn a lot about someone from the books on their shelf. If that's true, perhaps taking a look at the titles and subjects of your own books can reveal to you something about yourself. Or maybe they can help recall for You Now what You Then read, back when You Then had all the time in the world. In any case, the topics of your existing collection may suggest a related topic you can tackle when you write your next (or maybe your first) work of public writing. For example, you may be a reading teacher, and your top shelf may consist almost entirely of books on education, everything from inspiration to theory to exposés on the current state of educational inequity. However, one shelf below we find your trove of fly-fishing books—your burning passion once the school year ends. The very fact that you jump in the car the minute grades are turned in for your annual trip to the trout streams of Montana offers you a powerful clue: maybe your next (or first) piece of public writing will be on fly fishing, maybe even a piece describing how that particular avocation is similar to your vocation: teaching reading. It may seem far-fetched at first, but turning passionate avocations into break-out subject matter works. Just ask Norman Maclean, who spent his days writing and teaching Shakespeare to students of English literature at the University of Chicago, until he plumbed his love of fly-fishing to generate the Pulitzer Prize-nominated gem: *A River Runs Through It*, and, later, a film of the same name directed by Robert Redford and starring a young Brad Pitt. Is it too early to begin considering which Hollywood icon will play you in the movie made from your book? Probably, but you'll never know unless you write that overlooked text inspired by your hobby or avocation.

Finally, if the first two exercises fail to inspire a subject area for your next, self-assigned piece of public writing, think back to the careers you considered in elementary school, middle school, high school, and college. What did you imagine yourself doing for a living back then? In fourth grade, my career list would probably have read:

> Dallas Cowboys quarterback
> Gym teacher
> Geographer
> Historian
> Marine biologist

In a nutshell, my list boils down to sports, place, history, and fish . . . three of the four remain abiding writerly interests to this day. I'll leave you to guess which have stood the test of time.

GEO-LOCATING YOUR TOPIC

Public writers typically percolate several viable topics at once. Like practicing poets prone to seeing poems in everything from fruit market mangoes to middle school dances, public intellectuals see the world in multitude, often stockpiling topics as they move, fully awoken, through the world. Sometimes our ideas have staying power, such that we return often to them in mind, mulling them over, while at other times they lose their luster and recede from our consciousness. At other times our ideas strike like a bolt of lightning, sending us scurrying for our keyboard while the electricity still hums in the air. Much of the time it's a good idea to let even our most dramatic lightning bolts linger for a day or two to see if they still feel sufficiently charged.

There's no need to wait for lightning to strike, though. Instead, worthy ideas can be located systematically and developed intentionally, like a good seedbed or nursery stock. An excellent place to begin is with your community. Increasingly, it's not just the job we hold or the formal credentials we possess, but where we live and work that enlarges our expertise into something truly resonant. Place is central to demographics, an idea perfectly encapsulated in the term *geodemographics*. And the geodemographics of the places we live, work, and play shape our expertise and our experiences in crucial ways. For example, if we live in El Paso, Texas, or San Diego, California, our experience with immigration is likely much more immediate and proximate than that of a public writer who lives in Maine or Montana. If we live near a coast, our awareness of, and experience with, offshore oil drilling may be greater than that of our colleague who lives in the landlocked

middle of the country. And if we live in the nation's breadbasket, sur-
rounded by small farming communities, our zip code alone probably
better credentials us to comment on crop-growing and food-producing
than a fellow public writer living in the heart of New York City. Granted, zip-code-derived calling cards must be taken with a grain of salt, as
the commodity trader living near Wall Street may know more about
agriculture than the schoolteacher living in small-town Nebraska.

Take a moment, then, to consider the city, town, neighborhood, or
place you live in now or have called home in the past. What is it best
known for nationally, regionally, and locally? What traits do people
know it by? Has it been in the local, state, or national news recently?
Have you lived in your place a long time or a short while—either extreme may add juice to your piece. How do you feel about the place
in which you live? Are you its most spirited advocate, its best critic, or
a conscientious objector to the life lived around you? Whatever your
answer, it's important to think deeply about what your neighborhood,
city, state, or region is known for, as newspaper and magazine pieces,
in particular, are likely to be geodemographically "placed" by editors
whether we like it or not, in much the same way that most newspapers, and many magazines, acknowledge their host city or region in
their title.

Not long ago, I wrote an op-ed that called for colleges and universities to drop their celebrity graduation speakers in favor of commissioning those who do more unheralded work close to home. Initially,
I tried to pitch my piece of public writing to industry-standard publications in higher education and to a few metro newspapers in greater Chicagoland, where I teach, but to no avail. I was close to giving
up on the piece when it occurred to me that I really should send my
commentary to the *Los Angeles Times*. The greater Los Angeles metro
boasts more than two hundred colleges and universities, making it a
higher-education hub. LA is also a geographic hotbed for Hollywood
icons, including celebrity politicians like Arnold Schwarzenegger who
routinely demand five- and six-figures for commencement speeches.
The *Times* appreciated my piece and its timing, and chose to run my
op-ed early one May to coincide with graduation season.

I had been close to giving up on my anti-celebrity speaker op-ed,
when what I really needed to do was rethink the locus of my submission. In fact, many public writers make the mistake of thinking so hard
about their topic that they neglect the role that geodemographics play

in the publication potential of a piece of public opinion writing. Public writers able to connect current events with their own geodemographics stand the best chance of placing their piece in the highly competitive pages of the nation's metro newspapers. In most cases, the connections between author biography and author geography should reflect a synergy readily apparent to editors. For example, if a member of your family fights wildfires for CAL FIRE and you're a long-standing resident of northern California, you are an excellent candidate to write an op-ed, personal commentary, or news analysis piece tackling the politics of fire suppression in states known to suffer destructive wildfires.

NARROWING YOUR TOPIC

Let's call to mind Caleb, a youthful participant in one of my recent public writing workshops in Chicagoland who, if asked to list his current areas of expertise and deep interest, might produce the following list:

> Track and field
>
> Literature/creative writing
>
> Law
>
> Video Gaming
>
> Journalism
>
> Marketing/Business

Represented in Caleb's initial list is his college major (Literature with an emphasis in creative writing) and minor (marketing and business), his college co-curriculars (track and field and the collegiate newspaper), his hobbies (sports, reading, and video gaming), and potential career options that combine his love of the written word with his desire for its real-world application (hence journalism, marketing and business, and law). While still in his twenties, Caleb has achieved fluency in a number of these areas and certainly qualifies as a scholar by our definition. The notion that young people are too inexperienced to have developed an expertise in their field worth writing about is as preposterous as it is damaging to the ambitions and dreams of emerging writers. At universities where I have served as a professor I have known twenty-one year-old scientists who have co-authored important journal articles with their professors. Incredibly, a writing workshop I delivered in the California public schools included a thirteen-year-old who published his first book one year later.

Let's encourage Caleb to whittle down his list of potential areas of expertise as he ideates an article of informed public writing suitable for publication. Law, for example, should probably go. Having an older sibling who's a lawyer doesn't really qualify as expertise by firsthand experience or deep study. Such indirect knowledge might inspire a personal commentary written by a close family member that lifts the veil on the stress faced by young attorneys like Caleb's brother, but it probably won't suffice for an article- or chapter-length exploration. Similarly, we might recommend that he reconsider video gaming as a potential topic for an article of public scholarship. Being among the hundreds of millions of avid gamers doesn't necessarily qualify the writer as an expert. So far as I know, Caleb doesn't blog about video games, review new releases, or regularly attend gamer conventions or conferences, any of which might qualify as a true experiential credential.

I worked with a young man in his twenties once, Evan, who developed not just a love of gaming with his friends but also a passion for following the industry. By the time he enrolled in my workshops, video game companies were already shipping him gratis review copies, eager that he gift them with a positive review in one of several online publications for which he was then evaluating new titles. I encouraged him to write about the world of technology and gaming, though English, not Interactive Media or Computer Science or Digital Technology, was his academic major. And why not? Already, he possessed a knowledge of gaming's "canon" of important titles and its "literature" of classics sufficient to make many an English major envious. A few years later I received the happy news that Evan had been hired as the editor of an industry-standard gaming magazine. His field-adjacent expertise—his passion project and the subject of much of his public writing—had yielded unexpected fruit. Despite his technological savvy, he wasn't a defector from the ranks of English majors; indeed, quite the contrary, since his primary interest in his new field rested in his love of the narratives that gave first-person games their shape and substance. His academic emphasis—fictional and nonfictional narratives—had served to inform his developing area of professional expertise.

Let's return to Caleb now, our talented writer still looking for a topic to pitch for a proposed long-form article of public scholarship. Already, he has axed law and online gaming from his list, leaving him with journalism, literature, and business/marketing—all areas reflected in his choice of curricular and co-curricular study. What had begun as a half dozen areas of demonstrated passion and practice has been reduced to three core subjects wherein his experience is of a depth sufficient to successfully pitch a piece of credible public writing. He could certainly choose any one of these final three topics and examine an issue within it relevant to a wider public—for example the controversy over "fake news" fits nicely as a braiding of two of his listed areas of scholarship and practice: journalism and literature/creative writing. Or, realizing that in writing, as in cooking, the real juice is often in the fusion, he might instead look for a topic betwixt and between his final three: subject matter that represents a mash-up of professional writing and business/marketing. And where do the interests of professional writers and marketers overlap most clearly in Venn diagram fashion—in publishing, the business side of writing. Caleb has now located an area of interdisciplinary inquiry that fits the kind of in-depth, research-based exploration that is the stock and trade of public scholars. He's found a subject that all but requires him to move between disciplines as an interstate travels between states to move us to our destination. His geodemographic ties to the potential topic are compelling as well, since Chicago is a regional hub of the publishing industry and a storied city for journalists and journalism.

Next, we counsel him to tailor his topic still further, since publishing remains too broad an area to distinguish his pitch from countless others in the slush pile. The magazine or journal editor reading his query letter would surely want to know what aspect of publishing Caleb proposes to discuss, and what unique angle he plans to take on the subject; this would be especially true if he queries a venue not exclusively devoted to publishing, such as *Crain's Chicago Business*. Ultimately, he emerges from our workshop determined to explore the business of self-publishing and self-published authors, with greater Chicago as his chosen geodemographic case study. His newly narrowed topic represents an ideal blend of his skills and interests not to mention a topic whose research he is intrinsically motivated to complete, since he is also an emerging writer looking for alternate ways into print.

ADDRESSING ISSUES IN THE PUBLIC SPHERE

It's nice to dream about having the freedom to write about anything we want, but few working writers have such luxury, and fewer still really and truly want it. It's a grass is greener on the other side of the keyboard phenomenon: total freedom looks appealing until we've suffered an acute case of writer's block caused by having too many choices and not enough direction. For many of us, a higher-up at work assigns our topic and dictates our deadline. For others, perceptions of market demand determine subject matter; scribes like these sense a niche and write to fill it. Still others are moved by social conscience or motivated by a sense of societal injustice, like the writers for social change who exposed the hazards of lead paint in Chinese-made toys, or the journalists from the *Boston Globe* who uncovered the Catholic priest abuse scandal.

The sweet spot for a piece of public writing or scholarship is often one in which the writer has, or is resolved to acquire:

1. A formal or experiential credential in the subject field

2. A basic familiarity with that field's literature and research

3. An investment in the issues of that field as a scholar and as a citizen—in short, a citizen-scholar

If we can check off all three numbers above, we're well on our way to finding a wider audience. Still, the criteria don't quite completely capture it. One could satisfy them in spirit and still be opining about the neighborhood lemonade stand that now unfairly falls under draconian city regulations. Such topics meet the spirit of public scholarship, but perhaps lack the reach, research, and relevance for which most of us are aiming. Clearly, we need an additional criterion, something that addresses the big idea-minded disposition of the engaged public intellectual and citizen-writer. Our missing fourth criterion might read:

4. A willingness to address complex issues in the public sphere and interpret field-specific debates for a wider audience

In number four above, we arrive at a more precise description of public writing's most meaningful outcomes. A write-up in the local newspaper about the legalities of the lemonade stand wouldn't fully meet this criterion, as it's difficult (though not impossible) to imagine neighbor kids serving lemonade on a summer day as an issue with deep roots in an academic discipline. What would that discipline be? Food service? Law? Possibly, though not too many lawyers earn a living these days representing ten-year-old lemonade stand entrepreneurs. It's possible that a writer with expertise in urban and suburban sociology might tackle the phenomenon of the hard-pressed lemonade stand, though if they did they would surely have the good sense to apply the language and methodology of their discipline to produce an article for publication. Can't you just imagine it: "Fresh Squeezed: A Case for the Communal Values of the Lemonade Stand"?

A case in point is a physicist I met in one of my recent workshops. In the tradition of Carl Sagan or Stephen Hawking, Chris wanted to bring the airy language of science down to a more pedestrian level. While he might have chosen a topic more theoretical (particle physics, elliptical orbits, black holes), he chose instead to write about artificial intelligence—a subject so integral to our lives it comes with its own acronym—A. I. The prospect that computers might one day be programmed to develop their own general and emotional intelligence sufficient to enslave their makers is one that concerns us all, especially if we've seen *Terminator*. Chris has found a topic that meets or exceeds all of our topic-selection criteria, and he's off and running. Who better to weigh in on the potential threat posed by A. I. than a well-read theoretical scientist with the ability to address both the science of A. I. and at the same time address its legal and ethical quandaries? That's interdisciplinary scholarship and inquiry in action, coupled with the earnest concerns of an active and engaged global citizen.

WHAT AM I DOING IF I'M NOT ARGUING?

For generations teachers have harkened back to the good old days of the Greeks and Romans in an attempt to explain argumentation to their writing students. Certainly, any rhetorician worth their salt ought to be well-versed in classical rhetoric, but it's worth asking why so many otherwise well-intentioned and progressive teachers still slavishly adhere to the tenants of writing as practiced by men wearing togas in 50 BC.

Such teachers have drilled into their students' heads that rhetoric means the art of persuasion, a notion they further simplify as argumentation. Students are coaxed and cajoled into making arguments, analyzing arguments, countering arguments, and concluding arguments. They're given such a hard sell that a first-year student could hardly be blamed if instead of complaining about Comp 101, they slipped and called it Argument 101. In an argument-centric rhetoric, a paper is flawed from the first paragraph if it does not have an arguable thesis or debatable premise; and if it doesn't fail the argument standard by the end of paragraph one, it will surely fail by the end of paragraph four, where the teacher marks the paper down for lacking support of— what else?—its stated argument.

In fact, the word *essay* comes to us from the French *essayer*, meaning to try out, or to test. Moving beyond argumentation means writing our way into appropriately complex issues for which we do not always have an answer and for which a my-way-or-the-highway cocksureness seldom leads to a positive outcome.

The Greeks conceived of rhetoric as a competition—a quasi-gladiatorial contest of reason, logic, and style. Rhetoric, like debate, had winners and losers. Scores were kept, and the man—and regrettably back then it was nearly always a man—who fashioned the most artfully watertight argument for truth, wisdom, and virtue was declared the victor. Fortunately, we post-post moderns have transcended the notion that everything must be a competition, and that every competition must have a winner and loser.

Or have we? More than a millennia later, writing instruction still largely subscribes to the win-an-argument mentality, so much so that apprenticing writers often mistake "having an opinion" with "making an argument." Having an opinion comes easily to most of us, steeped as we are in user ratings and reviews. And it's not just students but wizened professionals, too, who want in on the opinion craze, adding the 997th review to a best-selling title on Amazon.com or being the 100th to post in the comments field following the latest controversial article in the *New York Times*. Why? Well, opinion is easy for readers to digest, and we're drawn to the binaries implicit in polemics. In my view, teachers who insist on beginning with "making an argument" or "having an opinion" get it backwards. For the public writer, positions are what we arrive at *while* we do the writing and the research.

The trouble with harping at writers to make an argument is that such heavy-handed coercion pushes them inexorably toward the very hot button issues that elicit strong opinions in the first place. It's ouroboros, the snake eating its own tail. Yet, conventional college paper topics such as abortion or euthanasia, which cannot be covered adequately in thousands of pages of jurisprudence let alone in a five-para-graph essay, continue to pervade rhetoric and composition classrooms.

So, what are we as public writers doing if we're not arguing?

In public writing we're analyzing, assessing, challenging, consid-ering, exploring, examining, interpreting, mediating, mapping, and questioning, and often we're doing not just one but each in turn. The trouble with argument as the be-all end-all is that it locks us down in bulldog fashion to a single modality, defining success as winning on the terms we have set forth in our thesis. Overzealous arguments are control freaks that too often leave the reader feeling left out or other-wise marginalized or manipulated. Imagine a business that unilater-ally wrote the contract (the thesis), fulfilled the contract (the body of evidence), discounted the opposition (stifling or slighting counter arguments), only to, in the end, reassert the binding nature of the con-tract (the conclusion) all without ever consulting the customer (reader).

By contrast, the verb *exploring* suggests a writer committed to learn-ing the lay of the land via a thoughtful mapping of the landscape—a sort of environmental scan. *Exploring* connotes an investigator reluc-tant to follow the first, most obvious path. By analogy, most of us would prefer a doctor who asks a series of thoughtful questions, takes our vitals, and runs the lab work before stating their thesis. We don't want our physician's assistant or resident intern to argue with us the minute we lay down on the examining table. Instead, we prefer that they take their time, contemplate all their options, and consult with the professional literature and with colleagues in their field before ar-riving at a conclusion that still leaves room for diagnostic uncertainty.

WRAPPING UP

Eschewing overheated winner-take-all arguments, public intellectuals explore their subjects: holding them up to the light; inventorying the case in its particulars; taking time to understand the positions of per-tinent stakeholders. When we examine, we look closely and with more than cursory scrutiny. We may have a hunch, hypothesis, or intention when we commence our examination, but we endeavor to keep an open mind as we explore multiple perspectives and reconcile conflict-ing data. Once the public writer is relieved of the burden of preemptive argument, they see new possibilities where before they sensed only the animal need for fight for flight—to bury the opposition before it bur-ies them.

4 Telling Smart Stories

The contemporary public writer's embrace of narrative strikes some as counterintuitive. With so much information at our disposal, and so many ways to disseminate it, why would today's public intellectuals and scholars return to a form that's as timeless as the troubadours? In his popular book *The Storytelling Animal: How Stories Make Us Human*, Dr. Jonathan Gottschall reminds, "The Human imperative to make and consume stories runs even more deeply than literature, dreams, and fantasy."[1] Gottschall insists that we are, in fact, "soaked to the bone in story," and that our inclination toward story is prehistoric in origin.

Gottschall's fascinating and timely treatment tracks the growing prominence of story in everything from first-person role-playing games (RPGs) to religious traditions to the mechanisms by which, as social psychologists point out, we swap stories to win friends and influence people. In a recent interview, Maria Konnikova of *Scientific American* asks Gottschall why he feels his book made such a splash if, as he insists, story is everywhere around us. His answer is revealing:

> I agree with the spirit of your question: If story is such a big deal in human life, why doesn't it get more attention? I think it's because, in general, we just aren't fully aware of it. In the same way that plankton isn't aware that it's tumbling through saltwater, we humans aren't aware that we are constantly moving through story—from novels, to films, to religious myths, to dreams and fantasies, to jokes, pro wrestling, and children's make-believe.
>
> Then there's the problem of academic boundaries. In universities, we chop story to pieces and spread it across departments. Psychologists get dreams. Musicologists get song. Literary scholars get novels. Anthropologists and folklorists get traditional tales. And so on. This keeps us from seeing

---

1. Jonathan Gottschall, *The Storytelling Animal: How Stories Makes Us Human* (Boston: Mariner, 2013), 19.

stories—from opera librettos to nightmares—as aspects of a unified mental process involving the construction of imaginative scenarios. And it keeps us from seeing how story infiltrates every aspect of how we live and think.[2]

Story is top-of-mind these days in business as well, according to a recent article in *Forbes* magazine. Narrative, it claims, is finally getting the attention it deserves as a business competency driving "emotional engagement" and "enhanced business performance."[3] The magazine declares story to be an ideal vehicle for creating an emotional attachment. "In today's age of brand experience, it seems that emotional engagement is proving to be more and more critical to achieving winning results and effective storytelling is at the heart of this movement," it concludes. Artful business-directed storytelling has become the coin of the realm, instigating a "revolution" in the way products are marketed and sold.

Experts in narrativity argue that as a species we're hardwired for story, so much so that writers who find genuine ways to translate their questions and investigations into narrative increase their chances of reader receptivity and information retention. Presidential speechwriters in the United States have utilized the power of story for decades to help connect with viewers at home. Decrying violence on the streets is one thing, but telling voters the story of a mother who has lost two of her children to tragic turf wars is many times more impactful.

In public writing workshops, it's often the quantitative and qualitative scientists that are the most resistant to the idea of infusing narrative elements into serious-minded, even scientific, writing. For them, story is something one leaves behind in middle school in favor of hard data. These skeptics see it as a gimmick, one that is somehow complicit in the "dumbing down" of research. Theirs is an understandable reaction, and I'm quick to point out they shouldn't feel obliged to "tell stories" in the strictly academic journals where they publish the results of their empirical research. Instead they might avail themselves

2. Maria Konnikova, "The Storytelling Animal: A Conversation with Jonathan Gottschall," *Scientific American*, April 19, 2012. https://blogs.scientificamerican.com/literally-psyched/the-storytelling-animal-a-conversation-with-jonathan-gottschall/.
3. Billee Howard, "Storytelling: The New Strategic Imperative Of Business," *Forbes*, April 4, 2016, https://www.forbes.com/sites/billeehoward/2016/04/04/storytelling-the-new-strategic-imperative-of-business/#a5975284d795.

of narrative strategically, saving it for occasions when they are trying to reach the largest possible audience. I urge them to think of story not as the province of creative writers, storytellers, and gifted raconteurs, but simply as a fundamental vehicle, or vessel, for information. The knowledge the writer seeks to convey may be the same regardless of the modality with which they choose to communicate it, but receptivity demands that they at least consider reader-friendly containers into which to pour their results.

Stories come in countless shapes and sizes. While they may be told off-handedly for amusement or entertainment, most are told to illustrate a point or to reinforce a worldview. A composition professor of mine preferred the term *likely stories* to the term *examples* or even *anecdotes*. In just two words his *likely stories* formulation reminded his students that the most compelling examples often function as stories in miniature.

The strategic use of story can also enhance our ethos as writers. Our willingness to share stories implies something positive about us, as storytellers are often seen as engaging, generous, and vulnerable before their listeners—in short, sought-after company. In choosing to avail ourselves of the unique container story offers, we as public writers and intellectuals get a boost from such positive associations. Who wouldn't wish for the ability to hold someone rapt with a compelling anecdote? The storyteller's gift is to infuse the seemingly insignificant or incidental with meaning, to fashion from mere data, fact, or circumstance something worth remembering or taking to heart. I ask skeptical quantitative and qualitative scientists to accept on faith what for them can be a difficult premise: that storytellers aren't charismatic faith-healers or snake-oil salespersons; instead, they're expert and artful conveyers of information. Storytellers are carriers, conveyers, and interpolators of meaning.

Too often, however, even skilled writers willing to concede the utility of narrative have difficulty finding and maintaining the narrative through line in their public writing, a fact Michael Pollan readily admits in an interview with *Writing on the Edge*:

> The main problems my students have are with how to structure a long piece and how to find a narrative in the midst of a sprawling subject. They're working on complicated pieces and there's a lot of exposition involved, a lot of issues involved, so you have to work to find the narrative. How do you situate

yourself in the story? Once you decide you're going to make yourself a presence in the story, how do you do it? You have to choose how to present yourself, which of your identities will work best.[4]

Narrativity challenges many intellectuals accustomed to lecture/exposition because it changes the way we present information, altering the modality of our expression from telling to showing. While exposition explains a known fact, narrative follows a series of events to an uncertain outcome (at least its outcome is uncertain to readers), unwinding a tale as if it were a big ball of yarn. The distinction between the two modalities can be difficult to discern, so let's break it down further with the help of the following chart courtesy of creative nonfiction teacher Bill Roorbach:

Narrative	Expository Writing
needs a time and place	ideas exist outside of time
tells a story	examines, explains
portrays events	analyzes events
exemplifies ideas	expresses ideas directly
puts a dream of events in a reader	uses events . . . for argument[5]

STORIES FOR SCHOLARS

How does one make a story of subject matter that appears on the surface to contain no intrinsic narrative? To answer that question it's worth returning to the narrative markers taught us by our elementary and middle school teachers. Back then (and still) a story was said to contain:

Character
Plot
Dialogue
and Setting

---

4. Pamela Demory, "It's All Storytelling: An Interview with Michael Pollan," *Writing on the Edge*, November 1, 2006, https://michaelpollan.com/interviews/its-all-storytelling-an-interview-with-michael-pollan/.
5. Bill Roorbach, *Writing Life Stories: How to Make Memories into Memoirs, Ideas into Essays, and Life into Literature* (Cincinnati: FW Publications), 2008.

Typically, our teachers listed these narrative markers exactly in that order, and for good reason: character really is the soul of story. No less an authority than F. Scott Fitzgerald once claimed of its preeminence "Character *is* plot." In Greek tragedies it's the tragic flaw of the hero that puts the plot into motion, not the other way around.

Admittedly, finding characters in serious or scholarly writing can be daunting at first, but locating the people involved in our chosen topic or issue helps embody and enliven research. Most writers cite their sources using MLA, APA, Turabian, or Chicago Style, typically beginning each citation with the last name of the author. Yet, as much as the scholar in us likes to separate the research from the researcher, behind every published theory, idea, or data set is a flesh-and-blood individual yearning to be acknowledged for their work. Viewed in this light, the typical APA references page isn't the dry, colorless recitation of bibliographic data it's made out to be, but a list of characters. Think of it as a *dramatis personae* of indispensable players in the real-life drama that is our chosen subject matter. If we believe that character engenders story, our task is to retrieve and liberate the personalities otherwise buried in the parenthetic citations or confined to the references page at the back of the book. It's to gather together the thinkers who make our work possible, and who toiled to better understand the selfsame questions we take up in our work.

Bestselling author Malcom Gladwell is a mensch at finding the characters hidden in the research, so much so that narrativity rests at the heart of his method. "I am a story-teller," Gladwell told Brian Lehrer of the *Brian Lehrer show*, "and I look to academic research . . . for ways of augmenting storytelling." In another interview with *Esquire* magazine, Gladwell, a long-time staff writer for the *New Yorker*, explains, "I'm not a thinker, a philosopher or any sort of visionary. I'm a storyteller, a translator of academic research." Instead, he expertly constructs what he calls "intellectual journeys"—quests for deeper truth and understanding that lend "intellectual sparkle to everyday subjects," as writer Sean O'Hagan puts it. For academic William Dembski, Gladwell's remarkable appeal is based on:

- A knack for raising interesting questions and drawing interesting connections (these being flip sides of the same coin).

- Ready access to interesting personalities, whom Gladwell describes in everything from informal conversations to formal interviews.

The real secret to Gladwell's success as a public writer, Dembski claims, is "the many colorful and fascinating people, people most of us would love to engage in conversation." He reports knowing one of the author's interviewees personally and vouches that Gladwell "nailed some things about this person that [he] sensed vaguely but had never precisely articulated."

Gladwell's ability to illustrate important public debates via compelling characters is on display in the first chapter of *Outliers: The Story of Success*. In "The Matthew Effect," Gladwell seeks to explain the phenomenon known as Relative Age Effect, an important theory in psychology. His introduction to the scholar responsible for popularizing it is straightforward enough, reading: "It wasn't until the mid-1980s, in fact that a Canadian Psychologist named Roger Barnsley first drew attention to the phenomenon of Relative Age."[6] Less skilled public writers would surely have left it at that, paying only token attention to Barnsley the man. But Gladwell knows that theories originate with people. In *Outliers* Barnsley is liberated from parenthetic citations and rescued from the relative anonymity of the notes, works cited, or references page to breathe new life. He becomes a character in the story the author aims to tell, so he is given a name, a short history, and calling card.

Gladwell expertly fleshes out the character behind the scholarship in the heart of his chapter. We're introduced to Barnsley, his wife Paula, and their two sons as together they view a hockey game in southern Alberta, Canada. Next comes the plot twist: while reading the roster of athletes Paula turns to her husband and asks whether he sees the pattern in the birth month of the hockey players listed therein; as it turns out the vast majority are born in the first few months of the year: January, February, or March. Gladwell renders the brief exchange between husband and wife in dialogue, in a scene set in the stadium, adding a quote from Barnsley in which the psychologist remembers the fateful night when the proverbial light bulb went off. When they return home from the game Roger and Paula gather birth date statistics for every player in the Ontario Hockey League to confirm their suspicions: a significant majority were born in the first few months of the year. The Relative Age Effect is born.

---

6. Malcolm Gladwell, *Outliers: The Story of Success* (New York: Little Brown and Company, 2008), 21.

Several pages later Gladwell writes: "Barnsley argues that these kinds of skewed age distributions exist whenever three things happn: selection, streaming, and differentiated experience." This sentence reflects the kind of formal summary many social scientists would content themselves with in a scholarly paper written primarily for colleagues in the field. Barnsley is a name who is only important to the extent that he is the vessel for an extraordinary theory. And what does the disembodied Barnsley do in the quoted passage? He "argues"—the verb of choice for what scholars do, and, it would seem, their sole function. Occasionally we allow them to assert, write, claim, or maintain, for instance, but seldom do we as writers allow them to do mundane things like attend sporting events, for example. We unfairly confine the scholars about whom we write to the drama of the mind, which is only a small but important part of the larger drama of life.

Consider the particular ways Barnsley emerges as a character in the mini scene Gladwell makes of the hockey game. We learn he is married with two kids; we learn that he likes hockey. We learn, contrary to the "genius" stereotype and its "egad!" moments, the truth of the Relative Age Effect is right there in front of Barnsley in the roster of the hockey team, but he still can't see it; it takes his wife to point out the pattern in player birth dates. From this anecdote we're reminded that so-called light bulb moments are seldom had alone in a lab, utterly removed from human contact. Instead, they're often arrived at serendipitously in pedestrian moments with colleagues, friends, or loved ones. From Gladwell's mini scene we learn that Barnsley is capable, much like us, of being obsessed with something other than his chosen field. In this case hockey is the passion that humanizes the man who becomes the chapter's protagonist.

Having introduced and developed a main character, however, Gladwell is now responsible for his care and feeding. From here to the end of the chapter the author must purposefully connect Barnsley to the plot at multiple points, bringing him back at least once if not several times to reaffirm his centrality and rationalize, ipso facto, his introduction into the narrative in the first place. Through Barnsley and his pathmaking scholarship, Gladwell has introduced us to the plot/conflict, "The Matthew Effect." If the age cutoff dates used in hockey and other sports lend a measurable advantage to older, more mature, more developed individuals in any given age class, how can society level the playing field in arenas as diverse as public schools, sanctioned sports leagues, and beyond?

Now there's a plot born of character.

INTELLECTUAL PLOTS

Plot surely ought to come with an asterisk where public scholarship is concerned, as many readers think murder, mayhem, and treachery when they hear the term. The plot in a piece of public writing is often considerably more staid. English novelist E. M. Forster claimed that plot was "a narrative of events with an emphasis on causality," an incredibly useful notion to which I would add *consequentiality*: plot is a narrative of events with emphasis on causality and consequentiality. The example Forster gives of this definition is a classic:

> STORY: The king died and then the queen died.
> PLOT: The king died and then the queen died *because* of grief.

Plot, then, has everything to do with the relationship between events and their consequences. Without such elements, the narrative devolves into a simple report . . . this happened, then this happened, then this happened. Readers looking for the plot in public scholarship will want to know what investigations the featured scholars or experts are pursuing and why, what theory is being tested, and what risk or consequence the results of the investigation may entail. Fortunately, public writing often features obsessed characters, and obsession, even when its object is primarily intellectual, spurs characters to action.

Bill Bryson's book *A Walk in the Woods: Rediscovering America on the Appalachian Trial* offers us an example of how plot works in Gladwell-styled intellectual journeys. Bryson's subtitle hints firmly at the purpose of his extraordinary participation: to rediscover a nation by walking one of its most iconic routes: the Appalachian Trail (AT). From the title alone we should be able to follow a clear cause-and-effect chain of events simply by inserting the word "because" between the major plot points in the chapter, "but" to indicate the twists and turns, and "until" to indicate the pivot points within the narrative.

> The action that precipitates the plot, sometimes called the "inciting incident," is Bryson's move from England back to New Hampshire

because

He wants to reconnect with his homeland

> *because*

He has lived as an ex-pat in Britain for more than twenty years

> *but*

Once home, he doesn't know exactly how to reconnect with the US

> *until*

He learns that the AT runs, quite literally, through his backyard,

> *but*

He procrastinates

> *because*

The trail's physical demands are daunting, and its risks are many

> *until*

His old high school friend Katz agrees to hike with him,

> *but*

when Katz arrives, he's woefully out of shape

> *because*

Katz has done some hard time fairly recently for drug and alcohol abuse and is killing his withdrawal by overeating

Using only three conjunctions—*because, but, until* (the latter of which can also be a preposition)—we've captured the causality of events. Notice the push and pull inscribed by the words *because, but,* and *until,* as together they trace a dramatic arc that leaves readers wondering what will happen next when our conflicted protagonist, once committed, takes the first irrevocable steps toward rediscovering America on the AT.

Though the story Gladwell documents is primarily intellectual, the events detailed in chapter 1 of *Outliers* should yield to similar analysis if indeed they constitute a plot of consequence. Let's see how the "story of success" reads through the lens of plot:

> the story of success is often portrayed as a story of intelligence and hard work; *but* many people who work hard and work smart will continue to fail in their quest to become conventionally successful *until* they learn the hidden psychological

and sociological factors that influence the odds of achieving their dreams.

As the example illustrates, intellectual adventures like Gladwell's possess strong plots, too.

One of the things I admire most about *A Walk in the Woods* is how, even in a book that avails itself of a strong and sometimes humorous "I" narrator, the consequences of the plot transcend individual interests in the way we've come to expect of serious-minded public writing. The author takes us through a litany of the risks he and others face who tackle the daunting 2000-mile-plus hike—crime, infectious disease, and bodily injury prominent among them—before detailing what for me is one of the book's ultimate plot points: if Americans don't interact with wilderness areas in a meaningful way, and if they continue to exhibit what public writer Richard Louv calls Nature Deficit Disorder, they are less likely to feel called to defend nature when it's imperiled. Once again we have a plot worth following, and one which promises to teach us about nature and ecology along the way. Bryson tells us:

> And there was a more compelling reason to go. The Appalachians are the home of one of the world's great hardwood forests—the expansive relic of the richest, most diversified sweep of woodland ever to grace the temperate world—and that forest is in trouble. If the global temperature rises by four degrees Celsius over the next fifty years, as is evidently possible, the whole of the Appalachian wilderness below New England could become savanna. Already trees are dying in frightening numbers. The elms and chestnuts are long gone, the stately hemlocks and flowery dogwoods are going, and the red spruces, Fraser firs, mountain ashes, and sugar maples may be about to follow. Clearly, if ever there was a time to experience this singular wilderness, it was now.[7]

This single paragraph contains a series of cause-and-effect relationships that together describe a personal plot of consequence (how easily we can become "dead inside" when we lead lives of quiet desperation) and a plot of national significance in the death and decline of

7. Bill Bryson. *A Walk in the Woods: Rediscovering America on the Appalachian Trail* (New York: Broadway Books, 2010), 4.

America's great hardwood forest. This larger plot—the consequences of our inability take better care of our natural resources—mirrors and at the same time clearly trumps the personal urgency Bryson feels to take better care of himself.

If our public writing feels static or rote, chances are good that we haven't yet identified distinct plot points—moments of action, reaction, and consequence—along the way to our characters' discoveries or epiphanies. Note too how nicely Bryson's smart stories conform to Gladwell's notion of public writing as, in essence, an intellectual journey. *Journey* connotes necessary movement, exploration, and serendipitous discovery, and an aerobically steep learning curve. As such, it's worth asking ourselves what journey the characters in our public writing have embarked upon, and *where* that journey takes them. As Rebecca Solnit reveals in her fine book of public writing *Wanderlust: A History of Walking*, the earliest Greek philosophers were forever on the move, treating learning and movement as mutually sustaining. Socrates, Plato, and Aristotle, she reminds, were all famous wanderers for whom travel, movement, and mobility stimulated the mind while opening it to new ways of thinking—broadening horizons. Their lesson still applies to the characters we deem central to our public writing narratives: if their intellectual pursuit doesn't, quite literally, also *move* them or *move* us as readers, then their quest is likely to fall short of the dedication requisite of the true lover of wisdom.

While most would consider the novelist and the scientist to be diametric opposites in terms of technique, it's worth noting that the five steps of the scientific method: Purpose/Question, Research, Hypothesis, Experiment, Data/Analysis, align fairly neatly with the five stages of plot (also sometimes called dramatic structure) we've studied since grade school: exposition, conflict/rising action, climax/ultimate test, falling action, resolution/revelation (denouement).

COMPELLING CHARACTERS

Early on in this book we inventoried a handful of very real differences between public writers and journalists. Unlike journalism, for example, most public writing does not require the conducting of original interviews, which are difficult to transcribe and even more difficult to book, especially if your interviewee is an expert in high demand, or a source living far away. Because of their degree of difficulty, however, interviews are highly prized, since they add texture and relief to our work, transforming it from monologue into dynamic dialogue. In his classic writing handbook *On Writing Well*, William Zinsser urges writers of nonfiction, "Get people talking. Learn to ask questions that will elicit answers about what is most interesting or vivid in their lives. Nothing so animates writing as someone telling us what he thinks or what he does—in his own words."[8]

Zinsser's advice rings as true now as it did in 1976, when first he penned it. While your piece of public scholarship may not contain an original interview with an expert in the field (you may, in fact, be that expert in the field), that doesn't mean it has to be devoid of the pleasure inherent in hearing the voices of real people having meaningful discourse. Once you've established the essential characters, settings, and plot points involved in the intellectual journey you hope to relay via narrative, you'll want to collect, if possible, some quotes from its key players, either transcribed from an in-person meeting with them (with their consent of course) or quoted, with proper attribution, from a previously published source, which might include an interview, lecture, or other public appearance published on a video sharing platform. If the discovery, theory, or idea about which we're writing is truly important, chances are good that its researcher-discoverer-author has been interviewed many times previously, creating a record of commentary that a savvy public writer can use to reconstruct a scene with integrity and veracity. And if the topic of your public scholarship concerns characters already in your immediate circle (friends, co-investigators, fellow researchers) then the voices your piece needs to really sing may be as close as your shared workplace. Remember, too, that in an age of synchronous video chat, an interview can be conducted from your computer with a source half a world away.

For his part, Gladwell depicts Barnsley and his wife speaking to one another, dialoguing back and forth as they might in a novel or a script. The "characters" take turns talking, signaled by a new paragraph for each change of speaker, and the speaker is indicated by what narrative writers call *dialogue tags*, that is, "Paula asked," "Roger replied." On first encountering this technique in intellectual nonfiction, many scholars protest, pointing out that they refuse to make-up dialogue for the sake of making their research more engaging. Theirs is

---

8. William Zinsser, *On Writing Well: The Classic Guide to Writing Nonfiction* (New York: Quill, 2001), 100.

false dichotomy, of course, for dialogue in public writing doesn't entail fabrication or invention. Instead, dialogue is collected from interviews, memoirs, newspaper stories, videos, journal entries, and the like, such that pure invention isn't necessary or welcome.

In the author's note that opens the best-selling book of narrative history *Devil in the White City: Murder, Magic, and Madness at the Fair that Changed America,* historian Erik Larson explains to readers what for him is a point of pride: "Anything between quotation marks comes from a letter, memoir, or other written document."[9] Larson's preface reminds us that our public writing needn't have long passages of dialogue to lend it the dialogic feel of stories well-told. Anything appearing in quotes adds vocal texture, whether it's a snippet of text previously published by one of our featured characters or a single uttered word that speaks volumes about the characters central to the issue we're exploring. The work of other authors and scholars, particularly if those authors and scholars are allowed to emerge as rounded characters like Roger Barnsley, also contributes to the sense of dialogic back-and-forth created via rich intertextuality. One simple measure of the amount of voice our public writing contains is the number and frequency of the quotes we employ. And because characters are defined in large part by the degree that they are voiced (think stage plays in which all thoughts must be spoken aloud or acted out to be manifest to an audience) the number and variety of attributed quotes in our public writing may also be an indicator of how much, or how little, our work is inhabited by voices other than our own. If we are seeking the American ideal of many voices joining together to form a chorus, the more characters, figures, or presences in our scholarly narratives the better.

CHARACTER TRAITS

Growing up, I loved to draw, and I loved my grandmother; why not, I reasoned, put those two loves together and sketch a portrait of her? I don't know how I convinced Gran, who was famously camera-shy, to pose for my project, but she did, perhaps because she loved me right back and was afraid her refusal would hurt my feelings. Permission granted, I sketched away lovingly for hours, vaguely aware with each new pencil mark that the picture emerging on paper wasn't as beauti-

---

9. Erik Larson, *Devil in the White City: Murder, Magic, and Madness at the Fair that Changed America* (New York: Vintage, 2004) xi.

ful as the beautiful woman in front of me; gradually it dawned on me that my portrait wasn't flattering at all. You should have seen the look on Gran's face when I finally revealed my awful masterpiece. Somehow she loved me still.

As most of us learned the hard way: describing people is a risky business. Most of the real-life characters we portray in our work won't be as forgiving of the pictures we paint of them as Gran was, especially where physical features are concerned. Often there's a sort of tacit quid pro quo between writer and the characters they depict; characters naturally assume that, as if in recompense for their time or participation, the portrayal the writer offers will be a flattering one.

Once public intellectuals begin to see their investigations as intellectual journeys viewed through the lens of story, the invitation to characterize can become intoxicating. Age, weight, height, skin color, voice, manner of speaking—for a fleeting moment the neophyte public writer reaches for every detail that will conjure their protagonist for the reader, no matter how irrelevant those traits may be. The same individuals who would never dream of detailing such superficial traits in polite company, now spill them onto the page in gratuitous detail.

One public writer who walks the character description gauntlet well is John J. Ratey, author of *Spark: The Revolutionary New Science of Exercise and the Brain*, and a clinical professor of psychiatry at Harvard Medical School. In chapter one of *Spark*, Ratey introduces his protagonist, high school physical education teacher Neil Duncan, as "a trim young physical education teacher." It's enough of a sketch to allow the reader to form a rough picture or to conjure a stock image from their brain to serve as a visual placeholder. Thus far, the description is generally complimentary; who among us wouldn't want to be described as trim and young? Next, we hear Duncan speak at some length as he instructs his gym class, and our image beings to crystalize a bit more. No further physical description of Duncan has been offered, but hearing someone teach speaks volumes about them. Ratey waits another full page before he drops another short physical description, this time providing an image of "the freckled and bespectacled Mr. Duncan" standing on the track. The image remains mostly neutral (there's nothing especially damning about being freckled and bespectacled, after all). With this new description we are nudged ever so slightly to begin to see Mr. Duncan as something other than the buff jock gym teacher stereotype. Beyond that, Duncan's appearance matters little to the story Ratey wants to tell, except that the reader is surely entitled to a basic description in order to see the narrative unfold in their mind's eye. A lengthier detailing of the gym teacher's appearance would feel gratuitous and tangential, no doubt distracting from the core content of the chapter: the idea that we learn more effectively after engaging in heart rate-elevating exercise.

In *Outliers*, Gladwell spills far more ink describing some of his profilees than Ratey spends on Duncan. The decision makes sense: *Outliers* is about exceptional people whereas Ratey's book, as the subtitle makes clear, is about the revolutionary connection between brain health and physical fitness. In "The Trouble with Geniuses," Gladwell describes one remarkably intelligent outlier, Chris Langan, a one-time game show contestant with a genius level IQ:

> He is in his fifties but looks many years younger. He has the build of a linebacker, thick through the chest, with enormous biceps. His hair is combed straight back from his forehead. He has a neat graying mustache and aviator style glasses. If you look into his eyes, you can see the intelligence burning behind them.

In most pieces of public writing, sixty words devoted to a subject's appearance would seem gratuitous, and it's true that Gladwell doesn't lavish such descriptions on many of his other characters. There is method behind the madness in this instance, as Gladwell clearly wants to humanize Langan, showing him as a flesh-and-blood person rather than the more reductive cultural view of geniuses as being, in essence, giant brains.

Ratey and Gladwell go about their sketches differently, but both take the time to describe their core characters' appearance briefly at least twice in their respective chapters, and both provide a description that's at least as long as the character descriptions on the dramatis personae page of a stage play. That's a good rule of thumb and a benchmark to aspire to, particularly if you're the kind of writer (and many of us are) who tends to prioritize the intellectual over the physical, to such an extent that we can come away from an interview or collaboration without noting the eye-color of our subject or collaborators. Many public intellectuals struggle to write extended character descriptions because their intense focus on ideas blinds them to other virtues.

SMART SETTINGS

Often overshadowed, setting merits at least a modest place in every public writing narrative. Sadly, the forgotten fourth marker of story amounts to little more than an afterthought for many public scholars. Perhaps the very ubiquity of the lab, office, or classroom intellectuals typically inhabit makes such places prone to neglect. Or perhaps the abject placelessness of much scholarly writing is grounded in the false notion that the mind is the only setting that matters. But the mind is a difficult place to make concrete for displaced readers seeking to place themselves in our work. Imagine, for example, a script that notes of its location—"Place: the author's mind. Time: the indefinite present." Such an indeterminate stage direction surely wouldn't be tolerated in contemporary theater, as it would give the stage designer virtually nothing to go on. Similarly, public writing whose only setting is the author's mind doesn't give the reader the best chance of taking their shoes off and staying a while.

In locating his discussion of Barnsley and the Relative Age Effect in a real-life place—a Canadian hockey game—Gladwell depicts an almost cinematic setting, generating an opening scene that helps ground the reader in an environment with which they're familiar. While public writers do not always conduct on-site interviews or research in the field the way deadline or feature journalists might, the principle is the same: fully explicating an issue means understanding that issue's key locus or setting. For example, in chapter two of *Outliers*, "The 10,000-hour Rule," the author introduces us to Bill Joy, the Silicon Valley icon who cofounded Sun Microsystems and rewrote the computer language Java. But "The 10,000-Hour Rule" doesn't begin with character— with Bill Joy the "gawky teenager" in 1971, but with setting instead, as we're given a detailed description (nearly a paragraph long) of the Computer Center at the University of Michigan in Ann Arbor, with its "beige-brick exterior walls and dark-glass front." Gladwell likens the capacious room that houses the oversized mainframes as something akin to the final scenes in the sci-fi classic *2001: A Space Odyssey.* The setting is critical because it's the place in which the boy genius, the sixteen-year-old Joy with his "mop of unruly hair," becomes addicted to computing during his first year at college. Sometimes setting rises to the level of character; such that the two are virtually inseparable from one another. For example, separating legendary Los Angeles Lakers star Kobe Bryant from L.A., or Martin Luther King Jr. from Selma and Birmingham, Alabama, would be a difficult, and probably self-defeating, feat.

Setting often precedes character even in character-centric public writing. For example, Ratey begins *Spark* not with a character description of Duncan, chapter one's protagonist, but with an evocation of "a slight swell of land west of Chicago" near a brick building which "harbors in its basement a low-ceilinged windowless room crowded with treadmills and stationary bikes."[10] Ratey reveals that this is the old cafeteria—its capacity long outgrown—that now serves as Naperville Central High School's cardio room. We can infer a lot from these brief scenic details: we are in the far western suburbs of Chicagoland, which suggest a fairly homogenous, relatively affluent population. From the fact the school's cafeteria has been outgrown and replaced we can infer that the action takes place in a booming burb that has likely experienced significant growth in recent decades. Other than the mention of the city in the name of the high school, Naperville isn't referenced on the first page. Why? Ratey writes for a national audience, and though Naperville is Illinois's fourth largest city, many readers outside the Midwest cannot place it, making any early mention of it by name more dislocating than locating.

In a book of such revolutionary ideas about physical and intellectual fitness, why would Ratey open with a description of the high school and the basement exercise room? Here the public scholar follows an almost cinematic protocol, one that offers a fly-over from Chicago, the nearest metropolis to Naperville, before we enter the building to discover our primary setting: the cardio room. In essence, Ratey offers us an establishing shot, so named because it establishes the setting for the action that follows. Many classic sitcoms begin with establishing shots to help orient viewers, for example, the exterior of Jerry's New York City apartment in *Seinfeld* or the exterior of the Dunder-Mifflin paper company in *The Office*. The initial exterior shot makes the interiors feel less claustrophobic, and it reminds us that we associate certain characters with certain settings in a way we find grounding, in much the same way that we often picture friends and family in their particular "spot" when we talk to them on the phone.

In a long-form work of public writing with a narrative thru-line, it's important to set the scene early, even if the location for the "ac-

---

10. John J. Ratey, *Spark: The Revolutionary New Science of Exercise and the Brain* (New York: Little, Brown and Company, 2008), 9.

tion" continues through the rest of the book or article. Nailing down a location early on is like sticking a push pin in a map; now we have a starting place, a home base we can reference as we move elsewhere. In *Spark*, Ratey sets the bulk of the first chapter in Naperville, then, when he's ready to move on, he provides his reader something akin to "driving" directions from his current location in the book. Thus, he begins the section "Good for the Body, Good for the Brain" with a transition not of time, but of place, writing: "About 135 miles south of Naperville, at the University of Illinois at Urbana-Champaign, a psychologist named Charles Hillman . . ." From this point forward, Ratey links each character and their research with a separate location, connecting setting and character in readers' minds: Mr. Duncan = progressive gym teacher = Naperville, Illinois; Dr. Hillman = psychology researcher = University of Illinois at Urbana-Champaign. In short, he uses setting to help structure, place, and pace events, much as we often link "chapters" of our personal lives with the places we lived in then.

If you're having trouble locating a relevant setting for your public scholarship, try a lab, office, or classroom. For example, in Simon Winchester's fine book of nonfiction *The Professor and the Madman*, the setting is Oxford University, and more frequently, the small outbuilding that serves as the headquarters for a group of obsessive bibliophiles endeavoring to piece together the world's most comprehensive dictionary. Just as in real life, visiting an individual's workplace helps us better understand, and empathize with, their daily reality. It only makes sense; the public writer can and often should take their readers on location, traveling to the source via words—to the researcher's laboratory, office, or classroom—to witness the characters in action. Setting asserts its relevance as a crucial part of the who, what, when, *where*, and why formula. If a group of colleagues came to town for a visit, wouldn't you be inclined to take them to your office, laboratory, research site, or workplace to share with them a slip of how and where you spend your days—in effect, showing them where the magic is made?

The setting in Larson's *Devil in the White City* is the titular White City itself, a reference to the electrified, Roman temple-like structures built by architect Daniel Burnham along Chicago's lakefront for the 1893 World's Fair. The opening pages of the paperback edition include two annotated maps complete with keys and legends, allowing the reader to see, from above, the lay of the land where Larson's historical nonfiction takes place. The author takes time to properly set the scene, writing:

> Anonymous death came early and often . . . Every day on average two people were destroyed at the city's rail crossings. Their injuries were grotesque. Pedestrians retrieved severed heads. There were other hazards. Streetcars fell from draw-bridges, Horses bolted and dragged carriages into crowds. Fires took a dozen lives a day. In describe the fire dead, the term newspapers liked most was "roasted." There was diph-theria, typhus, cholera, influenza. And there was murder.

Scientists and social scientists are prone to mislabeling scenic writing "creative writing" when it is actually closely researched nonfiction. They sometimes lament, "I couldn't write like that if I tried." They're entitled to their opinion, of course, though they would be wrong to dismiss Larson's method as creative writing, which suggests embel-lishment. Re-read the passage and notice in phrases such as "the term newspapers liked most," clues to Larson's scholarly methodology: in this case deep archival research and literature review in historical edi-tions of the *Chicago Daily Tribune*, which routinely reported on such gruesome incidences as the author describes. Seemingly melodramatic statements such as "fires took a dozen lives a day" may sound like they come from a novelist's quill pen, but they're facts easily verifiable in the city's death records and obituaries. Larson isn't inventing a lakeside metropolis in 1893 as a novelist would; instead he reconstitutes the gritty "black city" from historical record, much like an anthropologist or archaeologist reconstructs a lost civilization.

Because setting is so central to *The Devil in the White City*—so im-portant, in fact, that it's ensconced in the title—Larson begins Chap-ter 1, "The Black City," with a panoramic invocation of place, setting the scene before he introduces one of the chief historical characters, the murderous Dr. Holmes, that will soon come to call the burgeon-ing burg home:

> And in Chicago a young handsome doctor stepped from a train, his surgical valise in hand. He entered a world of clam-or, smoke, and steam, refulgent with the scents of murdered cattle and pigs. He found it to his liking.

Larson and Gladwell, two narrative-minded public writers at the top of their craft, manage to take their core disciplines and beats, history and psychology respectively, and distill from them smart stories that require no fabrication or fact-bending. Not all of us learned history and the social sciences in the cinematic ways these talented messengers manage to convey it, but don't we often wish that we had? Today, Larson's style is the rule more than the exception in history made palatable for broader audiences. To make one's subject matter come alive, to breathe life into it, is the task of nearly all public writers and intellectuals, regardless of discipline, and especially so in a world where competition for eyeballs is fiercer than ever. Public intellectuals based in the sciences know better than most that research and discovery are authentically dramatic; helping the reading public realize that "boring science" or "dry history" are in fact oxymoronic terms should be part of every public writer's creed.

To "I" or Not To "I", That Is the Question

For readers drawn to the intimacy of I-centric accounts, there is simply no substitute for the immediacy and intimacy of the first-person. Most public writers, however, eschew the pronoun, observing the prohibition against it insisted on by so many generations of public-school teachers.

Why such vehement resistance to an otherwise innocent pronoun? As they see it, the mere presence of an "I" narrator undermines the communicator's credibility as an objective scholar, needlessly shifting the focus from the message to the messenger. Many contemporary public writers continue to regard the subjective pronoun warily, using it cautiously and only in moderation because most seek to serve as interpreters of subject rather than as the subject itself. The risks inherent in the first-person may be better understood by analogy. Imagine if a translator in a high-level meeting between, say, the US and Iranian presidents began inserting their own views into what was intended to be a faithful transcription of the words used by the chief executives at the podium. Such intrusions and asides would doubtless be viewed as a distracting sideshow to what was supposed to have been the main event.

In many cases the public writer's desire to have a voice in the telling can be achieved in less intrusive ways than a litany of me-me-me. The writer's use of connotation can suggest their attitude toward their subject. A case in point is the series written by Charles Fishman and published by *Fast Company* to commemorate the fiftieth anniversary of the US moon landing in 1969. Fishman, the author of the *New York Times* bestseller *One Giant Leap*, certainly qualifies as an authority on his subject. Yet, he leads his *Fast Company* piece with the informal, somewhat cheeky headline "Apollo 11 really landed on the moon—and here's how you can be sure (sorry, conspiracy nuts)." The headline is willfully provocative and chock full of idiosyncratic voice. Clearly Fishman is among the roughly ninety percent of Americans who believe the US did in fact land on the moon, a majority which allows the author to poke fun at the expense of the "conspiracy nuts" he piques in parentheses. Since consumers of *Fast Company* are youthful, business-minded, upwardly mobile, and well-educated, one can assume that its readers share the author's dismissal of conspiracy theorists who persist in believing otherwise. Very early in his piece the author writes:

> Anybody who writes about Apollo and talks about Apollo is going to be asked how we actually know that we went to the Moon.
>
> Not that the smart person asking the question has any doubts, mind you, but how do we know we went, anyway?[11]

While Fishman uses the first-person on a couple of occasions elsewhere in his article, he artfully manages to avoid it in his opening salvo, first by using the workaround subject "anybody who writes about Apollo and talks about Apollo" when what he might have written is: "When I write about Apollo and talk about Apollo I'm always asked how I actually know that we went to the moon." Note that if he had written the alternative sentence he would have deployed a first-person pronoun (inclusive of the first-person plural "we") four times in twenty-two words, a frequency that may indeed strike readers as needlessly egocentric in a piece about the heroes of a lunar mission.

What's the difference between the published version and the first-person-heavy version offered above as a point of contrast? The alternate version not only sounds more subjective, and therefore potentially more unreliable, but it also risks sounding overly self-regarding, all but

11. Charles Fishman, "Apollo 11 really landed on the Moon—and here's how you can be sure (sorry, conspiracy nuts)," *Fast Company*, July 13, 2019, https://www.fastcompany.com/90375425/apollo-11-landed-moon-how-you-can-be-sure-sorry-conspiracy.

excluding the reader. By analogy, imagine if we attended a party and our hosts greeted us at the door not with "Nice to see you. Come in! How are you? Let me take your jacket," but chose instead to make it all about them: "I'm having a great night. Look at me. See how much fun I'm having!" On many occasions the public writer helps the reader make themselves at home by suppressing the "I" in favor of the "you" or the "we." At root it's a gesture of inclusion, humility, and deference.

Notice just how artfully Fishman implies in the passage that the reader and the writer are both "smart people" who know better than to believe lunar "conspiracy nuts," but who are curious about the lunar landing all the same. This is to be a discussion among friends of like mind and intellect, his words imply. The author continues with the first-person plural "we" and the indefinite pronoun "anyone" to highlight the difference between, as he sees it, reasonable, rational people and the folks he elsewhere calls "conspiracy-meisters." The middle of his piece is packed with historical evidence and a plethora of substantiating hyperlinks to, for example, reliable reporting done by the Associated Press.

Only when Fishman moves toward conclusion does he deploy the "I" pronoun extensively, opining:

> Anyone who wants to live in a world where we didn't go to the Moon should be happy there. That's a pinched and bizarre place, one that defies not just the laws of physics but also the laws of ordinary human relationships.
>
> I prefer to live in the real world, the one in which we did go to the Moon, because the work that was necessary to get American astronauts to the Moon and back was extraordinary. It was done by ordinary people, right here on Earth, people who were called to do something they weren't sure they could, and who then did it, who rose to the occasion in pursuit of a remarkable goal.

The author's well-substantiated proof of America's lunar exploration makes for an excellent example of how a public writer can create a strong sense of voice and tone while using "I" sparingly. It also serves as an apt illustration of how, with strategic use of pronouns such as "Anyone," "Anybody," "we," and "you," the writer succeeds in creating a conversational tone without leaning too heavily on the "I" crutch.

WHERE YOUR "I" WORKS BEST

In *Outliers*, Gladwell stakes out a middle ground between the familiarity of the first-person and the objectivity of the third-person, confining his use of "I" mostly to the preface and the opening pages of the first chapter. This have-it-both ways compromise, whereby the "I" is mostly relegated to introductory use, is an increasingly conventional choice among public scholars, as it allows the writer to establish early rapport with the reader before stepping aside for much of the duration to shine the spotlight on his or her subjects.

How does this move work in practice? Early on in Gladwell's first chapter, "The Matthew Effect," the man comes out from behind the machine to confess his aims: "In *Outliers* I want to convince you that these kinds of personal explanations for success don't work. People don't rise from nothing. We do owe something to parentage and patronage." Using "I" Gladwell owns his intention, reminding his audience that he will be presenting evidence in service to the larger claim of which he hopes to convince them. Note, too, that it's not just the use of the "I" that makes a sentence like this one subjective, but also the commissioning of the first-person plural "we." After this early intrusion, Gladwell all but disappears to become a translator and interpreter of information as he operates largely behind the scenes.

In Daniel J. Levitin's book *This Is Your Brain on Music: The Science of a Human Obsession* the author utilizes a similar meet, greet, and retreat strategy. His subtitle promises a scientific methodology while his background as a neuroscientist likewise anticipates a logical, rational approach. However, the author is also a musician, so it's natural for the artist in him to get personal with the audience in the introduction, descriptively titled "I Love Music and I Love Science—Why Would I Want to Mix the Two?" Levitin launches into several pages of fascinating and apropos personal history, beginning with the single sentence: "In the summer of 1969, I bought a stereo system at the local hi-fi shop."[12] The author packs this first sentence with meaningful autobiographical detail that signals more personal life story to come. From it we can infer that the author is a Baby Boomer, and one who was an early bloomer where rock and roll was concerned, buying a stereo system with his own money at an age when many of his peers were buying

---

12. Daniel J. Levitin. *This Is Your Brain on Music: The Science of a Human Obsession* (New York: Dutton, 2006), 1.

comic books. In American culture the Summer of 1969 is iconic, not only in the Brian Adams rock anthem of the same name, but because it encompasses the Summer of Love and Woodstock, not to mention the defining Hippie soundtrack of a generation, "Aquarius/Let the Sunshine In" by the Fifth Dimension. In just a few choice words of first-person autobiography, Levitin the scholar associates himself credibly with a powerful generational brand—American rock and roll and those alive in 1969 to witness firsthand its flowering.

In the pages that follow, the author describes meeting Paul Simon, dropping out of college, forming a rock band, and touring around California in the 1970s. He chronicles the break-up of the band and his transition to becoming a producer, which leads him in turn to a finer and more nuanced appreciation of sound. This newfound appreciation takes him next to Stanford University, and eventually to an advanced degree in cognitive neuropsychology, the core academic discipline invoked in *This Is Your Brain on Music*. In just a handful of pages Levitin goes from a simple sentence introducing his eleven-year-old self to a statement like this one: "Sound waves impinge on the ear drums and pinnae (the fleshy part of your ear), setting off a chain of mechanical and neurochemical events, the end product of which is an internal mental image we call pitch." In tone, subject matter, and syntactical complexity this latter sentence is actually far more typical of Levitin's work overall, demonstrating both the tonal chasm between the familiar first-person and the formal or even scholarly third, and the possibility of including both in proximity to one another, given proper separation and signposting. Public scholars choosing to invoke subjective and objective tones within an article or chapter of public writing typically find that being personal first works best. Nothing is more off-putting, and stereotype-inducing, than the tone-deaf scholar who begins robotically talking about their research before first telling the reader a little bit about themselves, their background, or their motivation.

A LARGER ROLE FOR YOUR "I"

In some cases, the extreme gyrations needed to avoid the "I" are more trouble than they're worth, leading the writer to exceedingly awkward workarounds that sound more like the Victorian Era than the Digital Age. When you find yourself resorting to anachronistic substitutions for "I" such as "one," "the author," or "this investigator," you'll know you've gone a bridge too far in your quest to avoid subjectivity at any cost. While public writing characteristically goes out to meet the world rather than dwelling on the self, there are occasions when self and world, inside and outside, cannot be so easily untangled. In such instances, the fully active, participatory "I" cannot be reasonably confined to a few pages in the preface or introduction but needs to infuse the piece as a whole. When that happens, one could decide to abandon the long-form article in favor of a public writing genre more unashamedly first-person or experiential, such as the op-ed, viewpoints piece, or personal commentary (more on these in upcoming chapters). Still, at just five hundred to seven hundred words these first-person forms are likely to be too brief and monologic for a public intellectual looking to explore deeply an issue or trend involving multiple characters.

The work of James McManus offers a case study in when to let your "I" roam freely. Many years ago, I had the pleasure of anthologizing Jim's fine article "Fortune's Smile," a piece the author originally wrote for *Harper's* magazine about the world of professional poker. *Harper's* paid Jim a hefty advance for his reportage, with the understanding that he, working as a freelance writer, would report on Binion's World Series of Poker (WSOP) in Las Vegas. Jim was already an accomplished amateur poker player, and the idea of merely reporting on events from the sideline seemed insincere to him, as if he was withholding an essential part of himself solely to maintain the appearance of journalistic objectivity. So, he took the $4000 advance for the article and used it to register himself for the WSOP tournament, and, in the ultimate beginner's luck braided with skill, played his way into the world finals. One imagines the happy if not somewhat anxious call he must have placed to legendary *Harper's* editor Lewis Lapham. "Um, Lew, you remember that sideline article I promised to write for you about women contestants at WSOP?" Well, I just played my way into the finals." Ultimately, Jim won $250,000 by playing his cards wisely, coming away with loads of money in addition to a piece that now needed to be first-person. The article eventually morphed into a work of cultural criticism and participatory journalism exploring the rise of high-stakes poker in Vegas entitled *Positively Fifth Street*.

Jim's example may sound exceptional, but authors whose direct experience or inseparable involvement with their subject matter causes them to turn emphatically toward the "I" are more common than one might think. In *Moonwalking with Einstein: The Art and Science of Remembering Everything*, Jonathan Foer, writing as a public intellectual, explores the art and science of memory, while at the time learning the techniques of "memory athletes" by entering himself into the United States Memory Championships. Because Foer's personal quest is so thoroughly intertwined with his intellectual exploration, his frequent use of "I" is both natural and inevitable.

You may not be a stud at five-card hold-em or a champion mentalist, but chances are good that you, as a public writer, know your subject well enough to have convinced your boss or editor that you're the writer for the job. In fact, you may already be an active participant, researcher, or competitor in the field about which you've agreed to write a piece for broader public consumption. If so, and withholding your personal experience with the issue feels dishonest to you, it's probably time to liberate your "I" and become a full-fledged character in your public writing. Imagine, for example, that you had agreed to write a piece about a series of proposed new FAA rules for private pilots and you were just a few air-hours short of earning your private pilot's license. You might reasonably write a brief informative news item about the proposed changes without mentioning your status as a pilot-in-training, but in a lengthier article you would probably want to mention that fact, involving yourself in the narrative. Doing so adds character to your writing, reinforces your ethos and credibility, and decreases the chance that you might be accused of a conflict of interest at a later date.

STORYTELLERS-IN-CHIEF

American presidents have for decades leveraged the power inherent in character and story to illustrate abstract principles and ideologies. While not known as a wordsmith, Donald J. Trump deployed a narrative strategy in his 2019 State of the Union Speech. President Trump echoed his earlier campaign promises to make America great again, and now he wanted to flesh out the concept of *American exceptionalism*: "Proudly [we] declare that we are Americans. We do the incredible. We defy the impossible. We conquer the unknown." The words aimed for inspiration but lacked embodiment (character) and exemplification (relatable anecdotes or "likely stories"). The President's abstract statements came alive, however, when he identified a World War II veteran in the audience, Sergeant Herman Zeitchiek, who stood, quite literally that night, for America's greatness as the themes of Trump's speech finally began to achieve momentum once embodied:

> I began this evening by honoring three soldiers who fought on D-day in the Second World War. One of them was Herman. But there is more to Herman's story. A year after he stormed the beaches of Normandy, Herman was one of the American soldiers who helped liberate Dachau.
>
> He was one of the Americans who helped rescue Joshua from that hell on Earth. Almost 75 years later, Herman and Joshua are both together in the gallery tonight, seated side by side here in the home of American freedom. Herman and Joshua, your presence this evening is very much appreciated. Thank you very much. Thank you.
>
> When American soldiers set out beneath the dark skies over the English Channel in the early hours of D-day, 1944, they were just young men of 18 and 19, hurdling on fragile landing craft toward the most momentous battle in the history of war.
>
> They did not know if they would survive the hour. They did not know if they would grow old. But they knew that America had to prevail. Their cause was this nation and generations yet unborn. Why did they do it? They did it for America, they did it for us. Everything that has come since, our triumph over communism, our giant leaps of science and discovery, our unrivaled progress towards equality and justice, all of it is possible thanks to the blood and tears and courage and vision of the Americans who came before.
>
> Together we represent the most extraordinary nation in all of history. What will we do with this moment? How will we be remembered? I ask the men and women of this Congress, look at the opportunities before us. Our most thrilling achievements are still ahead. Our most exciting journeys still await.

If Herman and Joshua survived the impossible—D-Day and Nazi concentration camps respectively—surely, the president suggests in sharing the story of these two inspiring characters, We the People can summon the courage to face the challenges before us.

GIVE YOUR RESEARCH A NARRATIVE INFUSION

Several years ago, a talented developmental psychologist enrolled in my workshop looking for tips on how they might reach a broader audience with their research on a fascinating subject: the science of adultery. Given a topic as sensitive as this, telling an "I"-based personal story, whether about oneself, a friend, or a family member, would prove difficult if not inappropriate. Still, they wanted to employ a narrative opener that communicated the life-altering impact infidelity can have on those who experience it. After a few false starts they came up with this:

> Elizabeth was thrilled when she married John, her high school sweetheart. Having two kids and a golden retriever was icing on the cake for her. The life that Elizabeth had pictured was finally coming true. As with any couple, Elizabeth and John had their arguments and fights; however, they were always able to fix things that had gone awry. The most significant catastrophe that hit the Edwards family was April 4th 1996 when their son Wade died in a car accident. Even through this, John and Elizabeth were able to overcome their troubles because their relationship was so solid.
>
> So why were . . . four words all it took for John to be unfaithful to his wife of twenty-eight years? Why didn't he just continue to walk into his hotel by himself? Why did he even think twice about the comment? What consequences would come as a result of his decision to commit an act of adultery?

As the author soon reveals, the man featured in the narrative opener is not some hypothetical John Doe but former senator and presidential candidate John Edwards, who, compelled by the four-word compliment given him by his campaign videographer ("You are so hot"), engaged in a long-term affair that would ultimately break up his marriage and wreck his presidential ambitions. In a footnote the author cites Elizabeth Edwards's book *Resilience: Reflections on the Burdens and Gifts of Facing Life's Adversities*, and later returns to this opening vignette or narrative through-line in the concluding section to book-end their article on the science of infidelity.

EVEN STORYTELLERS CITE THEIR SOURCES

If you're a public writer who is not also a professor or researcher, you probably can't remember the last time you used the sort of in-text parenthetic citations called for by most academic style guides—MLA, APA, and Turabian. That's because parenthetic citations are primarily applicable to formal papers, where they facilitate a quick ascertaining of the caliber, currency, and frequency of references to the work of touchstones in the field.

A case in point: while reading a book of public writing with a group of college students recently, I paused to ask where the in-text parenthetic citations were that we were so accustomed to seeing in work written by experts. The volume cited over a hundred sources in a notes section at the very back, but otherwise we found nary an in-text parenthetic citation in over 250 pages of text.

For a moment my question hung in the air, unanswered. These were students well-drilled in the routine: any serious work of scholarship needed in-text parenthetic citations, right? I decided to press my luck with a follow-up question. What rationale could an author or publisher possibly have for leaving them out?

Zack was the first to raise his hand. He's one of those students who doesn't participate much, except when the question is an especially tough one. He must have sensed I'd asked a stumper, because this time his hand shot up.

"They're ugly," he said.

I hadn't thought of it just that way, but Zack was right: in-text parenthetic citations *are* ugly, not to mention distracting when dozens of them rear their heads on a given page. Inarguably, an abundance of in-text citations, whether in the superscript numerals characteristic of endnotes or footnotes or the in-text parenthetical citations indicative of MLA or APA documentation, interrupts the visual and syntactical flow of the writing, cluttering the page with a list of what seem like odd bibliographic asides.

Zack's shot across-the-bow precipitated a veritable therapy session of long-repressed resentment of parenthetic citations. For nonfiction writers who work hard to cultivate character, plot, conflict, and setting, a sudden superscript number at a key point in the story can drop the reader out of the narrative completely, waking them from the necessary dream of a gripping story as surely as an alarm disturbs a pleasant slumber. In-text superscript numerals and parenthetic citations can also be tone-killers in work that aspires to any mood other than academically serious or somber. To drive home the point, imagine yourself leaving the following note on the kitchen counter:

I love you.[1]

That little "1" complicates the meaning of this otherwise earnest declaration utterly and completely, suggesting fine print to follow. Perhaps it comes with an expiration date or a caveat emptor like [1 when you wash the car]. Paired with the footnote, the three-word sentiment is more likely to elicit anger or incredulity than appreciation and affection. Or picture yourself reading a well-loved children's story aloud to your favorite toddler and suddenly coming upon a series of such notes challenging the math of Dr. Seuss's *One Fish, Two Fish, Red Fish, Blue Fish*. Narrative-minded public writers balk at parenthetic citations more than most, arguing persuasively that the last names of scholars in parentheses can feel almost parasitic, sucking the life blood from the story arc and ruining the pleasant bubble made by readers who give themselves fully to the tale being told.

The truth is, even professors who publish books with university presses these days seldom use in-text parenthetic citations when they submit their manuscripts. When publishing their work in daily newspapers and glossy magazines public scholars typically adhere to Associated Press (AP), while other intellectually-minded weekly, monthly, or quarterly magazines and journals often subscribe to a slightly modified version of the *Chicago Manual of Style (CMS)*. Most university press publications, whether books or journals, follow *CMS*, which means that no matter what their discipline, the writer-scholar will almost certainly be asked to abandon in-text parenthetic citations for footnotes (typically found at the bottom or the "footer" of the page), or, more commonly, endnotes (bibliographic entries at the end of a chapter or a book). Both footnotes and endnotes use superscript numerals to pinpoint specific places within the text where the author wishes to cite their sources. Such note systems are sufficiently effective at signposting the intellectual property of others that they are now ubiquitous in most works of popular scholarship.

Still, in papers, articles, or chapters where public intellectuals deal with a density of disparate sources, even the superscript notes prescribed by Chicago style quickly become cumbersome and distracting, cluttering the page and adding profit-killing heft and length to the "Notes" section in the book's back matter. I'm almost ashamed to admit that a book of popular history I once wrote contained nearly eight hundred endnotes in a volume whose text totaled roughly 450 manuscript pages. That density of citation—two notes per double-spaced page on average—isn't at all unusual in closely researched narrative history, but it's an example of how a lengthy work that draws heavily on primary and secondary sources soon grows by accretion to the point of unwieldiness. Even public scholars who aspire to keep notes to a minimum in deference to publisher wishes now routinely generate notes sections as long or longer than their books' most substantive chapters. In this book, I've endeavored to do better, eliminating the use of *Ibid.*, citing individual books only on first mention and with full bibliographic data, and avoiding multiple citations of the same text within the same chapter. These choices help me reduce the total number of endnotes from approximately 150 to 130 for a decrease of about fifteen percent.

Another way to combat citation creep in volumes that do not rely heavily on the intellectual property of others is employed by Gladwell in *Outliers*. So long as the author follows standard journalistic practice, attributing sources using author names and relevant book or article titles, (i.e., "According to psychologist Roger Barnsley's article 'Family Planning'") the notes section at the end of the book can be condensed. For example, after introducing us to Barnsley's work on the Relative Age Effect in the narrative, Gladwell's corresponding bibliographic entry in the notes section in the book's back matter reads:

> Barnsley and his team branched into other sports. See R. Barnsley and A. H. Thompson and Phillipe Legault, "Family planning: Football Style: The Relative Age Effect in Football," published in *International Review for the Sociology of Sport 27*, no. 1. (1992): 77–78.

While the bibliographic portion of the entry above closely resembles the citation template prescribed by the *Chicago Manual of Style*, Gladwell's notes section clearly follows an internal or "house" style guide specific to his trade publisher. Outside of the hallowed halls of academe, the key is not so much that your citations slavishly follow an academic style guide, but that a fellow writer, researcher, or reader fact-checking your work possesses sufficient bibliographic information to locate your sources expeditiously.

Other public writers and publishers wishing to avoid the *Chicago Manual of Style* endnotes system sometimes signpost back-matter citations using the page number followed by a short snippet of sample text used to locate the precise point to be attributed or credited. Larson uses this alternate system in *Devil in the White City*, where a typical entry in the notes section for Chapter 1, "The Black City," looks like this:

> 11. *"Never before*: Miller, 511.
> 11. *"The parlors and bedrooms:* Ibid., 516.

The "11" preceding each entry in Larson's modified citation can easily cause a writer accustomed to the *Chicago Manual of Style* to do a doubletake, as it looks like a duplication or a flat-out mistake. In the traditional endnotes system, the number at the far left is unique, as citations are numbered chronologically beginning with 1. In Larson's modified style the "11" on the left margin references the page number on which the identifying snippet of text ("Never before . . ." or "The parlors and the bedrooms") appears. "Miller" is the last name of the author, and "511" and "516" on the far right reference the page number in Miller's book where the cited material is found. Typically the complete bibliographic information for Miller's book would be listed completely on first mention, with "Ibid." (short for the Latin *ibidem* meaning "in the same place') used thereafter to indicate that the source is the same as the previous citation. Fortunately, elsewhere in the back matter Larson offers a comprehensive bibliography by which we can easily deduce that the Miller referred to in the endnote is Donald L. Miller, author of the book *City of the Century*, published by Simon & Schuster in 1996. The publisher's modified citation system works; we have successfully followed the bibliographic shorthand to the source.

Larson prefaces his notes section with an increasingly common disclaimer, one in which the public scholar announces their sincere intention to keep citations to a minimum. The author writes, "I have tried to keep my citations as concise as possible. I cite all quoted or controversial material but omit citation for commonly known facts that are widely known or accepted . . . . The citations that follow constitute a map. Anyone retracing my steps ought to reach the same conclusions as I." Larson's combination of a pared down notes section coupled with a generous bibliography is the method of choice for most publishers of book-length public writing. While it's natural for authors to make the case that one or the other—a notes *or* bibliography section—is enough, the two in combination are seen as ideal for scholarly content, as both back-matter sections perform a slightly different function. The notes section allows public writers to reference cited work at the exact point of its usage in the text, while the bibliography records the sources read and consulted in the researching and writing of the book, whether or not those sources are formally cited in the body of the book or article. For lengthy works that require the author to read hundreds of sources, a "selected bibliography" highlighting only the most significant works consulted is a welcome gesture of concision.

Public writers in doubt about how best to cite sources should check with their editor, who will very often refer them to the house style guide for recommended templates and frequently asked style questions. The *Chicago Manual of Style* is a fount of information for most other questions, no matter how peculiar, particular, or persnickety. Most public intellectuals consider the *CMS* a kind of Bible of the publishing industry, and most keep a copy within reach as they prepare their work for submission or publication. The University of Chicago Press also makes an abbreviated online guide available free of charge, including the most basic templates for endnotes and bibliographies, as well as a growing user Q & A database.

Still a complete unabridged copy of the *CMS* is worth its weight in gold. Once you've experienced for yourself the wealth of specifics it contains, you'll feel ill-prepared editing a manuscript without it. As you typeset the end matter for your first (or next) book of popular scholarship, for example, the *CMS* will tell you, when inevitably you forget, in what order your back matter should appear. Does the notes section come before the bibliography, or is it the other way around? If the acknowledgments page is to be placed in the back matter, does it appear before the subject index or after? What about the About the Author section, if there is one? Should there be an index? The *CMS* provides reliable answers to these and countless other questions. As most writers are also avid readers and bibliophiles, it's easy to assume that we know by heart the order of items in a book, but when it comes time to make for ourselves what others have previously cooked up for us, it's comforting to have an exhaustive recipe book near at hand.

Regardless of which style guide you employ, attributing your sources by first and last name on first mention in the body of the text (and last name thereafter) and, where appropriate, the name of the chapter, book, study, article, or report under discussion is good practice. Getting into the habit of weaving journalistic attributions into the sentence itself not only forces the public writer to better integrate their sources into a syntactical flow, it also ensures that the characters upon which our narratives depend are given a shout-out where they can live, and breathe, and act: right there in the heart of the chapter.

WRAPPING UP

Whether we choose to deploy it a little, a lot, or not at all, narrative writing should be an arrow in the quiver of every public writer aspiring to reach the widest possible audience. Character begets plot, and plot is a sequence of cause-and-effect events put into motion by a core conflict, complication, or question. Finding the narrative in our chosen topic helps combat the sort of lifeless expository writing that fails to connect with non-specialist readers. While the public intellectual may also be a character in the story they tell, narrative writing does not require use of the first-person pronoun and prescribes no fictionalizing. Instead "I" and "we" are deployed selectively to highlight an author's personal experience with the topic while underscoring ways in which the topic at hand impacts individuals personally. The "I" pronoun can help even the most erudite public intellectuals relay relevant aspects of their autobiography and explain the forces that help shape their perspective. For example, learning that neuropsychologist author Daniel Levitin was a 1970s rocker helps reassure readers of *This Is Your Brain on Music* that he understands and respects the artistic mind as well as the scientific method.

Nonfiction storytelling is not exempt from the rules governing citation and attribution, though increasingly it seeks to reduce citation creep. In-sentence journalistic attributions will prove sufficient for many public writers penning pieces for the popular press—newspapers, magazines, online news sites—while unobtrusive endnotes and other *Chicago Manual of Style*-based citation methods may be ideal for scholarly articles, chapters, and books published by academic and university presses.

5 Writing Like We Teach

Whether or not we teach for our day-job, most of us teach on a daily basis. We teach our children how to brush their teeth and to mow the lawn. We train our coworkers in new procedures and best practices. We teach community members new skills that stand to make them more safe, economically secure, and self-reliant. Sometimes we even succeed in teaching ourselves new tricks. If you've done any teaching at all in your life, you know that teachers invest in helping others achieve better outcomes. That instinct comes naturally to most educators, whether they're instructing an auto-mechanics class at the local community college or volunteering to teach Sunday school.

Like teachers, public writers hope to improve the lives of others by sharing what they know, what they've researched, and what has been shared with them in the past that made their lives that much richer. In the days of pocket protectors and old-fashioned card catalogs, many educators exclusively talked at (or down) to their students, the unwashed masses needing top-down edification. But just as teachers evolve, change, and update their teaching methods, so public writers change alongside them. The new public writer, like the new teacher, approaches learning differently than the lecturers of old, creating a conversation among learners while including them in shared solutions and collaborative breakthroughs.

RULES OF ENGAGEMENT: INTERROGATIVES, IMPERATIVES, AND HORTATIVES

Not long ago I was kvetching with an old friend who knows all too well the occupational hazards of befriending a pedagogue. Teachers are prone to lecture, and lecturers, lord knows, don't always make the most reciprocity-minded conversational partners. After patiently listening to me pontificate for what must have been ten minutes, my friend looked me squarely in the eye and said, "Okay, are you ready to ask me a question now?"

Ouch.

How easily we teachers standing at our bully pulpit forget our responsibility to engage in earnest inquiry alongside those willing to lend an ear to our bloviations. For many of us, breaking the lecture habit can be as simple as recalling a time when an interest in our fellow human beings trumped our need to convey information or teach a necessary skill. If that memory experiment fails to produce the requisite humility, perhaps a vexing home improvement quandary or difficult do-it-yourself project will find us penitent at our local hardware store, fully humbled and ready to ask questions of others.

Before I was a professor and a public writer I was a newspaper section editor with an innate love of, and interest in, people and what made them tick. I positively reveled in posing interviewees sincere questions, learning to construct my stories based as much on their public answers as my own private conclusions. Conducting hundreds if not thousands of interviews over a period of years, I learned that people generally like to be queried for their view or their experience, so long as the queries aren't of the gotcha or privacy-invading kind, and the more earnest the question the better. As a cub reporter my first assignment was to interview the widow of a young man recently deceased from Lyme's Disease. It was a heartbreaking story to report, and I can only imagine how the interview in that darkened, still-grieving house might have gone had I led with something flippantly rhetorical—"You must be feeling pretty bad, huh?"—or audaciously self-serving—"So, what's the scoop?"

Many naturally curious writers have had the questions drilled out of them by well-meaning teachers who preferred decided declarations to open-minded interrogatives. Too often, as the expert writing the paper, we are expected to assert and to declare. To ask a question is to show uncertainty, or an unwillingness to offer answers to the issues raised. So it is that when many of us write serious pieces, we issue statements rapid-fire as if pausing for an instant would render us vulnerable to attack or as if asking a question would make us seem wishy-washy or mealy-mouthed.

So, what can a question do that a statement cannot? Writing for *Fast Company* writer David Hoffeld answers that question in his article "Want to Know What Your Brain Does When It Hears a Question?" Hoffeld begins:

> What color is your house?

After reading that question, what were you thinking about? The obvious answer is the color of your house. Though this exercise may seem ordinary, it has profound implications. The question momentarily hijacked your thought process and focused it entirely on your house or apartment. You didn't consciously tell your brain to think about that; it just did so automatically.

Questions are powerful. Not only does hearing a question affect what our brains do in that instant, it can also shape our future behavior. And that can be a powerful principle in the workplace.[1]

Questions "hijack the brain," Hoffeld reminds us. They challenge our existing notions and complacencies, productively disturbing our certainty while opening us up to new learning. Moreover, they demonstrate the writer's interest in the reader, and signal their openness to reciprocal or symbiotic engagement wherein knowledge, interest, and concern flow both ways. Socrates, master practitioner of the eponymous Socratic method, believed that merely asking the right questions unlocked answers already hidden within us.

Questions galvanize readers as few other techniques can, stimulating our thinking while begging us to consider how our lives might change upon answering them. Skillful marketers in the publishing industry routinely use questions to engage would-be book-buyers and to advertise the valuable takeaways a reader can expect to find between the covers. Consider the editorial description on the back cover of the paperback edition of Harvard psychologist Daniel Gilbert's best-selling book of public scholarship *Stumbling on Happiness*. Even a cursory glance at the back jacket piques my interest via its provocative queries, including, among many others, "Why are lovers quicker to forgive their partners for infidelity than for leaving dirty dishes in the sink?" and "Why do dining companions insist on ordering different meals instead of getting what they really want?" Gilbert even promises to answer the imponderable, "Why do pigeons seem to have such excellent aim?" Most readers will be able to infer from Gilbert's academic expertise in social psychology, and the subject of the book itself—the

1. David Hoffeld, "Want to Know What Your Brain Does When It Hears a Question," *Fast Company*, February 21, 2017, https://www.fastcompany. com/3068341/want-to-know-what-your-brain-does-when-it-hears-a-question.

science of happiness—that the answer to the pigeon riddle hinges on individual perception. If we assume the winged rat is out to get us, then we have amassed another data point adding up to our existential unluckiness. Happier souls, meanwhile, are probably more likely to chalk up the cosmic accident to a statistical blip and continue on their merry way. The particular questions Gilbert and his book marketers chose to highlight are perfect because (a) they're relatable, (b) We've almost certainly experienced them before (who among us has never been so targeted by a bird?), and (c) it's possible to see at a glance how the book will follow through on its promise and answer the questions it poses to our delight and edification.

Hey, You

The second-person "you" is another favorite bugaboo for generations of schoolteachers, their collective disdain nearly sufficient at times to render its use extinct in formal reports and papers. Granted, any discussion of "you" must first acknowledge its liabilities, bringing us face to face with the very weaknesses that caused pedants of yore to treat it like the devil's own pronoun. First, *you* can be awfully presumptuous. In the sentence "You walk into a store and you feel all eyes on you," the writer presumes that the reader's experience has been the same as their own, though the reader may never have felt such unsolicited scrutiny. *You* also strikes formalists as a bit too informal a pronoun case, like saying "you guys," when what is meant is "esteemed members of the jury."

However, for all its liabilities, *you*, and the second-person possessive *your*, show up frequently in the work of accomplished public writers, including in Hoffeld's opening sentence above: "What color is your house?" In his second sentence he continues, "After reading the question, what are you thinking about?" The *you* in question is, of course, us. In this case and in others, *you* is a natural outgrowth of the conversation public intellectuals seek to simulate on the page, suggesting conversational rapport and, thereby, interest and empathy. *You*, not *he* or *she*, is the pronoun of choice when we sit down to dish, divulge, debate, and discuss in public. "Tell me how you're doing . . . . How'd your day go . . . . Are you ready to get out of Dodge?" In the twenty-first century, newly conversational teachers stop routinely to ask their students, "So . . . what do you think?"

IMPERATIVES AND HORTATIVES

Many serious-minded public intellectuals exist on a steady diet of declarative sentences the way college students of old existed on ramen noodles. In serious or scholarly work, the indicative mood rules the roost, since a declarative sentence makes a statement, gives an explanation, conveys a fact, or provides information. By contrast, an imperative issues a command, lending it something of a bad reputation. Few of us enjoy receiving directives, and even fewer of us choose to follow them—a frequent lament in teachers' lounges and faculty break rooms everywhere. We don't like to be told what to do, and especially so when the command is followed by an exclamation point.

Thankfully, the imperative serves a different function in public writing, where the kinds of commands issued to interested readers can be as gentle as "Think about it" "or "Consider." Often public writers, like teachers, turn to hortatives, from the Latin *hortari* meaning "to exhort" or "to urge." Hortatives encourage the reader to take action along with the writer or speaker. Even linguists lose their way in the exact difference between hortatives and imperatives, but most agree that an imperative issues an immediate or essential command, as if an exclaimation ("Look out!" or "Sit down!"), whereas the hortative urges further deliberation or action, as in "Try this," "Consider," or "Let's move on." In most cases the hortative, rather than the imperative, is more appropriate for public writing, where the modality is most often recognized by the verb "Let's" as in "Let us." Note that the implied subject in the hortative, like the imperative, is the second-person pronoun "you," making the hortative modality, like the second-person pronoun itself, an important marker of a kind of reader-focused, reader-friendly writing in which the "you" on the other end truly matters.

Public writer Daniel H. Pink is a master of such writer-reader rapport, engendering a conversation even as he teaches. In *Drive: The Surprising Truth About What Motivates Us*, Pink hopes to show the role intrinsic motivation plays in creating and maintaining crowd-sourced or open-sourced applications like Wikipedia. He writes:

> Fire up your home computer, for example. When you visit the Web to check the weather forecast or order some sneakers, you might be using Firefox, a free open-source Web browser created almost exclusively by volunteers. Unpaid laborers who

give away their product? That couldn't be sustainable. The incentives are wrong. Yet Firefox now has 150 million users.[2]

How does Pink manage to convey information on a serious subject while still sounding so off-the-cuff conversational? The answer lies in his use of a full palette of teacherly techniques, ranging from his use of the imperative (*Fire up* your home computer), to his use of the second-person (When *you* visit the Web . . ."), to his incorporation of interrogatives to acknowledge the questions readers are likely to have even as they're having them ("Unpaid laborers who give away their product?"). It's as if Pink has simulated a conversation between several different people in one short paragraph in which his is nevertheless the only voice.

ADDITIONAL TEACHERLY TECHNIQUES

Quiz Yourself

What else do the skills of effective public writers and effective teachers have in common? Thus far we've seen how merely asking your reader questions hijacks the brain in the best sense. But good teachers go beyond facile questioning to engage their audiences in more difficult problems, puzzles, and conundrums. Good teachers understand that sometimes learners learn most when they're forced to grapple with a problem or data set rather than being spoon-fed or force-fed answers. The diagnostic quizzes found in many check-out aisle glossy magazines (the type with the answers printed upside down at the bottom of the pages) serve a similar rhetorical purpose. Intellectuals may look down their collective noses at *Cosmo*-styled reader quizzes, but such self-diagnostics do more to engage the leisure reader in a task relevant to their life than just about anything else on the printed page.

In her bestselling book of public writing *Quiet: The Power of Introverts in a World That Can't Stop Talking*, Susan Cain wastes little time in engaging us on the value of introspection. She attempts to earn our buy-in in the introduction, where she invites readers to answer "true" or "false" to twenty questions, including, among others:

1. ___ I prefer one-on-one conversations to group activities

---

2. Daniel H. Pink, *Drive: The Surprising Truth About What Motivates Us* (New York: Riverhead, 2009), 22.

2. ____ I often prefer to express myself in writing

3. ____ I enjoy solitude

4. ____ I seem to care less than my peers about wealth, fame, and status

5. ____ I dislike small talk, but I enjoy talking in depth about topics . . .[3]

It's hard not to be sucked into Cain's quiz. It's quick, easy, and self-revealing. The last time I took such an introversion/extroversion survey I was a student. I remember testing as only the mildest of introverts back then, perhaps explaining how I summon the chutzpah to lead writing workshops now. Years later, though, I find myself answering "True," to the majority of Cain's diagnostics, suggesting that I've potentially grown a bit more introverted in the interim. While I may have begun Cain's book uncertain as to whether or not its focus on introversion would speak to me directly, by the time I've completed the quiz questions on page 13 I *know* that it does. That's the power of a brief yet targeted exam: to puncture the readers' false or misguided notions about themselves and replace them with something closer to an objective, undeniable truth.

Develop a Scenario

Engagement-minded public writers often find it helpful to develop scenarios for readers. In *Drive*, for example, Pink stops periodically to elaborate a kind of how-would-you-solve-this-problem thought experiment. This isn't self-help writing but, like a break-out group in a conference workshop with a puzzle or problem to solve, an attempt to engage thoughtful participants in finding their own answers. Pink writes:

> For a quick test of problem-solving prowess, few exercises are more useful than the "candle problem." Devised by psychologist Karl Duncker in the 1930s, the candle problem is used in a wide variety of experiments in behavioral science. Follow along and see how you do.

---

3. Susan Cain, *Quiet: The Power of Introverts in a World That Can't Stop Talking* (New York: Crown 2011), 13.

You sit at a table next to a wooden wall and the experiment gives you the materials shown below: a candle, some tacks, and a book of matches. Your job is to attach the candle to the wall so that the wax doesn't drip on the table. Think for a moment about how you'd solve the problem."

Next the author shares a black-and-white illustration of the set-up he describes in the passage, allowing us to place ourselves in the experiment. In so doing, he effectively recreates the set of experimental variables encountered by participants in Duncker's candle problem, giving us time to see how, and if, we would solve the conundrum. Only after a few hundred more words (and a second illustration) does Pink provide the answer to the creativity test: empty the tacks from the box, put the candle in the empty box, and tack the box to the wall. The difficulty inherent in this conceptual experiment, the author asserts, speaks to our tendency toward "functional fixedness"—thinking "inside the box," rather than outside of it.

Just as it's difficult for experts to slow down and ask sincere questions of the individuals they are otherwise prone to lecture, finding relevant scenarios to engage readers in useful problem-solving activities can sometimes feel like a chore to experts who already know their subject inside and out. Welcome to the world of teachers! Teachers spend hours reverse-engineering their existing knowledge, sometimes devising hands-on activities and experiments that will bring their students, slowly and deliberately, to the answers the educator has known for many years.

Admittedly, not every writer has room in his or her word budget for the kind of extended do-it-yourself scenario Pink provides over the space of several paragraphs. But through shorter thought-exercises, puzzles, and participatory prompts a similar level of engagement may be achieved in fewer words. In writing about Mihaly Csikzentmihalyi and his university of Chicago team of researchers, for example, Pink asks his readers bulleted questions about the ebb and flow of their personal motivation throughout the day, for example:

• Which moments produced feelings of "flow." Where were you? What were you working on? Who were you with?

While the candle-problem quiz took some 250 words to play out on the page, a series of bulleted queries like these take up a third of the space without any significant loss in reader engagement.

Social psychologist Jonathan Haidt uses a similar set of thought experiments and scenarios in *The Righteous Mind: Why Good People Are Divided by Politics and Religion,* opening his fourth chapter with the following scenario to pique the reader:

> Suppose the gods were to flip a coin on the day of your birth. Heads, you will be a supremely honest and fair person throughout your life, yet everyone around you will believe you're a scoundrel. Tails, you will cheat and lie whenever it suits your needs, yet everyone around you will believe you're a paragon of virtue. Which outcome would you prefer?[4]

Elsewhere in his thought-provoking book Haidt, like Pink, allows us to try our hand at some of social psychology's most relevant and revealing experiments, ranging from the Muller-Lyon illusion, to the Watson 4-card task, to the Necker Cube—all tricky visual puzzles undertaken by subjects whose results help scientists better understand perception.

In *Stumbling on Happiness*, Gilbert manages an even more difficult sleight of hand, simultaneously demonstrating how a classic bit of "magic" works while at the same time showing us how we fail to remember difference, which, as it turns out, makes us unreliable reporters of our own happiness. Gilbert shows us five face cards from a deck and asks us to pick a favorite, promising us that he will be able predict our choice. He delays the Reveal for five or six more pages, only to claim—wonder of wonders—that he knows our favorite and that he will subsequently remove our choice from the deck of six. The author fully embraces the role of magician, writing:

> A few pages back you chose from a group of six. What I didn't tell you at the time was that I have powers far beyond mortal men, and therefore I knew which card you were going to pick before you picked it. To prove it, I have removed your card from the group. Take a look at figure 5 and tell me I'm not amazing. How did I do it?[5]

Shortly thereafter the trick is revealed. Our favorite is missing from the deck because the second deck is fractionally different; none of the original cards are present, though the faces on the cards are the same.

---

4. Jonathan Haidt, *The Righteous Mind: Why Good People Are Divided by Politics and Religion* (New York: Vintage, 2012), 84.
5. Daniel Gilbert, *Stumbling on Happiness* (New York: Vintage, 2006), 48.

As Gilbert confesses, the ruse wouldn't work if we were shown both decks side by side. Instead he leaves the scenario for a few pages before returning to it. Because we're unable to compare the two decks on the same page, the switcheroo trick remains undetected. The scenario had to be developed, and delayed, for the riddle to properly register.

Characters and Case Studies

My dictionary offers two definitions for the term *case study*, a proven strategy educators (and didactic writers seeking to teach) use to get their points across. A case study is defined as:

1. A process or record of research in which detailed consideration is given to the development of a particular person, group, or situation over a period of time.

2. A particular instance of something used or analyzed in order to illustrate a thesis or principle.

Case studies enact a welcome winnowing effect, taking a phenomenon that can seem impossibly big and helpfully reducing it to a microcosm that exemplifies the larger pattern. Case studies come in all kinds and are used in many academic disciplines, so useful are they for controlling a topic and managing its scope. In his *New York Times* bestselling book *Moonwalking with Einstein: The Art and Science of Remembering Everything*, Joshua Foer examines the unique blessing and burden of near-perfect memory, sharing the case study of a man with a famously flawless memory: a journalist called "S," who's "the man" in the chapter title "The Man Who Remembered Too Much." Foer introduces the character at the core of his case study in narrative fashion: "In May 1928, the young journalist S walked into the office of the Russian neuropsychologist A. R. Luria and politely asked to have his memory tested. He had been sent by his boss, the editor of the newspaper where he worked."[6] S's memory is so complete he can recite lists of up to seventy numbers forward and backward, memorize math formulae without knowing math, and memorize Italian poetry without being able to speak the language. Despite all these amazing feats of recollection, the most remarkable thing about S—the thing that makes this case study resonant in the annals of abnormal psychology, is, as Foer

---

6. Joshua Foer, *Moonwalking with Einstein: The Art and Science of Remembering Everything* (New York: Penguin, 2011), 21.

puts it, "the fact that his memories seemed never to degrade." A patient teacher, the author has taken close to three full pages to develop a case study that illustrates the scientific premise he is about to tackle at length: the degradation of memory and the "curve of forgetting" operant in the memories of most normal humans. Had Foer done the opposite, begun with the graphs, tables, and hard science of the curve of forgetting, he would surely have lost many of his listeners/readers. In short, he wouldn't have been a very effective teacher. Later, Foer will offer another case study with an exemplary character at its center; a man named "EP," known for being "The Most Forgetful Man in the World." EP's memory is all but absent, encompassing only his most recent thought, making him, the author tells us, "one of the most severe cases of amnesia ever documented."

Sometimes a single case study serves as the touchstone for an entire article or book of public scholarship. Such is the case with Jared Diamond's Pulitzer Prize-winning *Gun, Germs, and Steel: The Fates of Human Society.* In the prologue Diamond, a professor of geography at UCLA, articulates his research question, namely which factors explain the vast historical inequalities between literate societies with metal tools and less literate hunter-gatherer peoples. That's the sort of Big Question educators love to hear their students pose, and public writers love their readers to entertain, but one whose scope is far too big for a lesson plan or short article. It's left for Diamond to find a character, and a case study, capable of embodying his big question. He recollects a man named Yali whom he met in in Papua New Guinea in the early 1970s. The resonant question Yali poses Diamond—"Why is it that you white people developed so much cargo, but we black people had little cargo of our own?"—becomes the impetus for the scholar's book.[7] The query, referred to in shorthand as "Yali's Question," cuts straight to the big mystery of human history—the origins of global inequality.

Story "Problems"

How often in our lives as learners have we been asked to solve what in elementary school we might have called "story problems"? For most of us the answer is often; in fact, virtually every standardized exam we've ever taken grafts interesting problems and questions onto narrative.

---

7. Jarod Diamond, *Gun, Germs, and Steel: The Fates of Human Society* (New York: W.W. Norton, 1999), 14.

Story problems encourage us to apply our theoretical knowledge to real-world contexts. In his chapter "The Rise and Fall of Motivation 2.0," Pink provides us with a story problem, too, though one that requires no particular mathematical acumen to solve, and one that he sustains longer than, for example, a shorter narrative scenario like the Duncker candle problem. This longer "story problem" begins:

> Imagine it's 1995. You sit down with an economist—an accomplished business school professor with a PhD in economics. You say to her: "I've got a crystal ball here that can peer fifteen years into the future. I'd like to test your forecasting powers."

Pink expertly deploys imperatives ("Imagine") and second-person pronouns to develop a mini-narrative complete with character and dialogue. The "you" in the passage, who serves as a proxy for us, the reader, continues the presentation for several paragraphs of dialogue, first presenting a traditional encyclopedia on compact disc followed by a second option, an online encyclopedia to be made by "a ragtag band of volunteers," and "hobbyists." Pink picks up the narrative throughline here:

> "Now," you say to the economist, "think forward fifteen years. According to my crystal ball, in 2010, one of these encyclopedias will be the largest and most popular in the world and the other will be defunct. Which is which?"

True to form, the story problem the author presents is a challenging one. In fact, it's the surprising or at least counterintuitive nature of the answer that stimulates our interest, knowing that the solution, once found, is likely to surprise and delight. In this case we learn that Wikipedia, the encyclopedia created almost entirely by volunteers, survived and thrived, surprising even the seasoned economists who predicted the crowd-sourced, crowd-funded reference would fizzle. The answer particularly pleases us if we're inclined to root for the underdog.

Callbacks

Another technique common to public writers and teachers alike is what my students and I have dubbed the *callback*—the referencing of prior knowledge to enhance learning via repetition. Educators use the callback every time they begin a lecture with "Yesterday we learned . . ." or a similar memory-jog. A callback rewards our attention, reminding us of the important knowledge we've garnered previously before segueing into what we can expect to study in the near future ("In today's lesson we'll be covering . . .").

Granted, the most efficient lessons maintain their forward momentum, moving forward briskly if not boldly. Yet, the most effective ones travel back periodically to touch on past progress, making education an iterative process. Callbacks can be as large as case studies returned to in the classic discursive fashion, which briefly and purposefully digresses from the main subject, argument, or narrative, only to return to it periodically thereafter. Callbacks can also happen in the smallest of spaces, including in single words that conjure a whole world of prior experience. Good friends, for instance, often use the callback strategy when they relive shared experiences. In referencing a mere word or two they manage to recollect days, months, or years of adventures together. For example, imagine that two of your best friends turn to one another and utter, in a somewhat conspiratorial tone: "One word: Vegas." For them, the mere mention of the glitzy desert city brings back a wave of memories. For Jared Diamond, reiterating the phrase "Yali's Question" takes us back to the core premise of the book as stated in the prologue.

Suppose I pause here to write:

> Remember Duncker's candle problem from earlier in this chapter? How did you solve it?

For most, a single mention of the candle problem will prove sufficient to call back previous information. Occasionally, memory triggers can be even more subtle, operating as if by analogy. For example, I might opine, "writing a textbook is an author's personal candle problem." Those familiar with Duncker's research would understand the analogy by context: the textbook author may have all the pieces, but now they must decide how best to put them together.

Analogies and Metaphors

Both teachers and public writers make liberal use of analogies to connect what audiences already know with something new yet analogous. Indeed, entire books of public writing have been founded on a metaphoric expression, such as Gladwell's *The Tipping Point*, which, by overarching analogy, examines "the moment of critical mass, the threshold, the boiling point."[8] On the back cover the ineffable "tip-ping point" is described as "that magic moment when an idea, trend, or social behavior crosses a threshold, tips, and spreads like wildfire." *The Tipping Point* is such an elusive concept, in fact, that three distinct metaphors are used in the prior quotation to explain it.

Experienced communicators turn to metaphor to explain especially tricky concepts, and those who use analogy go isolated uses of figu-rative language one better. Think of an analogy as a big metaphor under which smaller closely related metaphors nest. A good example is the oft-anthologized essay "Football Red, Baseball Green" by Mur-ray Ross. At pains to explain the underlying difference between two uniquely American sports, Ross deploys an umbrella analogy compar-ing football to war (archetypally Red) and baseball to the agrarian and pastoral (archetypally Green). The analogy may not be perfect, but it plays out in a series of metaphors within metaphors, nested like Rus-sian dolls. Once we accept the author's metaphoric premise: football = red = war, smaller metaphors cascade: if football is war, then the quar-terback is the general, the playbook is the plan of attack, the huddle is the battlefield meeting, and the play on the field is the battle itself.

Nick Saban, the celebrated coach of the University of Alabama's Crimson Tide football team, turns to sports analogy in an attempt to explain his life philosophy:

> Golf is a metaphor of life . . . . You have this beautiful hole, this beautiful opportunity to get a good score. You hit a beau-tiful drive. Well, I don't know how many times I've been 114 yards from the hole and made double bogey.
>
> Well, I hit a great drive, but it doesn't matter. It's only the next shot that matters. You could hit that in the water, which means now you have to overcome adversity. You put yourself in a hole, and it's, "Can I get up and down and still make bogey?" But that's how life is. Sometimes you don't control it. You don't control the negative things that happen. But you still have to overcome them. You still have to manage it. You still have to react the right way. It's not the problem. It's how you respond to the problem that is the key to the drill.[9]

8. Malcolm Gladwell, *The Tipping Point: How Little Things Can Make a Big Difference* (Boston: Back Bay Books, 2002), 12.
9. Chris Chaney, "Nick Saban: Golf Is a Metaphor for Life," *Swing U*, April 18, 2016, accessed October 15, 2019, https://golf.swingbyswing.com/life-

Via analogies the public writer effectively doubles the chance of reaching a reader. For example, a reader of Saban's interview may not care a lick for life philosophy or psychology or even football, but perhaps they know what it's like to hit a perfect drive in golf only to mess up an easy shot from the fairway. Conversely, a reader may hate golf, but love talking psychology or philosophy, so at least part of Saban's extended analogy works for them. Annie Murphy Paul, author of *The Key to Innovation: Making Smart Analogies*, explains the mechanics of how analogies work:

> A useful analogy reveals the deep commonalities beneath superficial differences. We can think of analogies as having two parts: the base and the target. The base is the thing you know about. The target is the thing that's new. Analogies are created by elaborating the similarities and the differences between the base and the target. When we use an analogy, we take what we know about the base and move some of it over to the target. Northwestern University psychologist Dedre Genter calls this process "bootstrapping the mind"—elevating ourselves into the realm of new knowledge, using the knowledge we have already to pull ourselves up.[10]

Given their shared talent for helping readers bootstrap to new knowledge, both teachers and public writers make liberal use of analogies in particular, and figurative language in general. Even a subject as difficult as brain science can be effectively illuminated via the use of metaphor as Harvard Med's John J. Ratey proves in his book *Spark: The Revolutionary New Science of Exercise and the Brain*. Ratey uses smaller metaphoric expressions throughout (Serotonin is "the policeman of the brain"; Glutamate is the "workhorse"; etc.), but his Big Metaphor portrays brain chemistry via an analogy to electrical circuitry. Early on he refers to neurotransmitters' role in maintaining "cell circuitry." The analogy is developed in subsequent pages, where synapses attract like magnets possessed of stronger voltages in their "resting state." Each of these single metaphors serves the larger analogy that makes the brain synonymous with a circuit. Several pages later the author concludes

style/nick-saban-golf-is-a-metaphor-for-life/.
10. Annie Murphy Paul, "The Key to Innovation: Making Smart Analogies," March 29, 2014, *Mindshift*, KQED, https://www.kqed.org/mindshift/34752/the-key-to-innovation-making-smart-analogies.

the section, writing "Far from being hardwired, as scientists once envisioned it, the brain is constantly being rewired. I'm here to teach you how to be your own electrician." Without committing early on to the development of the larger analogy, Ratey's conclusion wouldn't complete the circuit.

Sometimes analogies offer sufficient substance, and sustenance, to last an entire book. Asked to pen a preface to the paperback edition of *Guns, Germs, and Steel*, Jared Diamond leans on figurative language, titling his foreword "Why Is World History Like an Onion?" The answer: Diamond treats modern world history as surface, peeling back the layers all the way to the emergence of writing around 3000 B.C. while pointing out that the period from 3000 B.C. to the beginning of the human species represents ninety-nine percent of humanity's five-million-year history on earth.

Reenactments

The social studies and history teachers of my youth gloried in reenactments, coming alive when we would take field trips or role-play famous trials. On those days history positively lifted off the page to become tangible and real.

In reenactments and role-plays we were invited to walk in the footsteps of historical giants, feeling how they must have felt. I'm reminded that the first time I wore a tie came in Mr. Brown's tenth-grade government class, when I had the responsibility of role-playing a famous prosecutor of Nazi war crimes. (Mom tied my tie for me, and I slipped it around my neck so I could tighten it myself immediately before class.) The starring prosecutorial role helped me, a shy student, to gain confidence and poise. Already a pretty good close reader and a conscientious student, that single in-class exercise compelled me to grow more as an individual in a single day than a month's worth of teacher-centered lectures.

Public writers borrow from the playbook of dynamic educators when they breathe life into otherwise flat, two-dimensional subjects by embodying them. Reenactments on the page, like first-person role-playing games on the screen, give us agency, putting us in the driver's seat. Increasingly, popular museum exhibits do likewise, allowing both children and adults to relive and reenact historical events, whether that event is a grasshopper plague so thick it blocked out the sun or a stock market drop so steep it sent citizens scurrying to withdraw their life savings from the bank.

At some point, most American students have been put in the position of poor Harry Truman, the accidental president faced with the choice of whether to drop the atomic bomb on Hiroshima and Nagasaki, Japan, and end World War II through the use of a weapon of mass destruction, or to keep the all-powerful weapon in reserve only to risk the loss of tens or perhaps hundreds of thousands more troops in an invasion of Japan. History teachers have learned that the best way for students to understand Truman's awful predicament is to reenact the moment. Organizations such as the Constitutional Rights Foundation have turned to role-playing to help members of the public feel the full weight of the president's choice. They ask us to imagine ourselves as a member of the committee of advisers for President Truman, charged with debating the following options: (1) Continue the conventional bombings and blockade; (2) Demonstrate the atomic bomb; (3) Wait for the Russians; (4) Negotiate peace; (5) Keep the [Japanese] emperor; or (6) Use the atomic bombs.[11]

That's turning the bystander into an active learner, though, to be fair, the previous scenario still reads more like a lesson plan than language meant for a polished piece of public writing. Without much difficulty, however, the role-playing modality can be projected onto the page. Imagine a paragraph in a historical article that uses the second-person to turn an otherwise flat account into a walk-a-mile-in-their-shoes scenario like this one:

> You're the elected leader of the most powerful democracy on earth, and you face a dreadful choice. A new bomb in your arsenal packs the power to bring an entire enemy empire to its knees and to end an awful war of attrition that has cost your nation more than 400,000 lives. But dropping the new bomb means deaths of 200,000 or more in a single strike, the instant incineration of countless innocent civilians, and radiation so powerful its effects will linger for generations. Your cabinet members crowd around you, bickering amongst themselves, jockeying for your attention at an all-important historical moment. What do you do?

11. Constitutional Rights Foundation, "Choices: Truman, Hirohito, and the Atomic Bomb," accessed October 15, 2019, https://www.crf-usa.org/bill-of-rights-in-action/bria-15-3-b-choices-truman-hirohito-and-the-atomic-bomb.

Such role-plays on the page depend on stories for their ability to engage, and stories engender the narratives we're hardwired to receive. While text-based reenactments are not appropriate for all subject matter, public writers able to make the reader feel like a participant rather than a mere bystander are rewarded with greater engagement, attention, and enhanced learning.

TRICKSTER TEACHER TECHNIQUES

I don't remember much from my ninth grade English class beyond Mrs. Cook's righteous beehive and Dave Laughlin's leaning over to scratch his ankle every five minutes to check the crib sheet under his desk. But I do remember one day in particular. Mrs. Cook walked into class that day with an unusually distracted air; our normally ebullient teacher seemed troubled, and she opened with a solemn admission: she had just left a meeting in which the faculty had decided to "track" each and every student according to intelligence as measured by standardized test scores. "Smart" kids would exclusively take classes with other smart kids, mediocre pupils would be paired with other mediocres, and so on down the line. The dramatic announcement from our earnest teacher sent shock waves rippling through us, as we glanced anxiously around the room, wondering which of our friends we would be separated from when the tracking commenced. Mrs. Cook duly abandoned her lesson plan, and for the remainder of the hour we just talked—debating the ethics of the worrisome agenda. When the hour was nearly up, the beatific Mrs. Cook announced that there was no such proposal.

We had been duped!

But duped for an educative purpose. Educational tracking in all its various guises, from Honors programs to A.P. English, was only then gaining a foothold in our district, and she wanted us to share our opinions on the developing trend—opinions we doubtless would have withheld had we not been fooled into thinking we might be separated from our best friends forever.

As Mrs. Cook reminds, teachers reserve the right to play mischievous imp or court jester for educational purposes. My father, who attended two years of college in the late 1960s before dropping out to help my grandfather farm, often recalled an episode in his first-year psychology class when someone—a protestor perhaps—burst through the door of the lecture hall. The interloper shouted angrily at the assembled students, grabbed the American flag from the pole where it hung near the lectern, and left through the same door from whence he had come, this time with the purloined stars and bars stashed beneath his arms. The professor was deeply disturbed and asked my father and the other students if they could write down what they had just seen. Then, when Dad and his classmates compared notes to find they had radically different notions of the event, the cagey professor revealed that he had contrived the whole classroom-crashing incident as an experiment in the unreliability of eyewitness reports.

When individual figures we associate with earnest candor and solemn authority trick us, the object of the lesson sticks with us forever. Similarly, public writers who throw their reader a curve ball benefit from a bump in memory, retention, and engagement. Perhaps we lead our reader one way, then reverse course suddenly and lead them another. Perhaps we catch them out in a false assumption or presumption, pulling the rug out from under their preconceived notions. Sometimes we pull the proverbial wool over their eyes. In any case, the sudden shift leaves us in a state of suspension, of vertigo. As we struggle to get our feet back under us, endeavoring to replace a broken set of assumptions, or repair a faulty scaffolding, our learning curve shoots through the roof.

Fiction writers readily beget plots twists, but how do public writers pull an educative fast one on readers? Sometimes the trick happens via misdirection; a Gladwellian move whereby the script is flipped or the paradigm shifted. Remember Barnsley and the Canadian junior hockey league example? Early on, Gladwell writes "Success in hockey is based on individual merit . . . Players are judged on their own performance, not on anyone else's, and on the basis of their ability, not on some other arbitrary fact." The certainty of the author's assertions, seemingly gathering more surety and credibility as they're stacked one on top of the other, finds us nodding our heads in agreement, until Gladwell pivots in this dramatic single-sentence paragraph:

"Or are they?"

Every time I see a talented author pull off such an artful misdirection a dramatic "don, don, don" soundtrack plays in my mind. In the work of the most successful public writers, the misdirection technique has become familiar enough that writers have begun to use it with an even greater degree of meta-awareness of the cat-and-mouse game they're playing. In *Stumbling on Happiness*, Gilbert raises the misdirection ploy to a whole new level. Having introduced the notion that many are unreliable reporters of their own happiness, Gilbert titillates us by teasing a revelation yet to come ("Yes, and you'll find one in the mirror. Read on.")

But wait, there's more. After exhorting us to "Read on," Gilbert unexpectedly plays with our expectations once again in cat-and-mouse fashion. The next paragraph reads:

> Before you read on, I challenge you to stop and have a nice long look at your thumb. Now, I will wager that you did not accept my challenge. I will wager that you went right on reading because looking at your thumb is so easy that it makes for rather pointless sport—everyone bats a thousand and the game is called on account of boredom.

Gilbert manifests his trickster teaching persona here, being playful while gleefully performing as provocateur. One imagines he writes with the same, or similar, voice he uses while lecturing to his social psychology students at Harvard. And his engaged teacher voice is probably very similar to the one he might use delivering a TEDx talk, an oral presentation to colleagues (though in that instance he would no doubt use more jargon), or a speech to patrons at the local public library. These are all profoundly public venues where it's important for public intellectuals to be their most down-to-earth selves, talking informally, and establishing a rapport. And for the same reason that we often tell jokes to begin speeches—what is a joke, after all, but an initial misdirection climaxing with a resonant circling back we call the punchline—Gilbert occasionally plays the role of the trickster in his serious nonfiction. Note, however, that he doesn't wear that mask for long, which might undermine the seriousness of the more academic points he hopes to make. In fact, he abandons the bait-and-switch later in that same paragraph when he segues into a more scientific discussion of perception and cognition.

In *Quiet*, Susan Cain plays a different, though no less memorable trick, beginning her book with an extended case study of a young attorney named Laura who, in discovering her introversion, decides she should embrace it in difficult negotiations, quietly asking questions rather than playing the role of the bully. We learn a lot about Laura in the book's opening pages, following her through several career changes and epiphanies until we feel like we know her. That's when Cain admits to her educative sleight of hand in an adroit callback:

> If there is only one insight you take away from this book though, I hope it's a newfound sense of entitlement to be yourself. I can vouch personally for the life-transforming effects of this outlook. Remember that first client I told you about, the one I called Laura in order to protect her identity?
> That was a story about me. I was my own first client.

Don-don-don! The rhetorically tricky writer does it again, flipping the script in a way we won't soon forget. Perhaps the saying shouldn't be, "Fool me once, shame on you. Fool me twice, shame on me," but this instead: "Fool me once, and I'll remember what you say forever."

WRAPPING UP

Public writers and engaged teachers share an educative spirit as well as a set of proven techniques to engage learners. Given limited space and time, the most efficient way to communicate information is nearly always to tell, in lecture fashion, rather than to show. However, no matter how efficient the telling/lecture mode may be, it sometimes backfires, hindering engagement for participants who are hands-on, trial-and-error learners. Savvy writers and teachers learn to treat learning as a cumulative, iterative process that unfolds organically over time, via a provocative mix of statement, question, and directive. Where possible, engagement-minded public writers and teachers seek to provide real agency to learners, encouraging them to test the concepts under discussion for themselves. Sometimes that test consists of reprising an experiment, answering a series of questions, or completing a self-reflexive diagnostic. At other times, engagement occurs in the form of a role-play, reenactment, first- or second-person case study, script, or scenario adapted to the page. Especially crafty writers and teachers may even try a purposeful ruse, misdirection, or educative "white lie" meant to be sussed out by attentive learners. In each instance the learner emerges having interacted with the material in ways that cement deep learning.

6 Crafting Personal Commentaries

Many of my workshop participants are drawn to the idea of sharing their personal experience in newspapers or magazines. Usually, about a quarter of the aspiring public writers in any given group have at least written a letter to the editor. Many report being moved to write by something in the news that intersected powerfully with events in their own lives.

The letter to the editor serves as an important impetus for public writers, but it's limited as a genre in ways most influence-seeking writers find frustrating. Publications often cap letters to the editor at around two hundred words; others insist that the writer include their city of residence or email address, personal details that scare away privacy-minded contributors who nevertheless have something urgent to say. Most periodicals strongly prefer that letters to the editor be just that—a response to a piece that has appeared previously in their publication, effectively barring writers from setting their own agenda.

By contrast, personal commentary encourages writers to use their life experiences as anecdotal evidence to build a case for what they want readers to think, know, or believe. The most popular example of the personal or first-person commentary is sufficiently iconic as to have become synonymous with the genre itself: "My Turn." *Newsweek's* pioneering first-person public writing platform epitomizes the advent of a genre that foreshadowed blogs, citizen journalism, and many other related forms of public writing we'll discuss later in this book.

In the early 1970s, "My Turn" invested itself in what was then a radical concept: encouraging public writers to react to events through the lens of their own personal experience. Since the first column in November of 1972, in which journalist and cultural critic Bill Moyers lambasts President Richard Nixon for his insularity from the American people, "My Turn" has embodied the tagline "a personal page of commentary." Well over a thousand writers have bravely taken their turn.

"My Turn" and its ilk have been a boon for those looking to put personal and public selves into productive dialogue. The Irish poet W.

B. Yeats once wrote, "Out of the quarrel with others we make rhetoric; out of the quarrel with ourselves we make poetry." If so, first-person commentaries amount to a kind of personal poetry in prose written for a broader public, for in first-person commentaries we quarrel with ourselves as we broach larger societal issues of interest to others.

Many public writers yearn to share their poignant personal stories with the wider world, though that desire feels consistently thwarted. Many established professionals are afraid that delving into their personal lives and pasts will damage their business, their brand, or both. One of my most talented workshop participants of recent years enrolled after beginning a successful kettlebells business. For those who aren't familiar, kettlebells are cast-iron strength-training devices held in the hands, and my workshop participant had all but mastered them, placing as a top national finisher in multiple competitions. Lately they had made a business of helping others discover the sport as a vehicle for improved physical fitness. With a promising start-up just getting off the ground, they were understandably wary of using their legal name in a personal commentary that might be read by tens of thousands, or, in some cases, millions.

The fears of writers who have not yet made the difficult decision to surrender aspects of their personal and professional lives to wider audiences deserve the utmost respect. Many are understandably protective of the innocent bystanders in their lives—spouses, partners, children—whose trust might suffer in the process. Any writer who agonizes over the effect their personal commentary might have on others is a writer whose heart I am inclined to trust. However, in workshop I am quick to point out that the precious, poignant, and passionate things we fear sharing with others are often those that readers stand most to benefit from when shared. Society often valorizes creative writers for the bravery they display in publishing tell-all memoirs or autobiographical accounts, but in many ways the writer of "My Turn"-styled personal commentaries deserves equal respect for their courage, for in many cases they're willing to reveal difficult aspects of their past without the contractual promise of royalties, fame, or the built-in legal defense offered by major book publishers.

Writer Lewis Hyde writes powerfully about the selfless act of giving that defines the writer in his book *The Gift: Creativity and the Artist in the Modern World*. Hyde's text is something of a cult classic among writers, and it speaks to the anxieties and desires common to those in many creative fields. In it the author posits that a work of art or piece of writing possesses a worth well beyond its market value, and that it ought to be given away freely and be re-gifted perpetually. He writes:

> The spirit of a gift is kept alive by its constant donation. If this is the case then the gifts of the inner world must be accepted as gifts in the outer world if they are to retain their vitality. Where gifts have no public currency, therefore, where the gift as a form of property is neither recognized nor honored, our inner gifts will find themselves excluded from the very commerce that is their nourishment.[1]

Hyde writes in philosophic, almost mystical terms about the value of our thoughts and beliefs when we're brave enough to put them into the public sphere, though his message is simple enough: we should share our vision with others even when it's difficult or daunting, so that others, in turn, can pay that act of courage forward. It's an almost Buddhist notion, that in one's personal story is one's suffering, and in one's suffering resides the individual's and the reader's greatest potential for enlightenment.

Owning Your Own Experiential Credentials

How does the public writer of personal commentaries determine what they have to give and when and where to give it? I find it useful to make lists of what I call "experiential credentials"—not the degrees we hang on the wall that are the sum of our formal education, but the R-E-S-P-E-C-T earned in the school of hard knocks from which many of us graduate. Of course, such experiential credentials need not be unhappy experiences, though in many cases they represent difficult times with ultimately redemptive outcomes, since we tend to learn most from our losses and displacements. Experiential credentials often emerge from challenging times in our lives that educate us into greater personhood, and stand to educate others, too, when given as a gift.

Public writers open to getting personal should think first about what makes their lives unique. For example, perhaps the writer grew up with five brothers, spent their formative years living in a cabin in the woods, or served as the first female president of their high school

---

1. Lewis Hyde, *The Gift: Creativity and the Artist in the Modern World* (New York: Vantage, 2007), xix.

class. It's best not to think of such important existential artifacts as mere novelties or conversational ice-breakers, but as aspects of our lives that help distinguish us—the sorts of experiences that come bearing unexpected gifts. Often, generating such inventories proves a powerful experience, reminding us of elements of our personal or public struggles that we have long censored, repressed, or taken for granted, but which, in retrospect, endow us with real authority. For example, the writer who grew up with five brothers may be uniquely qualified to tackle the topic of toxic masculinity, sibling rivalry, or the sometimes stultifying effects of gender norms on childrearing. They may be able to comment authentically on the benefits and drawbacks of large families, or the ways in which elder siblings are sometimes pressed into service as proxy parents. Now suppose the writer with five brothers grew up to be a psychologist specializing in adolescent male psychology, as I encountered in one of my recent public writing workshops. In such cases, experiential and professional credentials join to make a powerful combination of relevant expertise that can be successfully applied to any number of contemporary cultural issues.

The case of the psychologist with five brothers is a timely one, as it segues into a prompt I pose to workshop participants looking to craft a piece of public-facing personal commentary: I ask them to make a list of the jobs (as well as volunteer posts and hobbies that rise to the level of avocations) they've held in their life, especially those they've held the longest, or held most recently. For example, my own incomplete list might read:

> Professor
> Radio producer
> Newspaper section editor
> Janitor/custodian
> Land conservationist and caretaker
> Children's librarian
> Bookmobile driver
> Author
> National commentator
> Playwright
> Maintenance shop worker
> Bowling alley cashier
> Mower/Landscaper

Making lists reminds us of the depth and variety of experiences we've had, of the tree rings we've amassed as we've aged, witnessed, and interacted with the world around us in ways that transcend professional pedigree. Until I stopped to complete the prompt myself, I had, for example, forgotten my three-plus years working on the crew of a maintenance department, or the summers I spent working as a janitor/custodian. I've noticed the same work-related amnesia among the diverse professionals who enroll in my workshops; too often in recounting our meaningful vocational experiences we conform to the cultural bias against blue-collar or manual labor, choosing to focus instead on the resume items likely to impress. Yet, the very life experiences we omit on a CV or resume are often the experiences that distinguish us from the millions of others who share our professional bona fides. A case in point: several years ago I found myself wanting to explore my feelings about the proposal to add to the physical wall erected on portions of America's southern border. I started a personal commentary, then stopped abruptly. What credibility did I have on immigration, living as I did then in a landlocked state in the middle of the country? What did I know about international borders and partitions? After several false starts and crumpled drafts, I realized I had quite a lot of relevant experience with borderlands and fencing. Earlier in my life I had lived for a time both in Las Cruces, New Mexico, and in western New Mexico, places experiencing a wealth of new immigrants. And in my time as a conservationist and land steward I had built many fences in the West and Southwest.

My personal commentary began:

> In over 20 years of fence-building from Iowa to New Mexico, I've learned that fences come with a built-in paradox. While they make it difficult to get in, they make it proportionally difficult to get out. On Western ranches, I've put up hundreds of feet of fence in ruggedly beautiful country. And with each post sunk, I've experienced a sinking feeling at the logic of willingly sacrificing the long view for the myopic and often mythic protections of a wall.

A month or so later my personal commentary appeared in New Mexico's largest-circulating newspaper, a publication with well over three million unique page views each month and a cumulative audience of over 300,000 readers for its Sunday edition. Three hundred

thousand may not seem like much to readers living on the more popu-
lous coasts, but it represents well over half of the population of Albuquerque. In fact, those 3.5 million average monthly page views at the
Albuquerque Journal represent approximately 1.5 page views on average per resident in a state with a population of just two million.[2]

Looking back, I'm grateful that I refused to surrender to the voices
in my head telling me I had no authority to speak and no relevant experience to share. If I had listened to them, I would have missed out on
a valuable opportunity not only to better articulate to myself my own
stance on the border wall, but also to reach several million readers in a
state where I had once lived and worked.

How about you? Now that you have your list of past vocations,
avocations, and volunteer positions and internships, do any potential
public writing topics announce themselves? Did you do what I did—
neglecting your manual labor or blue-collar work in favor of more
white-collar professional experiences? Now that you've remembered
the whole you—the one that's a blend of head, heart, and hands—do
you feel better suited to take your turn at writing a "My Turn"-styled
piece? Do any of the jobs you've had add credence or credibility to a
potential personal commentary informed by your professional experience? For example, if you once worked as an airline pilot or flight attendant, you likely have something to say about the rise of emotional
support animals on domestic flights. Or if you've cleaned houses for
a living, you have something important to contribute on the personal
vulnerability and predation experienced by those who work in others' homes.

In the past, so-called experts—doctors, lawyers, journalists, professors, teachers—dominated the personal commentary pages in most
journals, newspapers, and magazines. Their access to movers and
shakers, their professional degrees, and their existing record of public outreach (to patients, readers, students, clients, and the like) made
them especially credible in the eyes of the general public. In fact, when
Newsweek reviewed its "My Turn" column on the occasion of its twentieth anniversary they found that just eight professions accounted for
two thirds of all the "My Turn" columns.[3] After the writers, profes-

---

2. *Albuquerque Journal*, "2018 Advertising Specs & Info," 2018, https://www.
abqjournal.com/assets/pdfs/Albuquerque-Journal-Advertising-Solutions.pdf.
3. The *Newsweek* Staff, "Twenty Years of 'My Turn,'" *Newsweek*, November 8,
1992, https://www.newsweek.com/twenty-years-my-turn-196856.

sors, and journalists, who made up about fifty percent, came the lawyers, CEOs, editors, doctors, and teachers that made up the bulk of the
rest. Yet, "My Turn" had also served as a path-making forum for folks
with less traditional expertise, including welfare recipients, construction workers, law enforcement officials, firefighters, farmers, nurses,
prisoners, babysitters, welders, rabbis, bartenders, mail carriers, car-
penters, secretaries, factory workers, and film stars. That diversity has
only deepened since, so much so that personal commentaries are now
almost as likely to come from contributors with nontraditional professions as traditional ones.

LEMONS TO LEMONADE

Writing is a redemptive act, one capable of helping practitioners
mitigate, and sometimes overcome, grief, loss, and profound disap-
pointment. It's a wonderful, sometimes life-saving virtue of the craft.
Just as I urged you earlier to make a list of your vocations and avocations, I want to invite you now to inventory some of your biggest
disappointments.

Such lists are often too personal to share, but I hope you can see
that what we suffer, and what we manage to overcome and abide, con-
nects us to other people in powerful ways. Perhaps in the past we've
been divorced, been downsized at work, or been badly estranged from
a friend or family member whom we nevertheless dearly love. Personal commentaries written for broader publics often ask us to own
our personal or professional disappointments, declaring, in effect: *Join
the crowd!*

Had I been prompted to make a list of my own greatest private disappointments, I would surely have listed "Losing uninsured home to
a hurricane" somewhere near the top. It wasn't the loss of a loved one
or the decline of my own health, after all, though it certainly took its
toll on my well-being. For well over a year I kept the existential blow
almost entirely to myself, so deep was the internal wound it dealt. My
reasons for staying silent were understandable: honestly, I felt guilty
and cursed. I worried that by merely mentioning my loss to others I'd
come off sounding entitled, even though the place hadn't cost all that
much more than a top-of-the-line pick-up truck. Still, I had taken on
so much debt to buy the ill-fated house that I couldn't afford to properly insure it; several years later the hurricane hit and what remained

of the property ended up at auction. I stewed in my own private grief until the public trauma of Hurricane Irma slamming into the Texas Gulf Coast caused me to get over myself and reach out to others, writing about what it was like to have lost what you love in a hurricane. Drafting the personal commentary took every ounce of courage I could muster, though it came as something of a solace when *USA Today* picked up my piece on environmental gentrification, FEMA, and those like me unable or unwilling to re-build after a natural disaster; those whose only real choice was to fold and relocate. I think of that piece each time a natural disaster strikes, and how many of us there are out there silenced into submission by a blow that seems larger than ourselves.

YOUR JOB AND YOUR PUBLIC WRITING

Far too many of the industries in which we work exist behind a veil of secrecy requiring an almost cult-like adherence to the company line. Even professors who assert their own academic freedom sometimes find themselves censored, stifled, and threatened for their views. Corporate America can be even less tolerant of whistleblowers, cultural critics, contrarians, and conscientious objectors.

Understandably, then, writing from or about one's job or industry makes many would-be public writers anxious. It's one thing if the consequence of our opening up to the public about our personal life is a cold shoulder from friends or family; quite another if we feel our personal commentary, made public, might damage our career. It's a natural fear, especially when writing about one's personal or professional life, though I like to point out that pieces whose risk is sufficient to get their writer fired often yield unexpected dividends in the form of newfound respect from those who believe in speaking truth to power.

More often than not, editors selecting personal commentaries for publication will look for the unique intersection of personal experience and professional acumen, and, once they find it, they'll look for writers willing to go out on a limb. For example, one would expect a law enforcement officer to write in defense of cops who draw their weapons and shoot when threatened, but what about police officers with the courage to say that their colleagues are too quick to pull the trigger, especially when the target is black or brown? Often topics like these are sufficiently sensitive that they're best tackled by a writer who has recently left the field about which they are writing. A case in point is Redditt Hudson, who served on the St. Louis Police Department for five years before moving on to serve as the board chair of The Ethics Project and a member of the National Coalition of Law Enforcement for Justice, Reform, and Accountability. Hudson opens his first-person piece for *Vox* with a shot across the bow born of years of direct experience:

> On any given day, in any police department in the nation, 15 percent of officers will do the right thing no matter what is happening. Fifteen percent of officers will abuse their authority at every opportunity. The remaining 70 percent could go either way depending on whom they are working with.[4]

Given that a 2014 Gallup Poll placed police in the top five most trusted professions, an opening paragraph like this surely comes as a revelation to the citizen who believes that cops are cops because they're inclined to do the right thing. Hudson later claims that we fall victim to the "myth about the general goodness of cops," one that "obscures the truth of what needs to be done to fix the system." Despite his commentary's title, which begins "I'm a black cop," Hudson had moved on from the St. Louis Police force by 2016, when his commentary ran on *Vox*, graduating to civil rights and civil liberties work in Missouri and beyond. It would have been exceedingly difficult for him to write such a provocative piece had he remained on the force. Some of the personal stories he shares of the police brutality he witnessed in the streets of St. Louis would have utterly alienated him from colleagues exposed as racists.

Hudson found his personal and professional experiences as a former member of the St. Louis police force in unique demand in the days and months after the killing of African Americans Michael Brown and Anthony Lamar Smith in Ferguson and St. Louis, Missouri, respectively. In 2018 he contributed another similar viewpoints piece to *The Hill*, one in which he made many of the same points he'd made for *Vox*. This time, however, the news peg then in the headlines was a bill known as the Protect and Serve Act that proposed to make it a hate crime to "knowingly cause bodily injury to any person because of their

---

4. Redditt Hudson, "I'm a black ex-cop, and this is the real truth about race and policing," *Vox*, July 7, 2016, https://www.vox.com/2015/5/28/8661977/race-police-officer.

actual or perceived status as a police officer." The bill, Hudson claims, raises a "false flag that there is a war on police."[5] Killings of police officers and ambush attacks were at near historic lows, he points out, citing 2013 as the safest year for police officers in recorded history. Hudson's follow-up piece illustrates an important point about sticking with it, about the willingness to beat the same or similar drum more than once when one needs to be heard. Less persistent commentators would likely have balked at the prospect of publishing two commentaries on such similar topics in relatively close succession, fearing redundancy, or that the second would appear to be a knock-off of the first. Too often public writers with eclectic interests and virtuoso skills flit from topic to topic for fear of sounding like a broken record. But Hudson knows that the secret of topical commentators is often to adhere closely to the core passions that animate them, with what is most visceral and close to the heart. In this way, some of our most effective authors of personal viewpoints are a bit like the classics; rather than change to suit this year's fashions, they know that if they stay consistent the wheel will turn and the issues about which they care most deeply will become relevant again. The Protect and Serve Act represented just such a genuine opportunity for Hudson's enduring passions—racial justice and law enforcement—to return to the national spotlight, as did the tragic killing of George Floyd at the hands of Minneapolis police in May of 2020.

Often when we quit a job or leave an industry, our instinct is to put the pain behind us and to start with a clean slate. Yet, Hudson's work is also a prime example of how a conscientious objector who leaves a field or moves laterally within it can, given a little distance, speak truth to help heal it, thereby closing the loop. The author's commentary on the need for greater trust between law enforcement and the black community was shared over 1500 times, and elicited nearly a hundred comments on *The Hill's* website. The fact that the commentator had left the force years earlier did not damage his credibility in the eyes of readers; in fact, it likely enhanced it. For the public writer in particular, past jobs, positions, and posts can be every bit as relevant

---

5. Redditt Hudson, "Police don't need more protections—they need to build trust with black America," *The Hill*, May 16, 2018, https://thehill.com/opinion/criminal-justice/387897-police-dont-need-more-protections-they-need-to-build-trust-with.

as current ones, and sometimes more so, given the augmented vision hindsight often brings.

As employees dedicated to our industries, we assemble a body of varied professional knowledge, and much of it can be put to good use by public writers determined to make our jobs more just. Twenty-first century readers have shown themselves to be uniquely open to the busting of myths and the exposing of difficult truths. In 2018 the Labor Department had been investigating tech-giant Google for allegedly systematically underpaying women, but the results of a 2019 Google pay survey as reported by the *New York Times* found instead that men in the company were being paid less money than women doing similar work.[6] One can imagine the courage it would have taken for an underpaid male employee to write a personal commentary on the subject prior to the release of the study. Similarly, a female Google employee would be equally courageous in writing a viewpoints piece exposing the fact that the overwhelming majority of workers in her field are male (just short of seventy percent) and mostly white and Asian.

Of course, the public writer of personal columns must do more than blow the whistle on his or her stock and trade; they must also be attuned to the hidden or hidebound aspects of their industries that are too little publicized. My Uncle Wayne comes to mind. A former Air Force top gun from rural eastern Kentucky, he eventually settled into a good job with a major aerospace engineering firm in the Midwest, where he helped design electrical systems for commercial and military aircraft. Midway through his tenure at the company he began refusing to fly commercially, citing safety concerns. For years we gently ribbed him at family dinners about this irony, until late in his life he abruptly quit his post to serve as an expert witness in a legal action against the allegedly consumer-endangering practices of his former employer. Uncle Wayne wasn't a Judas or a traitor, slowly building a case for decades while deigning to cash his paycheck. On the contrary, he dedicated the best years of his professional life to honest engineering, repeatedly telling his supervisors of the errors and omissions until he had exhausted all routes for in-house accountability, and the urgent need to tell the public what he knew took precedence.

---

6. Daisuke Wakabayashi, "Google Finds It's Underpaying Many Men as It Addresses Wage Equity," *New York Times*, March 4, 2019, https://www.nytimes.com/2019/03/04/technology/google-gender-pay-gap.html.

GET PERSONAL, BUT BE BRIEF

Often when public writers begin to access the storehouse of personal and professional experiences they've been tucking away for years, the material comes tumbling out. Writing about one topic quickly gives way to another, until they become positively overwhelmed by their experiential feast of riches. A couple of hours of focused venting can produce 1500 words or more of compelling personal material, but the topics within those 1500 words are often divergent or digressive, lacking a coherent theme or framework. For this reason and others, *Newsweek's* "My Turn" wisely insisted that writers limit their contributions to around 750 words, and it's good practice for public writers of personal commentaries to write with a similarly firm word count in mind. A single newspaper column isn't a book-length memoir or autobiography, after all, but a highly focused attempt to bring an aspect of one's personal or professional life to bear on a limited yet resonant topic. In telling my personal story about having my nest egg ruined by a hurricane, for example, I had been tempted to give readers the entire backstory—how growing up in the landlocked Midwest had caused me to assume a major hurricane would never happen to me. I was tempted to broach, by way of context, my family's generations-long love affair with the Gulf Coast, a love sufficient to compel us to stay in cheap apartments just to plant our feet near the shore. Had I written a book on my experience, I would surely have devoted an entire chapter to deep background, but for my 750-word commentary I needed to stay grounded in the present, connecting my own personal and financial loss with the larger tragedies of environmental gentrification, the lack of flood insurance, and the many FEMA loopholes that leave individual residents and homeowners without federal assistance. In the end I bucked the media stereotype that valorizes hurricane victims who stay and rebuild on flood plains and marginal land, storms be damned, to detail how I decided to commence a painful leave-taking from the Gulf Coast.

Vox, the popular internet magazine known for its "Explainers" and "First Person" pages, is in many ways the heir apparent to the *Newsweek* "My Turn" section. *Vox* learned early on that the best way to explain a complicated issue to readers in a small amount of space is to allow them to see it through the eyes of a person with a powerful personal connection to it. Like many contemporary outlets for first-person work, *Vox* looks for a wide range of perspectives from writers

of every age, gender, race, class, sexual orientation, and political preference. In many ways they celebrate the growing topical diversity of
personal commentaries in the Digital Age, a multitude that goes the
groundbreaking breadth of "My Turn" one better. On the occasion
of the twentieth anniversary of "My Turn," *Newsweek* editors found,
for instance, that close to half of the columns run to date (465) had
been written on fifteen basic subjects, with national politics/govern-
ment accounting for more than 100 of those 465.[7] The rest of the top
five, totaling 202 columns, were devoted to business and the economy,
international relations and foreign policy, medicine and health care,
and education. Contrast that global focus with the more contemporary *Vox*, which has found greater reader interest in parenting, relationships, money, identity, mental health, and job/workplace issues.
During the COVID-19 crisis, *Vox's* "First Person" ran columns with
titles ranging from "Healing from a Suicide Attempt in Isolation" to
"I Work in a Nevada Brothel Shut-down in the Pandemic. Here's How
We're Getting By" to "1 Million Americans live in RVs. Here's How
we're coping with the pandemic." We'll talk more about the art of
titling your public writing in upcoming chapters, but for now notice
how expertly the titles of these viewpoints encapsulate their angle, appeal, and novelty. The site's editors, while careful to avoid the merely
gimmicky or sensational, have a knack for addressing reader curiosities. It's fair to say that many of us know someone who lives out of an
RV, for example, even if we haven't yet succumbed ourselves to the call
of the open road. But how many of us know someone who works in a
brothel? All moral judgements aside, it's an underrepresented perspective, and, prior to reading the *Vox* piece written by Chasen, an employee at Sheri's Ranch, a full-service sex resort, I didn't know that sex
workers in Nevada's fully legal brothels were not eligible to apply for
the stimulus loans offered by the Small Business Administration due
to a clause barring businesses deemed to present "displays of a prurient
sexual nature."[8]

In commentaries like Chasen's or Nathan Nichols's, who writes
about his decision to waive his tenants' rent during the pandemic, note
the shift away from grander topics related to politics and public policy

---

7. The *Newsweek* Staff, "Twenty Years of 'My Turn.'"
8. Chasen, "I work in a Nevada brothel shut down in the pandemic. Here's
how we're getting by," *Vox*, May 8, 2020, https://www.vox.com/first-per-
son/2020/5/8/21249630/coronavirus-covid-19-sex-work-nevada-brothel.

to those that are more intimate, familiar, and close to home. Today's readers are eager to know the man or woman behind the machine. They're more likely to view even well-known writers as equals—regarding them more like thoughtful, articulate friends than authority figures or distant experts. They're looking to trade intimacies, trusts, and disclosures in a you-tell-me-yours, I'll-tell-you-mine exchange of like minds and complicated lives.

WRAPPING UP

Finding the widest possible audience for our work all but demands that we bring ourselves down to earth, making ourselves vulnerable before the reader just as the reader makes themselves vulnerable before us. Personal commentary is a uniquely reciprocal genre and an opportunity for even the most serious-minded public intellectual to share some of the deeper, more personal reasons why they write on a given subject. In the past, researchers, intellectuals, scholars, and other prominent public figures often suppressed their personal views for fear of a perceived loss of objectivity or decorum, but in an authenticity-minded egalitarian era, introducing the personal part of the public self can itself be a sunshine cure.

7 Minding Your Tone

When I think about the challenge and promise of tone, I think about my nephew Ezra.

He's a brilliant guy who was reading three years above his grade level in elementary. Yet, at school Ez struggled mightily to be himself, noticeably withdrawing from his classmates as they chatted easily and well. Terrifically funny and witty outside the classroom, Ez was *verklempt* at school, responding to teacher questions, if he responded at all, in a clipped monotone that made him sound more like a robot-child than the fun, funny, and funky nephew I knew him to be.

The difference between Home Ez and School Ez was so pronounced that when I attended school with him once years ago, I left feeling sad that his teachers and fellow students didn't get to experience the boy I reveled in the rest of the day—the one who came out of his shell the minute we walked through the door to my sister's house. As a boy my father was the same way. In fact, I still have a copy of his report card from 1955 that reads: "Mike disturbs the whole class. His being nervous seems to create a slight stutter in his speech." Like my dad and my nephew, school made me anxious, too.

Most of us are a little like Ez, struggling to find our voice in environments in which we don't feel fully ourselves. Something about the anxiety of wielding language that doesn't feel as if it's our own makes us freeze up. When finally we muster the courage to speak, our voice inevitably comes out sounding stilted or strained.

Literary handbooks define tone as "an attitude of a writer toward a subject," but in my view that definition misses the mark. For me, tone is more directly described as how the writer or their writing *sounds*. Does the writer or the writing sound angry, wounded, self-satisfied, grateful, apprehensive, appreciative, concerned, or something else? Literary definitions of tone assign too much importance to author intention and not enough to reader perception. Just as writing and reading are a two-way street, so is tone. Often a reader responds to the writer's attitude with an attitude of their own. If the writer comes off sounding stuffy, or preachy, or superior, the reader will likely feel talked down to, or lectured at. This feeling in turn makes them want to put the book, article, or report away in favor of something more life-affirming. It's a big problem in public scholarship and higher education textbooks—I struggle with it here—and one with no easy solution. The irony is this: often the very things we hate when they're done to us as readers, we subject our own readers to when we're the author. While we may hate it when writers use needlessly big words to make themselves sound smart, cruel irony dictates that we fall victim to the same sin when it's our turn to wield the pen.

I've experienced this syndrome a lot as a teacher: anxious or insecure writers sprinkling their papers with ten-thousand-dollar words like "plethora" and "myriad" when they might just as well have said "many." During his two fraught years in college in the 1960s, my father (Dad ultimately dropped out to help my grandfather farm) deployed the word "conundrum" as often as he could to the delight and consternation of his professors. Once bitten by the gobbledygook bug, otherwise normal students come off sounding like high-brow Brits hosting *Masterpiece Theatre.* Conjunctive adverbs such as "thus" and "thusly" crop up routinely; throat-clearers like "alas" and "hence" occur with uncanny frequency. Still, we can hardly blame would-be scribblers for trying to talk the talk of their bosses and profs. As it turns out, trying to sound intelligent is a lot like trying to be cool: usually it backfires, and it's better just to be ourselves—or the most professionally appropriate version of ourselves, anyway.

As an undergraduate I had the good fortune of studying abroad for a year in Swansea, Wales. I hadn't the foggiest notion, really, of what Welsh culture might be like except what I had seen in the reruns of British sitcoms that ran on Saturday nights on public television. Naturally, I bought up all the rain-slickers and trench coats I could find at our local Salvation Army store before leaving for my year abroad, stuffing them into my already overstuffed suitcase pre-departure. Who cared if my newly acquired arsenal of outdoor gear reeked of old-man woolens? Come hell or high water, I would be prepared for the comically awful weather I had seen on TV.

Of course, when I arrived on campus I learned very quickly that none of the students were wearing old-man trench coats, and I realized it rains every day only in Hollywood's version of the UK. In fact,

I found the weather along the Welsh coast to be a good bit more hospitable than it was back home. Duly ashamed, I kept the trench coats hidden away in my suitcase for the remainder of my time overseas. I was like the dutiful American student who had completed all the exercises in his *Parlais Francais* workbook, only to realize, upon arrival in Paris, that the French he'd practiced in his workbooks was already fifteen or twenty years out of fashion. Similarly, in our serious work we often write with an affectation that insinuates itself into our natural voice like a parasitic infection or an alien worm. Like my stuffy London Fog trench coats, such affected writing conforms to stereotypes more than it acknowledges real life. Students may imagine profs wearing tweed and elbow patches, for example, or perhaps even swishing to class in their Oxford gowns, but most of the professors I know wear jeans to work.

Where tone is concerned, balance is the order of the day. Granted, a jeans tone may be a bit too informal or youthful for serious-minded intellectual inquiry; certainly a shorts-and-flip-flops tone would be too causal. By analogy, a slacks-and-button-up tone turns out to be just about right for most public writing: easy enough to move around in, but still formal enough to retain some decorum.

Dogs of Tone

Tone beguiles, so much so that once we've thrown off the shackles of the stilted language we once felt compelled to invoke in our reports and papers, we sometimes swing too much toward what I call the "cool man tone." It's so rewarding to find ourselves writing sans inhibition that often the writing we craft in subsequent, post-liberation drafts amounts to too much of a good thing. Accessible public writing doesn't require the colloquial nor the chatty, nor the dropping of slangy phrases like "nowadays" and "back in the day." Accessible writing is often just that—the kind of business-casual that could, following the analogy, be as appropriate for a Friday night as a Sunday morning. Overstylized, hyper-liberated public writing can often feel like wearing a burlap sack to a board meeting; it's bound to get noticed, but not necessarily for the reasons we might want.

One of the best examples I know of too much tone comes in a 2017 *Chicago Tribune* piece by Christopher Borelli. I like Borelli's writing well enough, and certainly one doesn't get to be a features reporter/columnist for one of the best newspapers in America if one doesn't have excellent chops. But in his homage to Chicago's famous "Depression Dog" (essentially a hot dog wrapped with fries) and the restaurant that serves it, Gene's and Jude's, Borelli exemplifies too much of a good thing. Let's take a look at portions of this over-the-top write-up, with the firm hope that the next time our own exuberance gets the better of us, we'll say "Depression dogs" three times to ourselves, click our heels, and come back down to earth. Borelli's article begins:

> The acting teacher Stella Adler once said that life will beat you down and crush your soul and art reminds you that you have one. Keep that in mind right now. January is terrible. The third week in January is the most depressing week of the year. A researcher in England in 2005 (who has since become a life coach) did decide that the third Monday of January is the most depressing day of the year—a claim that led to Blue Monday gaining traction, a pseudo-holiday promoted by public relations firms too obtuse to recognize the third Monday of January is often Martin Luther King Jr. Day. But let's split the difference: Third week of January, most depressing week of the year.[1]

Stop right there. Already Borelli has far too many balls in the air—acting coaches, Stella Adler, January, researchers in England, depression, Blue Mondays, Martin Luther King Jr.—and we're still in the first paragraph. We empathize with the writer surely: his tastes are eclectic, and his enthusiasm for his subject is so off the charts he can hardly help spilling it all over the page. The trouble is we're already 125 words into the piece—a lifetime in newspaper journalism—and the subject of the write-up hasn't yet come up. We could chalk it up to prose style—an artful or purposeful deviation from the norm of ordinary usage—but there's no denying the first paragraph is a bit too spastic to be coherent. If Borelli plays this fast and loose in the all-important lead (often spelled "lede" in newsrooms), how can he serve as a reliable narrator elsewhere?

---

1. Borelli, Christopher, "We've got the antidote to your January blues: The Depression Dog," *Chicago Tribune*, January 19, 2017, https://www.chicagotribune.com/entertainment/ct-depression-dog-sad-art-ent-0120-20170119-column.html.

Let me be clear: first paragraphs, even in newspaper journalism, don't have to slavishly adhere to the who, what, when, where, and why. It's perfectly okay to try a misdirection that keeps the reader on the hook until they have that "aha . . . so *that's* where you were taking me" epiphany. Sometimes, it's fun and even satisfying to be fooled, detoured, or coyly delayed by an expert writer with a big bag of tricks. In this case, however, Borelli's first three lines would surely prove sufficient as a misdirection if that's his jam. So it's January in Chicago. We're cold. We're depressed. It's awful. Got it, now let's move on.

Instead, paragraph two gives us more of the same stagnancy, this time with a side of Chi-town politics:

> The holidays have become a memory, credit card statements arrive; the weather is fog and rain and snow and cold and mud and loneliness. This year, this week, the most unpopular president-elect in recent history will be sworn in. Same day, a new M. Night Shyamalan movie opens that you probably don't want to see.

The writing in paragraph two likewise bristles with voice. The syntax is apt (for example, I admire that first compound sentence, with its graceful parallelism and enviable concretion), but the original problem persists—more gratuitous cultural references, more moody snark, more words—55 more to be exact—and still no hot dogs. Several more cheeky single-sentence paragraphs follow until, five paragraphs in, we belatedly arrive at what journalists call the nut graf—the fact-based paragraph that typically follows a teaser lede. In a piece written for the Poynter Institute, Ken Wells, then writer and editor at *The Wall Street Journal*, describes the nut graf as "a paragraph that says what the whole story is about and why you should read it. It's a flag to the reader, high up in the story: You can decide to proceed or not, but if you read no farther, you know what that story's about."[2]

I don't begrudge Borelli his emo-poetic tone, which works well for him in spots. For example, shortly hereafter he comes up with a memorable simile comparing the neighborhood around Gene's and Jude's, close to O'Hare International Airport, to "a place where even in the bright sunlight the sky looks like an old mattress in an empty lot." My

---

2. Chip Scanlan, "The nut graf tells the reader what the writer is up to," *Poynter Institute*, May 19, 2003, https://www.poynter.org/archive/2003/the-nut-graf-part-i/.

beef with the piece is that Borelli is clearly overreaching, projecting his own January blues onto everything he sees, making him an unreliable narrator. In literature, the same tonal hyperbole is called, for good reason, the pathetic fallacy. Let's sample a paragraph from nearer the middle of the opus to see where pathos obscures and at the same time oversaturates the prose:

> The line at Gene & Jude's isn't for philosophizing. It's a working-class line, with old men in oversized tinted eyeglasses who maybe should be retired by now wearing work jackets zipped down to their stomachs. No one eating here looks as though his world is at ease; even the people who roll up in new Volvos appear to [be] escaping something, if only for the time it takes to eat. The employees at the counter in matching white T-shirts put your Depression Dog in a brown sack and leave a crater in the center of the bag that lets your food breathe. You take the sack and eat in your car, or you eat on the thin linoleum ledge that serves as a table. There is no rest, or seats, for anyone here. You lean elbows on the ledge and stare out on the only view, a large parking lot bordered by sand-colored homes that appear untouched by whatever economic prosperity has been celebrated recently. Picture Hopper's "Nighthawks," drained of every drip of romance.

I like the *Nighthawks* reference that concludes Borelli's otherwise over-the-top paragraph, but, my goodness, the presumptions that need correcting! Is it not possible that a thinking person could indeed be philosophizing in line while waiting for their Depression Dog, or must those queuing up for their comfort foods be, by default, tired and hungry working stiffs, as the author implies? How does Borelli know what the customers are thinking? Do women eat hot dogs, too, or is it only bespectacled men wearing jackets? Who is the author to say the guys in line maybe should have retired years ago? And what about the Volvo driver versus the proletariat conflict the writer conjures up without evidence?

So many stereotypes, so little time!

The piece takes further tonal liberties as it careens toward an ending. The writer has made the piece so thoroughly about himself, his preoccupations, and his chosen melancholic, mind-of-winter blues, that the reader, if indeed they've stuck with the piece, has little choice but to surrender to Borelli being Borelli. The writer's hyper-liberated tone will go where it wants, and the reader either follows along passively on the writer's joyride, or quits in protest at the scribe's implicit my-way-or-the-highway ultimatum. Next, a mere snippet of Frank Ocean music wafting from one of the pick-up trucks pulling up to Gene's & Jude's sends Borelli into several paragraphs of an ecstatic, artistic dither that's nearly all tangent:

> The [Frank Ocean] music is a languid sigh. Everyone, artist, listener, seems served. It's not so different from new music by The xx, or, say, Jenny Hval, a Norwegian singer whose acclaimed album from last year sounds like it was made at 3 a.m., after everyone went to bed and she was left with unsettled thoughts. January is for morose. The downbeat "Rogue One: A Star Wars Story" plays better in the gloom of now than the sparkles of the holidays. "Homesick for Another World," the new story collection by on-the-rise writer Ottessa Moshfegh, is terrific and bleak, offering few pats on the head. The protagonist in one story is in a bar on Christmas night, and Moshfegh's description rings of parody and truth: The floor was parquet, and my footsteps squeaked as I walked haltingly toward the bar. There was no music on, nothing. A small cat slunk by, then rubbed itself against a stack of old newspapers. A radiator hissed and sputtered. . . . A middle-aged woman stood behind the bar, smoking a cigarette. Otherwise the place was empty."
>
> Gene & Jude's works much the way sad and depressing art works in January—as paradoxical relief from sadness and depression. Like music and books and movies, it's set, unchanging.

Errors of *logos*—fact and logic—crop up in abundance, as Borelli gets the name of the restaurant wrong (it's Gene's and Jude's not Gene & Jude's) in addition to making the head-scratching declaration that music and books and movies (read: art) are unchanging.

I hope my critique of the Depression Dogs article doesn't sound disrespectful or holier-than-thou. I've been this writer; I suspect we all have. Let's remember: many less exuberant writers would give their last gel pen to have an ounce of the panache Borelli possesses, or to experience, just once, the enviable problem of too much voice.

To borrow the old saying, I'm laughing *with* the piece, not at it. I can't help but chuckle when I imagine a hardboiled editor at the *Trib* putting Borelli's piece down and saying gruffly and in that inimitable Chicago accent, "Okay, Shakespeare, now tell me about the goddamned hot dogs!"

Writing Ages

In their classic handbook *The Elements of Style*, William Strunk and E. B. White advise "not [to] effect a breezy style." "The breezy style," they write, "is often the work of an egocentric, the person who imagines that everything that comes to mind is of general interest and that uninhibited prose creates high spirits and carries the day."[3] Strunk and White point a finger at the "aging collegian" type who purposefully drops phrases like "dishing the dirt" and "howzabout" and "primo" to sound cool. While the examples are a bit dated, their message holds: no need to write like a youthful hipster if you're a graying middle-aged professional who heads directly to bed after a late dinner. As any son or daughter will tell you, there's nothing more painful than seeing a "parental unit" or other such "old person" trying to pass as "with-it."

We might be tempted to revise Strunk and White's sixty-year-old counsel to read: "Write like the age you are not the age you wish you were," and yet that otherwise sage advice wouldn't work so well for many traditional-aged college students and youthful corporate hires. Let's be honest; in many ways younger writers are at an inherent disadvantage where professional discourse is concerned. Their reports and papers practically require them to age their diction and syntax to reach more seasoned audiences. Consider: according to a recent Pew Study, only thirty-two percent of the consumers of the *New York Times* are between the ages of eighteen and twenty-nine, and the *Times* boasts one of the highest percentages of younger readers among popular print and broadcast media.[4] The rate drops to a mere twenty percent for news magazines overall and to seventeen percent for public writing-

3. William Strunk and E. B. White, *The Elements of Style* (East Rutherford, NJ: Penguin, 2007), 106.
4. The Pew Research Center, "In Changing News Landscape, Even Television is Vulnerable," September 27, 2012, https://www.pewresearch.org/politics/2012/09/27/section-4-demographics-and-political-views-of-news-audiences/.

friendly magazines like the *New Yorker, Harper's,* and *The Atlantic.* If undergraduate public writers are asked to imagine a reader the age of their eldest sibling, they're still often writing "too young." Even graduate students must learn to write for audiences significantly more aged than themselves. In the increasing youthfulness of their student body, the University of British Columbia in Vancouver is typical. There the average age for a Masters student recently tallied 29.3; while for Doctoral students the average age clocked in at 33.3.[5] In 1991 50.89 percent of Masters students were twenty to twenty-nine; in 2018 that number had increased to 64.24 percent for the same age group.

Anxious young professionals eager to climb the corporate ladder often feel the need to "write older" on the page when called upon to produce reports for senior team leaders, managers, and supervisors. It's inherently unfair, and possibly ageist, but then again no one ever cited office dynamics as paragons of equity. Instead of complaining about the unfairness of it all, a young professional might instead consider it an opportunity to flex their sense of audience awareness. North America has a remarkably low PDI or Power-Distance Index, a fancy way of saying North Americans don't defer to age and authority as much as, for instance, the Japanese or Koreans. Hence, a young public writer's willingness to tailor their writing to the interests and needs of an older audience may be seen as a mark of respect or deference in addition to a savvy gesture toward audience awareness.

Why aren't there more readers in the eighteen to twenty-nine age bracket? Young people are busy; many are taking classes, holding down a job, and establishing a relationship or a family. Most young readers haven't yet reached their peak earning years, meaning they often don't have the discretionary income to spend on the kind of books, magazines, and journals that feature public writing. Yet, well-crafted and engaging public writing has the power to change all that, welcoming younger readers with at least a modicum of the subject matter, tone, and content a rising generation seeks. Online, magazines like *Fast Company,* with 17.2 million monthly page views, is going venerable, older business publications like the *Wall Street Journal* and *Forbes* one better. Defining its brand with words like "innovation," "world-changing ideas," and "design," the 1995 start-up prefers lan-

---

5. The University of British Columbia, "Demographics–Age," accessed October 15, 2019, https://www.grad.ubc.ca/about-us/graduate-education-analysis-research/demographics-age.

guage that speaks to the young and the young at heart. According to its website, *Fast Company* "inspires readers to think beyond traditional boundaries, lead conversations, and create the future of business."[6] They urge potential advertisers to "align with *Fast Company's* society of change amplifiers, fast adopters, and ambitious rebels." Thinking beyond chronological age to focus instead on the virtues or attributes of our ideal reader, a la *Fast Company*, is one way to transcend the ageism baked into the publishing industry.

Interestingly, for all its youthful vibe, the median age of the *Fast Company* community member tops forty, and with a median household income in 2019 of over $187,000, its readers achieve a significantly higher income stream than the average wage-earner in their early forties. Sixty percent say they're tasked with making decisions within their business and forty-three percent report being in "top management" at their workplace.[7]

The popular science news site *Live Science* offers another compelling example. Though *Live Science* doesn't publish its age demographics online, it's a well-known fact that its readers skew young. The site has become extraordinarily popular with science-vested readers in their twenties and thirties, in particular, who have helped it net thirty-eight million monthly page views and an impressive eighteen million new monthly users. Like *Fast Company*, *Live Science* signals its youthful vibe in an "About Us" page that reads: "For the science geek in everyone, *Live Science* breaks down the stories behind the most interesting news and photos on the Internet, while also digging up fascinating discoveries that hit on a broad range of fields, from dinosaurs and archaeology to wacky physics and astronomy to health and human behavior." In choosing signifying words such as "geek" and "wacky" the editors hope to synergize with open-minded spirits and nimble minds. The challenge for *Live Science* and its ilk is twofold: (1) overcome the established lack of youthful readers on stand-alone news sites and (2) choose youthful language without alienating older readers. Remember the "face mites" NPR story we examined in an earlier chapter? Writing for *Live Science*, Brandon Specktor covered it, too, under the

6. *Fast Company*, "Spotlight," accessed October 15, 2019, https://spotlight.fastcompany.com/.

7. *Fast Company*, *2019 Media Kit 2019*, accessed October 15, 2019, https://images.fastcompany.net/image/upload/v1549315273/fc/Mediakit_2019_1.18.19_j8z8qc.pdf.

disgustingly memorable headline "Face Mites Live In Your Pores, Eat Your Grease, and Mate on Your Face While You Sleep." Specktor is an admirably concrete writer with a keen sense of audience, but for me his lead paragraph "ages down" a bit much, potentially leaving older readers feeling left out, or grossed out:

> Don't freak out, but you probably have a few dozen arachnids grinding up on the tiny shafts of hair lodged inside your face, quietly gorging themselves on your natural oils.[8]

Specktor's is visceral writing except that, in expressions like "grinding up on," it may take the cult of youth a mite too far.

The lesson holds: if you're a writer who desires the largest possible audience, learning to age your writing up and down (but mostly up), where and when appropriate, is an important step toward greater engagement and accessibility.

DRUNK ON LANGUAGE: LATINATES

In many cases the language of jurisprudence isn't willfully tone-deaf; it's just born that way. Much of the super-serious language of our legal code comes from a "dead language," Latin, associated with higher learning, law, medicine and theology. Words derived from the Latin (Latinates) tend to be built from many meaning-obscuring syllables (polysyllables) whereas the more direct language families (the Germanic languages from which much of English is derived) are often more plainly monosyllabic.

I learned to appreciate the difference between Latinate and Anglo-Saxon roots working at a bowling alley that stayed open until the wee hours. To keep ourselves awake one slow weekend a coworker and I challenged ourselves to come up with as many synonyms for drunkenness as possible. Ours may have seemed a silly game dreamed up by the sleep-deprived, but our list spoke to the incredible variety of word origins or *etymologies* (itself a Latinate and before that a Greek word) describing the all-too common condition of inebriation.

Some of our words—such as *inebriation* and *intoxication*—were clearly Latinates, given away both by their gratuitous syllable count

8. Brandon Specktor, "Face Mites Live In Your Pores, Eat Your Grease, and Mate on Your Face While You Sleep," *Live Science*, May 22, 2019, https://www.livescience.com/65533-your-face-mites-never-poop.html.

and their telltale prefixes and suffixes. Alternately, words like *drunk* and *blitzed* clearly belonged in the Germanic language family. In fact, most of the dozens of drunken synonyms we concocted on our late shift made no pretense about the ugliness of drunkenness itself, whether they were colloquial speech or words to be found in a regular or slang dictionary—*schnockered, hammered, soused.* Of course, if you're arrested, the charge will be for the euphemistic Latinate *intoxication* rather than for being plainly *pickled* or *plastered* in public. Latinates lend dignity and cover.

Years later I learned that wordsmith Ben Franklin had published his own Drinker's Dictionary in the *Pennsylvania Gazette* on January 6, 1737. Franklin prefaces his rather comical list thusly: "The Phrases in this Dictionary are not (like most of our Terms of Art) borrow'd from Foreign Languages, neither are they collected from the Writings of the Learned in our own, but gather'd wholly from the modern Tavern-Conversation of Tiplers."[9]

Franklin wasn't kidding about the tonal richness of his barstool lexicon. Here's just a taste of his Drinker's Dictionary for letters B and C. Notice how many of the expressions sound like drunkenness feels or looks—an important lesson in language's mimetic capacity—*mimesis* from the Greek word meaning to imitate. A word's mimetic quality allows it to sound like the thing it hopes to mime, and, in that mimicry, to convey an accompanying tone. In Franklin's book, a drunkard could be said to be:

> Biggy, Bewitch'd, Block and Block, Boozy, Bowz'd, Been at Barbadoes, Piss'd in the Brook, Drunk as a Wheel-Barrow, Burdock'd, Buskey, Buzzey, Has Stole a Manchet out of the Brewer's Basket, His Head is full of Bees, Has been in the Bibbing Plot, Has drank more than he has bled, He's Bungey, As Drunk as a Beggar, He sees the Bears; He's had a Thump over the Head with Sampson's Jawbone; He's Bridgey; He's Cat, Cagrin'd, Capable, Cramp'd, Cherubimical, Cherry Merry, Wamble Crop'd, Crack'd, Concern'd, Half Way to Concord, Has taken a Chirriping-Glass, Got Corns in his Head, A Cup to much, Coguy, Copey, He's heat his Copper, He's Crocus, Catch'd, He cuts his Capers, He's been in the Cellar, He's in his Cups, Non Compos, Cock'd, Curv'd, Cut, Chipper,

9. Steven Grasse, *Colonial Spirits: A Toast to Our Drunken History* (New York: Abrams Image, 2016).

Chickery, Loaded his Cart, He's been too free with the Crea-
ture, Sir Richard has taken off his Considering Cap, He's
Chap-fallen.

If we are sometimes deadly serious and formal before a judge wielding
Latinates, we are, by contrast, more relaxed and uninhibited while in
our cups, as the tone of the Drinker's Dictionary demonstrates.

Sound Produces Tone

In a long career, public writer and journalist Susan Orlean has artfully
translated to the broader reading public everything from the botany
of orchids to the sublime difficulties of taxidermy. Not surprisingly,
she's a master of musicality in public prose. She achieves her lyrical
effects both by including as many impactful single-syllable words as
possible (monosyllabic nouns and verbs practically guarantee punchy
prose) and via the use of hard consonants such as p, t, k, b, d, g and, for
me, the hard c. Note how many of these so-called plosive consonants
crop up in the first paragraph of Orlean's portrayal of former president
George W. Bush's hometown of Midland, Texas:

> In Midland, Texas, it's not the heat; it's the lack of humid-
> ity. . . . Midland has the kind of air that hits you like a brick.
> After a few minutes, your throat burns. After a few days, your
> skin feels powdery, your eyelids stick, your hair feels dusty
> and rough. The longer you spend there, the more you become
> a little bit like the land—you dry out and cake and crack. Not
> until I spent time in Midland did I fully appreciate the fact
> that the earth has an actual crust, like bread that has been
> slowly baked. I became convinced that if I stayed for a while I
> would develop one, too.[10]

It's easy for the soft-spoken and sentient scholars, specialists, and
experts who generate much of today's public writing to forget that it's
okay to sound their sonic drum, just as Orlean creates a backbeat with
hard consonants and percussive (plosive) sounds. Public intellectuals
often conflate reasonability and civility with softness of sound, to the

10. Susan Orlean, "A Place Called Midland," *The New Yorker*, October 16,
2000, 128, https://www.newyorker.com/magazine/2000/10/16/a-place-called-
midland.

extent that the words they choose serve as an unintentional lullaby for many undergraduates and casual readers. Many of these same intellectuals have grown accustomed to assuming the attention of their audience. They talk; others listen. But too often, and over time, this presumption leads to the kind of droll, punchless delivery that risks making even well-chosen words flat and forgettable.

SENTENCE LENGTH: THE LONG AND THE SHORT OF TONE

Experienced public writers know when to challenge their reader (with longer than average complex sentences) and when to give them a well-earned breather (with shorter than average simple sentences). Length, then, is closely associated with tone in the minds of readers, with pieces punctuated by shorter sentences more likely to be perceived as having a tone that is "accessible" or "reader-friendly."

What's average? In his book *Indlish*, Jyoti Sanyal notes: "Based on several studies, press associations in the US have laid down a readability table. Their survey shows readers find sentences of 8 words or less very easy to read; 11 words, easy; 14 words fairly easy; 17 words standard; 21 words fairly difficult; 25 words difficult and 29 words or more, very difficult."[11] Elsevier, a global publisher of scholarly journals in health and the sciences, recommends that writers craft sentences of 12–17 words, while noting that sentences in peer-reviewed scholarly journals often average between 25–30 words, with some of longest outlier sentences topping fifty words. Journalism, with a mean sentence-length (MSL) of 10–12 words on average, is the most concise of all.

It may sound superficial, or even self-evident, but lay readers are likely to ascribe a higher degree of difficulty or complexity to pieces of public writing with long sentences, while inferring greater ease, or simplicity, to those featuring shorter more digestible ones. Wider margins and longer paragraphs are also visual cues to the kind of complexity general readers find daunting. In fact, if one could design a publication of public writing whose pages invite rather than dissuade perusal by lay readers, it would look very much like a newspaper, with its narrow line widths, easy-to-read columns, and agreeably short sentences.

---

11. Jyoti Sanyal, *Indlish: The Book for Every English-speaking Indian* (Viva Books: New Delhi), 49.

While public writers often write sentences that fall within the twelve- to seventeen-word average recommended by Elsevier, the most effective among them aren't afraid to mix it up to prevent monotony, varying their sentence lengths at will. The most merciful have the good sense to follow their longest, most acrobatic sentences with shorter, simpler ones. I call the short end of this long-short oscillation the "chaser"—a brief palette-cleanser. Just as a veteran teacher will often follow a difficult lesson or exercise with a break, so the public writer learns to follow especially long or complex sentences with those that are more direct and readily digestible. The next time you find yourself wading through a particularly long sentence written by one of your favorite popular scholars, see if the theory holds true and they follow with a bracing chaser.

My go-to writer for sentence variety and mixed diction is the late-great David Foster Wallace. At times, Wallace's ability to move between sentence lengths, vernaculars, and even academic disciplines is almost hyperbolic, as in the following excerpt from his classic essay "Consider the Lobster":

> And an arthropod is an invertebrate member of the phylum Arthropoda, which phylum covers insects, spiders, crustaceans, and centipedes/millipedes, all of whose main commonality, besides the absence of a centralized brain-spine assembly, is a chitinous exoskeleton composed of segments, to which appendages are articulated in pairs.
>
> The point is that lobsters are basically giant sea-insects.

The first sentence comes in at nearly fifty difficult, polysyllabic Latinate words, before the chaser sentence of nine words brings the whole thing comically down to earth in the rhetorical appeal known as *bathos*. Wallace offers a prime example of a fact with which most prose stylists would readily agree: while it's more fun to inflate the balloon it's just as satisfying, in the end, to burst a bubble and bring it back down to earth.

In his fine book *Writing Tools*, journalist Roy Peter Clark of the Poynter Institute covers the long-short paragraph two-step under the category "special effects," treating it as something of an exceptional move, though in my book it's fundamental. Either way, Clark and I agree that the technique, as he puts it, "packs a punch."[12]

---

12. Roy Peter Clark, *Writing Tools: 50 Essential Strategies for Every Writer* (New

WRAPPING UP

If we've ever been told by an indignant conversational partner, arms folded across their chest, "Don't take that tone with me!" we know that a reader's or listener's objection to our attitude, or even the mood underlying our statements, can cause them to dismiss our point completely. Tone and audience awareness can make or break even our most earnest attempts at communication. If a public writer's fundamental goal is to incent others to take the time to listen, then minding our tone is essential.

Naturally, tone depends very much on intended audience, as Ben Franklin's list of drunken synonyms sampled from tipplers at local taverns makes clear. Effective public writers are above all adaptable and responsive to audience needs, modulating tone and pitch as the rhetorical occasion demands. While we have an obligation to project our voice, and to interest if not to engage, we must also listen for moments where our writing becomes too breezy or needy, more focused on how it (or we) will be received than on the message our prose means to convey.

York: Little, Brown and Company, 2006), 95.

^{8} Knowing Your Audience

Writers willing to make the effort to better know their audience—their demographics, their desires, even their dreams—often find that the reader they've previously only imagined gets real in a real hurry. When I teach the concept of audience to college students, I sometimes ask them to imagine they've had a wicked accident while doing donuts in a parking lot—no bodily injury, thank goodness, but their car is now a twisted pretzel that might as well be totaled. Next, I ask them to imagine the different approaches they might take retelling the story of their accident to each of the following audiences:

> The policeperson who took the accident report
> The insurance company
> Their parents (who bought the car)
> Their best friend
> Their girlfriend or boyfriend

Very often, knowing exactly whom we're writing to determines the words we choose and the attitude or mood those words convey.

RESEARCH THY READER

How do we as public writers garner information on that mythical beast—our reader—we most likely will never meet in person and yet spend our entire professional lives imagining? If we are considering potential submission venues for an in-progress piece of public writing, we might reach out to the editor of that publication, who's likely to know loads of specifics about who buys their publication. Some magazines, newspapers, and journals make such information accessible to the general public, though often it is hidden under the "advertise with us," "for advertisers," or "media kit" link. Advertisers believe in highly targeted segment marketing as part of their creed—the more they know about the consumer the more efficiently and economically they're able to convince would-be advertisers of real rather than imagined synergies.

Under the advertising link, we often find information about gender, age, education level, and median income of readers with whom we seek audience. Sometimes a deeper dive into actual reader demographics proves dispiriting. For example, readers with the money to subscribe to top periodicals and journals and the time to read them are often far less diverse as we might like. The *New York Times* and *The New Yorker* offer cases in point. Publishers of much of the best public writing, these Big Apple-based periodicals closely guard their audience profiles. Still, a little research online from venerable sources like the Pew Research Center yields telling results.[1] Readers of the *New York Times* are three times as likely to have a postgraduate degree and twice as likely to make more than $100,000 per year. Approximately fifty-six percent of its readers are men. Nearly sixty percent are college graduates and nearly forty percent are high-earners. Nearly two-thirds of the regular readers of magazines in which public writing appears, venues such as *The New Yorker, The Atlantic* and *Harpers*, are college graduates, as are sixty-three percent of readers of the *Economist* and *Bloomberg BusinessWeek*. More than half of the regular readers of the *Wall Street Journal* (fifty-six percent), *New York Times* (fifty-six percent), and news magazines in general (fifty-three percent) are college graduates—nearly double the percent of all Americans who have earned their degree circa 2020. Information as detailed as this allows us to make an educated guess as to appropriate tone.

And what do demographics tell us about the politics of *New York Times* readers? Only thirteen percent identify themselves as Republican, with similar percentages holding true for *The New Yorker* (nine percent). Compare this figure with the minority of Republicans (twenty percent) who read the *Wall Street Journal* and *USA Today* or the majority sixty-five percent who listen to *The Sean Hannity Show*. Statistics as lopsided as these would surely dissuade us from submitting to *The New Yorker* if we were a conservative public writer pitching a piece about, say, the benefits of trickle-down economics. Conversely, we might feel emboldened if we were percolating a piece on the positive political legacy of the late Supreme Court justice Ruth Bader

1. The Pew Research Center, "In Changing News Landscape Even Television Is Vulnerable," September 27, 2012, https://www.people-press.org/2012/09/27/section-4-demographics-and-political-views-of-news-audiences/.

Ginsburg. A recent Gallup poll shows, among those who do identify with a major party, there is a double-digit Democratic advantage at each age-point from eighteen to thirty-five.[2] Publications whose readers skew young are generally more likely to favor liberal- and progressive-minded topics and approaches.

Public writers do well to consider the youth, or lack thereof, of the readers of their target publication, especially when the target venue is a news magazine. An earlier Pew Research poll found the readership of most news magazines aging faster than the population overall.[3] Among the seven magazines studied (*The Atlantic, Jet, Newsweek,* the *New Yorker, Time, U.S. News,* and *The Economist*), the outlets most likely to publish long-form, in-depth public writing—*The Atlantic* and *The New Yorker*—logged average reader ages at or just below fifty. By comparison, *Jet's* average reader was approximately thirty-three years-old in 1995 and just over forty years of age a decade later in 2005. The average reader age statistics reflect a uniquely volatile period in the publishing industry, as magazines struggled to monetize online platforms and draw younger consumers. Still, the striking age discrepancy among subscribers of particular periodicals should cause any public writer to stand up and take notice. In 1997, for example, the average reader of *Jet* was nearly seventeen years younger than the average reader of *The Atlantic,* approximating a generational gap. It's the difference, for instance, between sharing a story with our friends, and spinning it to our parents.

Bodice-Ripping Romance Writers Get Their Audience

Few are more keenly aware of the demographics and desires of their readership than those much-maligned scribblers of "bodice rippers": romance writers. Scoff if you must, but raconteurs of love stories get their audience, and the audience gets them back. Look at recent Nielsen tracking statistics and at surveys conducted by the Romance Writers of America and it's easy to ascertain that romance readers are unusually

---

2. Frank Newport, "Party Identification Varies Widely Across Age Spectrum," *Gallup.com,* July 10, 2014, https://news.gallup.com/poll/172439/party-identification-varies-widely-across-age-spectrum.aspx.
3. The Pew Research Center, "Median Age of Readership by Magazine," March 12, 2007, https://www.journalism.org/numbers/median-age-of-readership-by-magazine/.

loyal.[4] Thirty-five percent have been reading the genre twenty years or more . . . longer than some of my youngest public writing students have been alive. Think romance readers are naughty? Think again. The top two tropes in romance lit are more pure than prurient: (1) friends to lovers and (2) soul mates/fate.

The statistics say that romance readers, wrongly stereotyped for their love of trashy novels, actually rank the quality of the story more highly than the name recognition of the author. They're more likely to buy books from a brick-and-mortar bookstore than a virtual shop online, and they are nearly as likely to browse their local Walmart for their next good read as they are the neighborhood Barnes and Noble. Defying their reclusive cat-lady stereotype, romance readers are uniquely well-connected. Seventy-six percent of readers discuss the romance books they're reading with friends and acquaintances. According to Nielsen's Books and Consumer Tracker, women still make up more than eighty percent of the market, though their market-share is dropping as more men discover the pleasures of this uniquely reader-responsive and rapidly diversifying genre.[5] Romance book buyers in the US are most likely to be between thirty and fifty-four years old, are highly concentrated in the South, and boast an average individual income in excess of $55,000.

Facts like these help debunk harmful stereotypes writers sometimes hold about their readers and help identify reader interests and needs with greater accuracy and fidelity. As the statistics cited above demonstrate, we as writers are badly missing our mark if, in drafting our debut story of two friends turned soulmates, we assume our readers to be poor shut-in Southerners with few friends with whom to discuss their favorite reads.

REMEMBER THE RECEIVING END

Let's face it: it takes an ordinate amount of ego-strength to put our thoughts down on paper. A sturdy ego gives us impetus to express ourselves in public as well as to steel ourselves for the reaction. Ironically,

4. The Nielson Company, "Literary Liaisons: Who's Reading Romance Books?", August 10, 2015.
5. Romance Writers of America, "About the Romance Genre," accessed October 15, 2019, https://www.rwa.org/Online/Romance_Genre/About_Romance_Genre.aspx.

however, the same powerful "I" that compels us to write often blinds us to the needs of the reader with whom we seek audience.

A case in point: Remember the long letters or emails we once wrote to the people we loved back home when we were younger? The ones we dashed off in a dither from the drama of summer camp, or study abroad, or a first year at college? We went on for pages that, when boiled down to their essence, read: me, me, me, and more me. In our defense, we may have been baited into our egotistical ways by the inherent limitations of the genre; unless we were composing our missives on social media or some other synchronous chat platform, we had little choice but to monologue. Since we were writing to someone who couldn't be there with us, and therefore couldn't grow visibly sleepy, or disinterested, or impatient as they listened to our unilateral recounting, we had tacit permission to make the conversation one-sided. In our letters and emails home we acknowledged the lives and the worlds of those on the receiving end, surely, but we typically did so rhetorically, with a short-but-sweet "So how are things with you?" thrown mercifully into the third page of our diatribe, as much to give the exhausted writer a needed rest as to salve the guilt we felt for making our communiques all about us.

Sometimes my workshop participants and I retrieve one of those early personal letters or emails and count up how many question marks we used in them. Usually we come back with tallies of zero, or perhaps one or two at the most. There must be something about writing, we conclude, that tempts us toward self-centeredness and solipsism. It's almost as if the more emphatically we resolve to be the author, the more we begin to ignore the feelings of others for fear they will knock us off course or distract us from our stated purpose. On the positive side, being allowed to monologue, to sustain a train of thought for many paragraphs without interruption, allows us to achieve coherence and momentum. Such undivided focus can be intensely therapeutic—like being allowed to vent on a long road trip where our copilot does nothing more than interject an occasional question when our stamina begins to flag.

To combat the me-syndrome, I encourage us to think of the act of writing as a conversation more than a lecture or monologue. In a recent workshop we generated the following diagnostic list of good conversation descriptors. For us, a dynamic conversation is:

- Engaged

- Reciprocal
- Coherent
- Relevant
- Respectful

By *engaged*, we meant that a conversation implies some sort of mutual investment and interest; absent that, it tends to end rather quickly.

By *reciprocal*, we wanted to convey the back-and-forth, give-and-take of mutually satisfying discourse. For us reciprocal means more than providing a token few seconds in which the reader/listener obligingly responds. Reciprocity means achieving a natural rapport in which the reader-listener has important lines of their own to deliver, and meaningful work to do to meet the writer halfway.

By *coherent*, we signified that a conversation should have a train of thought—two or more people willing to stay on-topic long enough to respond to one another's comments and queries before indulging tangents and non-sequiturs.

By *relevant*, we meant to say that a conversation, if mutually satisfying, is typically mutually relevant. If the subject of the discourse lacks relevance to one or more party, that party is likely to tune out altogether.

By *respectful*, we intended to communicate that public discourse should be guided by a sense of decorum if not dignity. While we might disagree wholeheartedly with our conversational partner, or with the methods they use to make their point, we acknowledge that they have the right to say it, so long as they do so with a modicum of respect. This elusive quality—the willingness to agree to disagree while nevertheless engaging in conversation—we once called civility.

Reviewing our list of descriptors, we find that the thing most of us have been having in our papers, articles, and reports isn't a conversation as much as the me-monologue we mastered as needy teenagers. Just as our long-ago letters and emails lacked question marks signifying sincere interest in, and responsiveness to, others, so too our most recent publications and reports neglect the agency of our readers.

Other than the obvious ego-trap, what prevents us from crafting reader-serving writing isn't meanness or pettiness but, more often than not, a core uncertainty about whom we're writing to. Taking the time to get to know our readers really isn't all that different from the investment we routinely make in those we love, like, or have no choice but to work with. We learn to "read" them (hopefully we read them sympathetically) because we have good reason to care about their satisfaction, whether that reason is a potentially poor performance review, a below-average rating on Goodreads, or a disgruntled review board at the agency or institute that funded our work. Engaging in a true conversation on the page, establishing a compelling so-what factor, respectfully acknowledging a reader's time, intelligence, and autonomy—all these are part and parcel of public writing that seeks to serve.

The Five "Es:" Why Readers Read

Apprenticing writers are often asked to keep their audience in mind, but without fleshing out the person on the other end, such advice sounds like platitude. The truth is most of us haven't the foggiest notion of who's on the other end, mainly because reading remains a somewhat anonymous and hermetic act. When writing for our particular workplace we often know our limited readership all too well—so well that we often feel hamstrung by our advance knowledge of their particular likes and dislikes. But for true public writers—those who reach an audience beyond friends, family, and coworkers in their field—meeting readers in person is a relative rarity. Perhaps they introduce themselves to us at a conference; or they send us an email or follow us on social media. Short of such exceptional outreach, however, our readers often remain unknown and at-large.

The enjoinder to keep our audience in mind is often marginal advice until we drill down on whom that audience actually is. "But I don't have an audience yet!" we might reasonably reply, exasperated on hearing the cliché counsel to "know our audience" trotted out yet again. In such a context "audience" sounds big and impressive—suggesting legions of adoring fans hanging on our every word—when in fact we what we more often have is an audience of one: our professor, mentor, or work supervisor. And all we really know about that slighty grumpy reader is the half-baked inferences and half-boiled assumptions we've been able to make thus far about them—their likes and dislikes, their ideologies, a whiff of their politics, a cursory sense of their pet peeves and don't-go-theres. At its most heightened, our sense of audience might extend to an intuitive knowledge of how this or that authority figure would likely respond to any point we might make in our writing.

For student writers, a teacher often serves as a focus-group-of-one, and that audience is, by definition, nonrepresentative. At the exact moment when emerging writers need to broaden and diversify their audience, they find themselves thrown back to the writing-for-one paradigm, where the one they're writing for is often a middle-aged, middle-class, liberally educated scholar. Writers looking to better their craft need more varied input than that. Instead of calling to mind a single idiosyncratic reader secure in their ivory tower, faculty lounge, or administrative office suite, why not imagine a wider and more dynamic audience for our work, honing in on the characteristics of that broader readership in aggregate? Isn't that how successful businesses develop a sense of their customer base, and politicians their constituencies? But when such demographic data isn't readily available, what, if anything, can we conclude about the audience for our public writing?

When I begin to lose sight of my audience, I find it helpful to remind myself of the diversity of reader motivations with a homegrown mnemonic—"The Five Es." For me, the Five Es amount to a recitation of why most of us read, and what we as writers hope to give readers by way of a complete package:

> *Education.* We read to learn what we need to know or want to know. Every textbook, every training manual, every continuing education article seeks to teach us something we need to perform our job more expertly. Even self-improvement is driven by our need to learn a better or different way.

> *Entertainment.* We read to be entertained in much the same way that we might tune into a smartly written sitcom or a compelling documentary. We download a thought-provoking podcast for the comfort and the company of hearing an intelligent voice with something compelling to say.

> *Escape.* We read in order to get away from the burden of self, from the confines of our everyday lives, and from the stifling and deadening effects of routine and status quo. As a motivation, escape often comes with an unfairly negative connotation, but what reader isn't willing to testify to the life-giving power of disappearing into the world of an engrossing account?

Engagement. We read for conversation and communion, not just between reader and writer, but with the like-minded souls who care just as passionately about the world around them. Often texts themselves become the locus of this communal spirit when we join books clubs and discussion groups for those need-to-talk-about texts and ideas. Timely and thought-provoking narratives have the power to draw us out into the world, causing us to face beautiful and sometimes damning truths about the society we have been complicit in making.

Empowerment. We read because we want to be able to change our own life or the lives of others. Long ago our teachers taught us that editorials, op-eds, and letters to the editor ought to include potential solutions to the problems we flag. It's a corollary to the golden rule: those who complain the loudest ought to be willing to offer the brightest and boldest solutions. Readers often want to leave a text with an empowering takeaway—the sense that they can do something with the knowledge or awareness gained. With learning comes the desire to better control outcomes, whether that outcome is selling more units, breaking a habit cycle, or making more ethical choices. Empowerment via another closely related "e"—enlightenment—may explain why the best-selling nonfiction book of all time is the King James Bible. Sales in the billions for a holy book testify to the wisdom and guidance readers find therein.

The Five Es speak to high-minded reader motivations, but we read for visceral reasons, too: to become more successful (at our work, in our personal life, in our love life, in our chosen sport or hobby), more wealthy, more attractive, more beautiful, and many other motivations that might seem less intrinsically noble than the intentions inscribed in the Five Es. While intellectuals may scorn anything that seems remotely "self-help," the lay reader often reads for more immediate exigencies than the scholar accustomed to taking the long view. Curing ourselves of cancer, for example, strikes the sufferer with a terminal diagnosis as far more urgent than David Foster Wallace's ethical treatise on the live-boiling of lobsters.

When the subject matter for public writing truly rings the reader's bell it's likely to ping both high-minded and visceral motivations. A great example is Gladwell's *Outliers: The Story of Success,* which consistently comingles intellectual discourse with personal growth narratives. "Who among you wants to be less successful?" I often ask my workshop students early in our time together. It's a rhetorical question, of course, and one I, too, must answer. Personally, I would like to be more successful as a son, a partner, and an entrepreneur. And the list goes on.

Gladwell has Needy Me at the word *success.* Yet, he also has High-Minded Me with the promise of an intellectual inquiry into why some succeed famously while others fail to thrive. A first-generation college student who grew up in poverty, I'm open to hearing Gladwell's sociological and psychological case studies explaining the obstacles that prevent some talented people from rising to the elite echelons of success, and how we as a society might ensure them a more equitable opportunity.

MIND YOUR JARGON

We writers are expert in sniffing out others' jargon but pretty much hapless when it comes to detecting our own. To make the point, I invite my public writing workshoppers to return to previous papers and articles they've written for a team leader, supervisor, or professor. Then I ask them to find a jargon-laden passage that, in retrospect, excludes rather than includes the average reader.

One, a marketer in training, locates this snippet in some of their previous disciplinary scholarship: (I've bolded some of the jargon for ease of discussion.)

> Another advantage of this methodology is that industries can market products on **media platforms** where the company's **target audience** would most likely be made aware of it. For example, Primark may have an advertisement online rather as opposed to newspaper, because their main **target audience** is young female adults and very few people of that **demographic** read daily newspapers. In essence, a corporation can more efficiently **budget finances** and **appropriately advertise** their product.

This passage may not scream corporate vernacular at first glance, perhaps because marketing's language, like psychology's, has so thoroughly infused our everyday lexicon that coinages such as "target audience" and "media platform" seem as if they belong to the culture at large. But read more closely into the passage and it's easy to see how heavily it tilts toward those who share the writer's field.

If this writer's dalliance with discipline-specific discourse seems tame, read the sample below another aspiring public writer, an organic chemist, wrote in the abstract of their lab report:

> ***Directly synthesizing*** *a* **carboxylic C-O bond** *into an* **ester** is a challenge in **catalytic chemistry**, as well as **synthetic organic chemistry**. The only methodology currently available requires the use of *heavy metal salts* . . . . Recent research has shown **radical based syntheses** *to be effective in forming* ***carbon-oxygen bonds*** from **aliphatic carboxylic acids** *without environmental or personal concerns. Successful studies have been done using the* **aliphatic carboxylic acid, naphthyl acetic acid**. The goal of this study on ibuprofen was to determine if a **radical based strategy** would be effective on a more **complex aliphatic carboxylic acid**. Ibuprofen was chosen because of its low cost, availability, and its more **complex carbon backbone** than **naphthyl acetic acid**. An **NHPI radical synthesis and a DCC Steglich esterification coupled radical synthesis** *were run, in which were both successful in producing the desired* **carbon-oxygen bond** to form an **ester**.

Doubtless, the lab supervisor who received the report understood its meaning perfectly, yet this writer wasn't at all happy with the jargon of their passage when viewed through the lens of public writing. In fact, they felt downright guilty for assuming that their audience knew, for example, what acronyms like DCC (N,N' Dicyclohexylcarbodiimide) and NHPI (N Hydroxyphthalimide) stood for. Buried in the acronyms and chemical compounds is the writer's real subject: heavy metals such as arsenic, cadmium, chromium, lead, and mercury that hold enormous public health significance. Metallic elements of exactly the kind the report describes are known to induce organ damage even at lower levels of exposure. They're classified by the EPA as human carcinogens.

After our workshop, the author duly resolved to write chemistry in a way the general public could understand. As the heavy metal example demonstrates, the difference can mean life or death.

COMPLEX TIMES CALL FOR SIMPLE SPEECH

During the COVID crisis, scientists who could convey their knowledge jargon-free became minor celebrities. One such mensch was Dr. Emily Landon, an infectious disease expert at the University of Chicago. Landon's televised remarks struck many as an example of humane, empathetic talk from a medical doctor. Where others failed, Landon succeeded in personifying the virus as a merciless thief in the comments that follow, making the illness less abstract and more palpable, all while building up to the Big Ask, appealing to healthy individuals to stay home:

> This virus is unforgiving. It spreads before you even know you've caught it. And it tricks you into believing that it's nothing more than a little influenza. For many of us, it may not be much more than the flu. And so it could be very confusing as to why schools are closed, restaurants are shuttered.
>
> And now, the virus is taking what's left of our precious liberty. But the real problem is not the 80 percent who will get over this in a week. It's the 20 percent of patients, the older, those that are immunocompromised, those that have other medical problems who are going to need a bit more support—some oxygen or maybe a ventilator, life support.
>
> We do amazing things like this to save patients in our American hospitals and across the world every single day. But we can't take care of everyone at once. And we can't keep that low mortality promise if we can't provide the support that our patients need.[6]

Landon makes liberal use of the familiar personal pronouns—"I," "We," and "You"—not the more formal third-person we might expect form a medical official dispensing advice. In the middle of her remarks this expert in infectious diseases digresses to humanize the information she dispenses, putting a face to the illness when she describes the sacrifices her son, a fifth grader, is making, staying home from sports, science fairs, and school bake sales to keep others safe. The takeaway: if

6. Emily Landon, "Dr. Emily Landon speaks about COVID-19 at Illinois governor's conference," March 20, 2020, https://www.uchicagomedicine.org/forefront/coronavirus-disease-covid-19/emily-landon-speaks-about-covid-19-at-illinois-governors-press-conference.

an eleven-year-old can see past their own immediate needs to sacrifice for the greater good, we can too. Landon continues with a question:

> How can soccer or a book club be so dangerous? Why ask so much of people for just a few hundred cases? Because it's the only way to save those lives. And now is the time.
>
> Because the numbers you see today in the news are the people that got sick a week ago. And there are still people today who got sick today, who haven't even noticed that they've been sick yet. They picked up the virus, and it will take a week to see that show in our numbers. Waiting for hospitals to be overwhelmed will leave the following weeks' patients with nowhere to go.
>
> In short, without taking drastic measures, the healthy and optimistic among us will doom the vulnerable. We have to fight this fire before it grows too high. These extreme restrictions may seem, in the end, a little anticlimactic. Because it's really hard to feel like you're saving the world when you're watching Netflix from your couch.
>
> But if we do this right, nothing happens. Yeah. A successful shelter in place means that you're going to feel like it was all for nothing. And you'd be right. Because nothing means that nothing happened to your family. And that's what we're going for here.
>
> Even starting now, we can't stop the cases from coming fast and furious, at least for the next couple of weeks and in the short term. But with a real commitment to sheltering in place and a whole lot of patience, we can help protect our critical workers who need to use public transportation in order to safely get from where they need to go.
>
> We can give our factories time to ramp up production of all that PPE, so that we have enough masks to last. And we can make more medications and learn more about how we could use them to help save more lives. Even a little time makes a huge difference.
>
> And I know we'll get through this together and find a way back to the life that we used to live. Public health and hospitals have been working hard for a long time. And now,

it's your turn to do your part, a huge sacrifice to make, but a
sacrifice that can make thousands of differences, maybe even
a difference in your family, too.

Familiar pronouns, eye-opening metaphors, conversational rapport,
straight talk from a real person rather than an empty suit or lab coat—
Landon's sincere remarks conjure the bedside manner of the trusted
family doctor, coupled with the skill of a consummate spokesperson.
Unabashed talk about the virus has become commonplace, but when
one recalls that president Woodrow Wilson never delivered a single
dedicated speech about the Spanish Flu pandemic that killed nearly
700,000 Americans, one appreciates even more the candor of a new
generation of public officials concerned with inclusive, and effective,
messaging.

WRAPPING UP

Writers eager to be read and to be understood shouldn't be afraid to
research the specific demographics of their readers. While more intuitive scribes may find artistic satisfaction in attempting to divine
who's on the receiving end, such clairvoyance isn't necessary and can,
in fact, lead to erroneous, stereotypical, or misguided decisions when
we make false or stereotypical assumptions about who's reading our
work. Learning the specifics of subscriber demographics from advertising and marketing departments can, in fact, give us a concrete idea
of who we're reaching, and, perhaps more importantly, who we're failing to include.

   When experts use excessive amounts of jargon in their communications, lay readers and listeners often come away feeling stupid,
overwhelmed, or just plain annoyed that the communicator-on-
high—the man or woman behind the machine—won't come down
from their pedestal or ivory tower. Public officials and spokespersons
willing to forego their professional jargon altogether, or to deploy it
modestly and only with accompanying context and explanation, inevitably attract larger followings than those who communicate exclusively to their colleagues. Jargon-adverse public intellectuals may find
it easier to "win friends and influence people," to paraphrase the classic
how-to text by Dale Carnegie.

   Writers in highly technical fields will find it especially important
to keep their audience in mind, since members of the public may be

predisposed to seeing such experts as pompous know-it-alls. Specialists who learn to temper their technical expertise with the bedside manner of the iconic family doctor should take solace in this abiding fact: in times of crisis the voice of the down-to-earth expert is often the voice of reason.

9 Getting Rid of Gobbledygook

T he idea that language can have life-and-death consequences stands at the center of President Barack Obama's Plain Language Act of 2010. The law requires that federal agencies use "clear government communication that the public can understand and use."

For decades rebel bureaucrats working within the government have crusaded for clearer and more accountable language in government communications. One of the pioneers in the resistance, John O'Hayre, an employee at the Bureau of Land Management (BLM) Western Information Office in Denver, published a shot across the bow of obtuse wonks and bureaucrats in his treatise aptly titled *Gobbledygook Has Got to Go*. More than a half century after he penned the slender yet useful book, it endures as a cult classic among those who care passionately about the transparency and accuracy of government outreach. The cover of my personal copy, printed by the US Government Printing Office at a cover cost of 40 cents, shows a stern Uncle Sam pointing a threatening finger at a sword-wielding dandy who's scampering away in terror. Who's the bespectacled, feather-hatted fop, you ask? Why, none other than O'Hayre's chosen foil in the book, Mr. Gobble D. Gook, Esquire. Naturally, the author makes his nemesis a lawyer. The book's preface is priceless and, for our purposes, perfectly on point:

> The Bureau of Land Management (BLM) is people, a scattering of persons in nearly one hundred towns across the continent. We become an organization only when we work intelligently together to reach common goals. And we can work together this way only when we understand each other, when we communicate clearly.
>
> Our communications have sometimes failed because of a fascination with the traditions of officialese, an in-grown compulsion to be impressively ornate rather than simply direct, to be "proper" rather than personal. We've had costly false starts because of false notions about written communications

because of our failure to read our own writing through the other fellow's eyes.

If we are to succeed in these times of new technologies, new demands and new attitudes, we must improve our communications radically. We must abandon soggy formality and incoherence in favor of modern personal communications . . .

No longer can gobbledygook be allowed to clog communication lines. Every BLM employee, regardless of rank or position, must adapt to the philosophy of simple, direct, personal communications.[1]

"It's past time government writers realized that a revolution has taken place in American prose," O'Hayre bully pulpits a few pages later, "a revolution that started years ago and is operating today at fever pitch. Newspapermen, magazine writers, and fiction writers have joined in this revolution that demands simple, concise, clear prose." Government writers are far too slow to join the cause in O'Hayre's estimation. "Jargon is the gobbledygook that passes for communications in government 'has gotto go!' It's too out-of-date to renovate; it's too expensive to tolerate." Elsewhere O'Hayre saves some of his heaviest artillery for the evil of jargon and its practitioners, calling them "flossy, pompous, abstract, complex."

True to his word, the author spends the next hundred pages with his axe sharpened to a razor's edge, ruthlessly cutting out complexity and pomposity wherever he finds it in case after case of government legalese. Fancying himself something of an aggrieved superhero, he battles his nemesis gamely at every turn to keep the insidious Gobble. D. Gook, Esq. on the run. O'Hayre saves many of his most concise before-and-after examples for the middle of the book, as our gratuitous syntax slayer and unsparing word-cutter turns his attention to a BLM fire report from Nevada penned by one of his esteemed colleagues, which reads:

FIRE REPORT: Heavy rains throughout most of the State have given an optimistic outlook for lessened fire danger for the rest of the season. However, an abundance of lightning maintains a certain amount of hazard in isolated areas that have not received an excessive amount of rain. We were

---

1. John O'Hayre, *Gobbledygook Has Got to Go* (Washington DC: US Government Printing Office, 1966), 2.

pleased to have been able to help Nevada with the suppression of their conflagration.

Certainly, I've read worse in workplace memos, but nothing escapes the chopping block of Mr. O'Hayre, who says this of the poor chap whose work he's about, almost literally, to decimate. "The curious thing about this stilted, stuffy, unnatural, puffed up and pompous piece is that the fire officer who wrote it is an educated, dignified, uncomplicated, easy-going, unpretentious, plain-talking fellow, who wouldn't be caught dead talking like he writes." The problem that afflicts the state fire officer who so earns the author's ire is the same that afflicts many of us when confronted with a workplace writing assignment: "We become somebody else and usually that somebody else is an aristocratic dandy of some past century." Here's Uncle Sam's attempt at combatting "writing evil caused by big word pomposity":

> Fire readings are down throughout most of the State. But a few rain-skipped areas are dry, and lightning is a hazard there. We are glad we could send some of our people to help Nevada put out their recent range fire.

It's not a perfect rewrite—for example, "fire readings are down" in the first sentence could certainly be concretized and clarified—but at fifty percent of the original length the revised version would certainly be a more digestible read for busy firefighters and fire officials on the front lines.

GOBBLEDYGOOK ISN'T GONE, BUT IT'S GOING

Thanks to the tireless efforts of the O'Hayres and Obamas of the world, Gobbledygook is still on the run, as evidenced by the 2020 Census. Faced with woeful questionnaire return rates caused in part by the COVID-19 crisis, government wordsmiths went back to the drawing board, sharpening their pens to craft clear, connotatively charged appeals to the American public. I confess to being one of the poor souls deemed derelict in their duties. My first overdue notice arrived in the form of a tidy black and white postcard whose big bold type encouraged me to "Shape the future." The message on the flip side read:

Dear Resident:

> It is not too late to respond to the 2020 Census. Make sure you are counted.
>
> Please respond now at my 2020census.gov or complete and return the paper questionnaire we sent you earlier. If you are unable to respond online or need assistance, please call toll free . . .

Uncle Sam strikes all the right notes in this first reminder, appealing mostly to the self-interest of its recipients—it wasn't too late for *me* to be counted; *I* could still shape the future. They would make it easy for me.

By the second notice, the government scribes recognize that laggards like me require a new approach:

> Dear Resident:
>
> Recently you should have received instructions for completing your 2020 questionnaire online. Local communities depend on information from the Census Bureau to fund programs that promote the well-being of families and children as well as equal employment opportunities for you and your neighbors. If you have not already responded please complete your short 10-minute 2020 Census questionnaire now.
>
> Your response is important to your local community and your country. By law, your response is required and your answers are confidential. If you do not respond, we will need to send a Census Bureau interviewer to your home to collect your answers in person.

In this second reminder, the Census Bureau swaps out the earlier appeal to self-interest in favor of community spirit. Now our procrastination or outright refusal to complete the form could have unintended consequences, hurting our family or our community. The tone of the follow-up missive is informative rather than accusatory or passive aggressive. One imagines the team of writers in Washington who drafted it figured this second notice might be read by someone else in the household; someone other than the individual who ignored the first notice.

Like tens of millions of other Americans during that first winter and spring of COVID-19, I'm ashamed to say I required a third notice, one which echoes the content and tone of the prior communique closely. This time, however, the writers attempt a different approach. While the prior notice highlights abstract qualities such as well-being and equality, the third and final notice tries a new tack, referencing benefits more tangible and concrete: "such as helping to put in roads, parks, and hospitals where they are needed most." However, the carrot of improved infrastructure and health is carefully counterbalanced by the most explicit stick yet in the following statement, placed smack dab in the topic-sentence position where it can't be missed: "You are required by law to respond to the 2020 Census."

Believe me when I tell you I didn't delay returning my questionnaire for the purpose of bettering this rhetorical analysis, but if it was necessary for me to receive three notices in order to comply, I am pleased to find in my unconscionable delay an object lesson in informative, clear, and respectful government communication.

AND THE WINNER OF THE NO GOBBLEDYGOOK AWARD IS . . .

Each year the government's regulatory language continues to grow by accretion, bogging down the bureaucracy with over 200,000 pages in the Code of Federal Regulations alone at last count. Gobbledygook is so thoroughly ingrained in our jurisprudence it's proven impossible to weed out in the half century since O'Hayre demanded in no uncertain terms that it go. What choice do we have, then, but to celebrate smaller, incremental gains in clarity and concision, however modest, wherever we find them?

One of the more dramatic contemporary examples from the Plain Language Initiative website is this before-and-after comparison of drug labels that won the No Gobbledygook Award presented by Al Gore.[2]

---

2. Tamar Nordenberg, "New Drug Label Spells It Out Simply," *FDA Consumer*, July–August 1999, 31.

Allergy Tablets

INDICATIONS: Provides effective, temporary relief of sneezing, watery and itchy eyes, and runny nose due to hay fever and other upper respiratory allergies.
DIRECTIONS: Adults and children 12 years and over—1 tablet every 4 to 6 hours, not to exceed 6 tablets in 24 hours or as directed by a physician. Children 6 to 11 years—one half the adult dose (break tablet in half) every 4 to 6 hours, not to exceed 3 whole tablets in 24 hours. For children under 6 years, consult a physician.
EACH TABLET CONTAINS: Chlorpheniramine Maleate 4 mg. **May also contain** (may differ from brand): D&C Yellow No. 10, Lactose, Magnesium Stearate, Microcrystalline Cellulose, Pregelatinized Starch.
WARNINGS: May cause excitability especially in children. Do not take this product unless directed by a physician, if you have a breathing problem such as emphysema or chronic bronchitis, or if you have glaucoma or difficulty in urination due to enlargement of the prostate gland. May cause drowsiness; alcohol, sedatives and tranquilizers may increase the drowsiness effect. Avoid alcoholic beverages, and do not take this product if you are taking sedatives or tranquilizers without first consulting your physician. Use caution when driving a motor vehicle or operating machinery. As with any drug, if you are pregnant or nursing a baby, seek the advice of a health professional before using this product. Keep this and all drugs out of the reach of children. In case of accidental overdose, seek professional assistance or contact a Poison Control Center immediately.
Store at controlled room temperature 2°-30°C (36°-86°F).
Use by expiration date printed on package.
Protect from excessive moisture.
For better identification keep tablets in carton until used.

Made in U.S.A.

N3 111111 11111 8

Note that the "before" example isn't too bad. Bolded all-caps indicate the most important information; bolded lowercase suggest secondary importance. Beyond the bold headings, however, this is a crowded page, one that visually implies that recommended dosages and drug warnings are as important as whether or not the tablet contains the common food coloring D&C Yellow No. 10. There's a potentially tragic irony here when we realize that a person suffering from a debilitating cold, flu, or allergy is unlikely to have the focus to comb through a swarm of text to get the information they need in time for their dosage.

When we compare the "before" example with the "after" example that follows, it's easy to see a bright contrast.

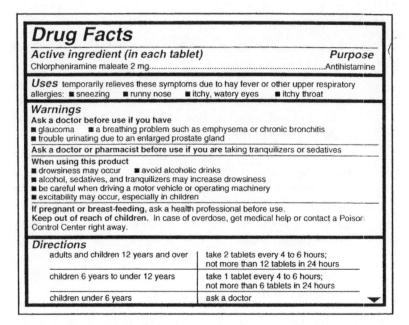

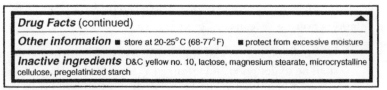

In this new-and-improved version the most crucial information has been bulleted in decreasing order of importance after the fashion of the inverted pyramid style preferred by journalists. Additional white space has been created by moving the least important information (proper storage temperature, etc.) and inactive ingredients (those least likely to cause an adverse reaction) to a bottom or side flap. The government bureaucrats also strike the right tone in the revised wording of the new-and-improved version. The tweaks in diction may seem small—for example, the difference between the admonition "Use caution" and the improved "Be careful." Yet, most of us would be more comforted by "Be careful" than "Use Caution." Why? "Use Caution" sounds like a robot-caregiver compared to the more humane and parental "Be careful."

In announcing the first round of No Gobbledygook Award winners, Vice President Al Gore spoke at length, peppering his speech with before-and-after examples the newly implemented executive order had helped create:

> Today, I am proud to announce—on behalf of the President—a new initiative that will go a long way to making government easier to understand. The President is issuing today an Executive Memorandum to the heads of all executive departments and agencies, directing them to begin writing in plain language to the American people.
>
> Here is a general guide to plain language: short is better than long; active is better than passive; everyday terms are better than technical terms, and—you can use pronouns like "we" and "you;" in fact, you should. As many of our departments and agencies are already finding out: when you apply these rules, a 72-word regulation can shrink to six words; the title of a regulation can change from "means of egress" to "exit routes." And letters to customers can create understanding, instead of confusion and frustration.[3]

Later in his speech, the Vice President quoted what, in his view, was one of the more egregious uses of Gobbledygook in an old OSHA regulation covering "Means of Egress":

> Ways of exit access and the doors to exit to which they lead shall be so designed and arranged as to be clearly recognizable as such. Hangings or draperies shall not be placed over exit doors or otherwise so located as to obscure any exit. Mirrors shall not be placed on exit doors. Mirrors shall not be placed in or adjacent to any exit in such a manner as to confuse the direction of the exit.

And this Plain Language Initiative fix:

> Exit routes: An exit door must be free of signs or decorations that obscure its visibility.

"That's it. From 76 words to 14," Gore commented, before adding, "But we still might be able to make it a bit better. The words 'obscure

---

3. "Plain Language Initiative Announcement," Plainlanguage.gov, accessed October 15, 2019, https://www.plainlanguage.gov/examples/awards/gore-speech/.

its visibility' are a little like the old gobbledygook." How about: 'Don't put up anything that makes it harder to see the exit door.'"

In other cases, Plain English, or lack thereof, can quite literally be a matter of life and death. *The National Law Journal* describes the sobering case of a judge who told jurors that a murder conviction required "malice aforethought," a torturously tangled phrase the jury misinterpreted to mean that the murder had to have been committed with a mallet. The Plain English Initiative cites several compelling studies pointing to a tragic flaw in the legalese that characterizes many states' jury instructions, among them:

- According to a study by the Northeastern University's Capital Jury Project, forty percent of capital jurors wrongly believed that their jury instructions required them to accompany a conviction with a death sentence.

- According to a study of Washington DC jurors, more than fifty percent of jurors defined "preponderance of the evidence" as a "slow and careful pondering of the evidence." More than fifty percent of jurors could not define "speculate," and about twenty-five percent did not know the meaning of "burden of proof," "impeach," or "admissible evidence."

After revisiting and rewriting its garbled instructions to jurors, California compiled its own before-and-after examples to share with members of the Plain Language Action and Information Network (PLAIN), a community of federal employees dedicated to the idea that citizens deserve clear jargon-free communications from their government.

Before	After
Proof beyond a reasonable doubt	Proof that leaves you with an abiding conviction that the charge is true
A preponderance of the evidence	More likely than not
Failure of recollection is common. Innocent misrecollection is not uncommon	People often forget things or make mistakes in what they remember.

In each and every instance the "after" example is not only more clear but emphatically more plainspoken; maybe it is more clear *because* it is more plainspoken. As the old hymn reminds, "It's a gift to be simple."

More concretely, the difference between the Befores and Afters are revealed in syllable counts. For instance, the "before" version of the third jury instruction takes more than twenty syllables to convey, while the "after" takes a mere seventeen. That's concision—making the point without extraneous or gratuitous words. The new-and-improved version also humanizes itself by inserting a subject ("People") while invoking the kind of time-tested common-sense language parents might use. (i.e., "People often . . . make mistakes"). Compare this to the opaque "before" language—"Innocent misrecollection is not uncommon"—a phraseology so convoluted only a lawyer could have dreamed it up.

PRESIDENTS WHO PASS THE BUCK

President Warren G. Harding was notorious for *pleonasm*, a word that signifies using more words than necessary to make your point, from the Greek *pleonasmos*. Harding's long-winded and wordy manner of speaking is part and parcel of his pleonastic oratorial style; little wonder that he also liked to use the term *bloviate* to describe his dubious art, a word that has come to be synonymous with politicians blowing hot air. Indeed, any discussion of the urgent need for plain language from government officials would be incomplete without a brief inventory of some of the more egregious examples of political bloviation— talking a lot while saying precious little.

President Bill Clinton infamously bloviated his way through this grand jury testimony in 1998, testifying that he wasn't fibbing to his aides when he told them, about his alleged extramarital affair with his young White House intern Monica Lewinsky, "There's nothing going on between us." Under oath, Clinton clarified (or perhaps purposefully muddied) that original statement, saying his testimony:

> It depends on what the meaning of the word 'is' is. If the—if he—if 'is' means is and never has been, that is not—that is one thing. If it means there is none, that was a completely true statement. . . . Now, if someone had asked me on that day, are you having any kind of sexual relations with Ms. Lewinsky, that is, asked me a question in the present tense, I would have said no. And it would have been completely true.[4]

---

4. Timothy Noah, "Bill Clinton and the Meaning of 'Is'", *Slate*, September

In 2020, Donald Trump found himself in a similar linguistic thicket over Coronavirus testing in the White House, bloviating, "I tested very positively in another sense. I tested positively toward negative, right? So no, I tested perfectly this morning. Meaning I tested negative. But that's a way of saying it. Positively toward the negative."[5] Reporters and citizens alike were left scratching their heads at the prez's gobbledygook.

Earlier, Trump stepped into another controversy caused by his diction, appearing to imply that household disinfectants such as bleach and Lysol might be effective against COVID-19 if injected into the body. The media outcry was vociferous though mostly unfounded, as the Poynter Institute discovered when they fact-checked the transcript of the president's speech. Even so, poison control centers throughout the nation reported a spike in calls, and Lysol saw fit to issue a statement that read in part, "As a global leader in health and hygiene products, we must be clear that under no circumstance should our disinfectant products be administered into the human body (through injection, ingestion or any other route)." A closer read of the transcript shows that the president's potentially tragic miscommunication originates in a series of incomplete thoughts and uninformed word choices:

> A question that probably some of you are thinking of if you're totally into that world, which I find to be very interesting. So, supposedly we hit the body with a tremendous, whether it's ultraviolet or just very powerful light, and I think you said that hasn't been checked, but you're going to test it. And then I said supposing you brought the light inside the body, which you can do either through the skin or in some other way. And I think you said you're going to test that, too. Sounds interesting, right?"
>
> And then I see the disinfectant, where it knocks it out in one minute. And is there a way we can do something like that, by injection inside or almost a cleaning, because you see it gets in the lungs and it does a tremendous number on the lungs, so

13, 1998, https://slate.com/news-and-politics/1998/09/bill-clinton-and-the-meaning-of-is.html.

5. Justin Wise, "Trump on his latest coronavirus test: 'I tested positively toward negative'" *The Hill*, May 21, 2020, https://thehill.com/homenews/administration/498990-trump-on-his-latest-coronavirus-test-i-tested-positively-toward.

it'd be interesting to check that, so that you're going to have to use medical doctors with, but it sounds interesting to me. So, we'll see, but the whole concept of the light, the way it kills it in one minute. That's pretty powerful.[6]

Later in his remarks the president clarified to a reporter: "It wouldn't be through injections, almost a cleaning and sterilization of an area. Maybe it works, maybe it doesn't work, but it certainly has a big effect if it's on a stationary object." The record shows that the president did not in fact advise injecting household cleaners into the body, but instead of pointing out that fact, Trump and his advisors later claimed he was merely being "sarcastic." Shortly thereafter, the administration announced that Trump would cease delivering what had been his daily Coronavirus briefing.

Trump wasn't the only world leader to miscommunicate about the emerging crisis. French President Emmanuel Macron said this in his speech to the French people, "Were we prepared for this crisis? On the face of it, not enough. But we coped. This moment, let's be honest, has revealed cracks, shortages." *Cracks? Shortages?* To some Macron's mea culpa was watered down in egregious euphemism, understatement, and what George Orwell calls Doublespeak (originally "Doublethink") in his dystopian novel *Nineteen Eighty-Four.* The so-called small cracks Macron references did not adequately address the spread of a disease that, even at the time of his speech, had accounted for nearly 15,000 deaths and 100,000 confirmed cases in France alone according to official estimates, numbers that surely suggest more of a cliff or a chasm.

COVID-19: A Study in Government Messaging

Early in the outbreak of COVID-19, America struggled to find a language for the common-sense precautions it asked citizens to take to keep themselves safe, resulting in a proliferation of descriptive terms, each with its own problematic connotations.

Shelter-in-Place seemed to connote a natural disaster or nuclear war. Some feared the term would only heighten the growing public

---

6. Daniel Funke, "In Context: What Donald Trump said about disinfectant, sun and coronavirus," *Poynter Institute*, April 24, 2020 https://www.politifact.com/article/2020/apr/24/context-what-donald-trump-said-about-disinfectant-/.

panic over the pandemic, especially for younger generations that had never endued the once ubiquitous nuclear fall-out drills. *Stay-at-Home Order* connoted paternalistic overreach to many, signifying the all-seeing, all-knowing State telling citizens what they must do. Those who argued against its use pointed out that it could lead the public to feel as if they were being punished, like unruly teenagers, for bad behavior. *Safer-at-Home* softened the sentiment somewhat by implying that while citizens could move about by their own free will, they would be safer at home. Critics of the term charged that it was blatantly euphemistic since *safer-at-home* offered politicians and other public officials linguistic cover for stay-at-home orders. Others pointed out that the term *safer* was in fact a monumental hedge, belying the fact that no place was safe from the virus, and that the best We the People could hope for was to stay *safer*. *Government Lockdown*, meanwhile, rankled those who felt it falsely connoted martial law, fascism, and the inevitable compromising of citizens' civil rights. Unsurprisingly, the term, initially used by the media to describe government-imposed stay-at-home orders in Italy and Spain, was not widely adopted by public officials in America, for good reason.

In their communications with concerned residents, America's mayors attempted to win the public's support via an appeal to the common good. In northern California, mayors throughout the greater San Francisco metro area followed up the Bay Area shelter-in-place order with direct outreach to residents. In Menlo Park, mayor Cecilia Taylor wrote a heartfelt letter addressed to residents just days after one of the nation's earliest and most strict stay-at-home orders went into place. Her plainspoken, jargon-free missive reads in part:

> As individuals, it is important for each one of us to minimize our own risk of being infected by taking preventative measures within and outside our homes. It is as simple as washing your hands frequently, not touching your face, coughing or sneezing into a tissue and then throwing the tissue in the trash, avoiding crowded places if you are at a higher risk, and staying home if you are sick. For a full list of the actions you can take, visit the Centers for Disease Control and Prevention (CDC) coronavirus disease prevention and treatment website.
>
> As a community, we can demonstrate values of compassion and decency by not spreading misinformation, educating

ourselves, taking care of our most vulnerable residents, and not shaking hands.

As your Mayor, I will communicate with you regularly about COVID-19 in the coming weeks and months in coordination with city staff. My goal is to communicate accurate information, raise awareness and support your needs. I am more than hopeful we will get through this together.[7]

Taylor's letter to concerned citizens avoids needlessly invoking medical buzzwords while successfully projecting the calm, poised, reasonable tone one expects of a leader in the midst of a crisis.

New York governor Andrew Cuomo likewise earned plaudits for his efforts to put an incomprehensible tragedy into terms the public could understand. As New York took its first halting steps toward a phased reopening after a lengthy stay-at-home order, the governor took the podium to say:

This is about facts and science and data these decisions are being made as a matter of math . . . . You start to increase economic activity, you have more people coming out of their homes, more people contacting other people and then you measure the impact of that increase with numbers—not with opinions, not with politics, not with partisanship. With numbers . . .

You have 30 tracers ready for every 100,000 residents. That comes from the experts, and then you watch the infection rate and you make sure that you don't get near 1.1 on the infection rate. It's math and there's a liberation in that. At a time of such division in politics and elections and all this garbage this is an exercise in science and math and it's data that we can all share and we can all participate in. I encourage people to go look at the data and look at what's happening in your region because that's how we're going to get through this—on the numbers on the math, on the facts.[8]

7. Cecilia Taylor, "Letter from the Mayor addressing the novel coronavirus," City of Menlo Park, March 9, 2020, https://www.menlopark.org/CivicAlerts.aspx?AID=465.
8. "Amid Ongoing COVID-19 Pandemic, Governor Cuomo Announces State is Bringing in International Experts to Help Advise the State's Reopening Plan," New York State, May 18 , 2020, https://www.governor.ny.gov/

Cuomo's staccato delivery fell short of poetic, but the public appreciated the governor's plainspoken, straight-shooting attempt at translating into layperson's terms the input received from medical advisors. He was successful enough, in fact, that respondents to a Sienna College Research Institute poll reported trusting the governor over President Trump by a 78 to 16 percent margin.[9]

Elsewhere in America, however, confusion grew around such fundamental terminology as "self-isolation," "self-quarantine," and "social distancing," prompting the US Department of Health and Human Services to offer their own set of definitions:

> Isolation separates sick people with a contagious disease from people who are not sick.
>
> Quarantine separates and restricts the movement of people who were exposed to a contagious disease to see if they become sick. These people may have been exposed to a disease and do not know it, or they may have the disease but do not show symptoms.[10]

Still, confusion over the new government-speak and its attendant epidemiological jargon abounded, raising further questions. If someone claimed to be "self-isolating," they could either be symptomatic, asymptomatic, or perfectly well, the H.H.S. definition appeared to suggest.

As a new lexicon born of the disease began to take hold, government bureaucrats and medical officials renewed their commitment to the kind of clear, unambiguous language called for by Obama's Plain Language Act of 2010. Wordsmiths at the CDC would surely have made O'Hayre proud with this example of clear, unadorned, unpre-

---

news/amid-ongoing-covid-19-pandemic-governor-cuomo-announces-state-bringing-international-experts.

9. Lynsey Jeffrey, "Conservative New Yorkers Trust Cuomo Over Trump On State Reopening, Poll Finds," National Public Radio, April 27, 2020, https://www.npr.org/sections/coronavirus-live-updates/2020/04/27/846223674/conservative-new-yorkers-trust-cuomo-over-trump-on-state-reopening-poll-finds.

10. U.S. Department of Health and Human Services, "What is the difference between isolation and quarantine?" HHS.gov, https://www.hhs.gov/answers/public-health-and-safety/what-is-the-difference-between-isolation-and-quarantine/index.html, accessed May 30, 2020.

tentious prose written from government officials to citizens, written in response to the question: "What is social distancing?"

> Social distancing, also called "physical distancing," means keeping space between yourself and other people outside of your home. To practice social or physical distancing:
>
> - Stay at least 6 feet (about 2 arms' length) from other people
> - Do not gather in groups
> - Stay out of crowded places and avoid mass gatherings
>
> In addition to everyday steps to prevent COVID-19, keeping space between you and others is one of the best tools we have to avoid being exposed to this virus and slowing its spread locally and across the country and world.
>
> Limit close contact with others outside your household in indoor and outdoor spaces. Since people can spread the virus before they know they are sick, it is important to stay away from others when possible, even if you—or they—have no symptoms. Social distancing is especially important for people who are at higher risk for severe illness from COVID-19.
>
> Many people have personal circumstances or situations that present challenges with practicing social distancing to prevent the spread of COVID-19. Please see the following guidance for additional recommendations and considerations for:
>
> - Households Living in Close Quarters: How to Protect Those Who Are Most Vulnerable
> - Living in Shared Housing
> - People with Disabilities
> - People Experiencing Homelessness[11]

In fewer than two hundred words, the CDC expertly defines its terms, while indirectly calming the fears of citizens who might misinterpret the guidance to say that they must remain six feet from others in their own household—a practical impossibility for most. The

---

11. Centers for Disease Control and Prevention, "What Is Social Distancing?" https://www.cdc.gov/coronavirus/2019-ncov/prevent-getting-sick/social-distancing.html accessed June 1, 2020.

government communication specialists who crafted the finely tuned message are careful to be inclusive, preferring the official term "household" to more subjective terms such as "family" or "loved ones" that may not apply to all those who shelter together. Importantly, they preference the phrase "people experiencing homelessness" over the more imprecise, impolite, and impolitic nomenclature "homeless people."

Wrapping Up

Given the significance of their subject matter, public writers err on the side of formality and dignity, though increasingly the most useful official communications aren't weighted down with obscure Latinates and other needlessly polysyllabic words. The COVID-19 crisis obviated the need for clear, consistent, concise government messaging, reminding the public of the deadly consequences of inexact, inexpert, or just plain inept use of language in a time of crisis.

It's fitting that we conclude this chapter by returning to the visionary federal employees that are part of the Plain Language Action and Information Network (PLAIN). They insist on the radical notion that government documents be readable by the very people whose lives they govern. For these PLAIN speakers, an effective government document was one that helped readers:

- find what they need,
- understand what they find; and
- use what they find to meet their needs.

Whether we write for the government or simply in the public interest, we as public writers would do well to affix the preceding list to our keyboards as a constant reminder that our writing aims not just to communicate coherently, but, like the most dedicated government officials and public servants, to help reader-citizens meet their needs, solve their problems, and better their lives.

10 Establishing Ethos, Embracing Inclusivity

Awriter, speaker, or public servant makes an appeal by ethos when they convince their audience that they are worth listening to. The credibility of a speaker or a writer relies on their authority on the subject matter as well as on how much they personally are deemed worthy of respect. The Greek's idea of ethos can be boiled down to a nutshell: ethos is a good person writing well.

Given the Greeks obsession with ethics and character, it's easy to see why a concept as enduring as ethos would fall out of fashion among some post-post-moderns. What is a "good person," really? And if such a thing exists, how do we define it? Even the definition of what constitutes good writing is hotly debated among today's scholars. Whether or not one uses the term *ethos*, it's clear that authorial credibility and character can determine whether our work is read, and if so, how it is perceived.

For many public writers being a good person is synonymous with being a good citizen. Drilling down on the unique attributes of good citizenship, therefore, offers us one reasonable way to arrive at a contemporary definition of ethos—a good person writing well. Whom better to ask than Canadians, a people admired the world over for their neighborliness and global citizenship. For Canadians responding to national surveys good citizens are those who (1) actively participate in their community, (2) help others, and (3) are tolerant of others.[1]

It's easy to see how an active citizen-writer could come to epitomize ethos in an era many perceive as sorely lacking in civility. Because public writers seek to serve while making their words relevant to a wider community, ethos is central to their success. Like politicians and other public servants, public writers rely on ethos to move an audience.

---

1. The Environics Institute, *Canadians on Citizenship: Final Report*, February 2012, https://www.inclusion.ca/site/uploads/2016/10/Canadians-on-Citizenship-Final-Report-Mar-1.pdf.

Gender-Inclusive Language

Many seasoned public writers feel falsely confident in their use of gender-inclusive, non-binary language, but the effects of sexist language are insidious and ethos-wrecking. Like unintentional bias, bigotry creeps into the language of even the most mindful practitioners, and all of us need more and better training to weed it out completely. A case in point is the city of Berkeley, California, which adopted a gender-neutral language policy for its municipal code in July of 2019. The comprehensive edit would eliminate gender-preferenced language throughout, as indicated in the strikethrough words below:

> Section 4.39.110 Gender.
>
> "Gender." Whenever a personal pronoun is used in the neutral ~~masculine~~ gender, it shall be deemed to include the feminine and masculine also. <u>"They/them", shall indicate a singular individual,</u> unless the context indicates the contrary.
>
> Section 5. That Berkeley Municipal Code is amended to read as follows:
>
> Section 11.08.050 Construction of genders.
>
> The <u>neutral</u> ~~masculine~~ gender includes the feminine and masculine ~~neuter; the feminine, the masculine and neuter; the neuter; the masculine and feminine.~~ "They/them" shall <u>indicate a singular individual, unless the context indicates the contrary.</u>[2]

The Berkeley city manager and city clerk also confront the sexism implicit in what they describe as "commonly encountered titles of office, employment, and descriptors." Consider the image conjured when you read the word *architect*. Do you picture a man? If so, you may be right (according to recent statistics published by the National Council of Architectural Registration Boards, women account for just over thirty-five percent of newly registered architects), still the responsibility to use gender-inclusive language transcends statistics. Put another way, if one wrongly assumes the masculine gender and uses

---

2. City of Berkeley, City Council Report, June 16, 2019, accessed October 15, 2019, https://www.documentcloud.org/documents/6205125-Berkeley-gender-neutral-language-ordinance.html#document/p8.

the masculine pronoun, one marginalizes and minimizes the work of nearly two in five licensed female architects.

Readers frequently gender professions with their built-in bias. For example, if in the newspaper you read that a maternity nurse named Morgan delivered a healthy eight-pound baby, you might gender the nurse as female despite their gender-neutral name. It isn't that your conclusion is illogical (less than ten percent of nurses nationwide are male) but that such a presumption is potentially inaccurate and harmful. In fact, travel back a few sentences to the description of Morgan as a "maternity" nurse, and one finds another term rooted in gender exclusivity, since *maternity* itself comes from the Latin word *mater*, meaning mother. A public writer fully committed to gender-inclusive language might opt instead for "labor and delivery nurse," "obstetrics nurse," or "perinatal nurse."

Inclusivity-minded writers can and should push back against sexist language not only by using the they/them neutral singular recommended by the city of Berkeley, but by taking care not to perpetuate the gendering of professions. For example, a writer developing a hypothetical example about an architect might consider using the pronoun "her" to remind equity-minded readers that nearly two in five licensed architects are in fact women. For example:

> Suppose a leading architect for a boutique firm designs a multi-use retail space; she will want to be conversant with local zoning requirements, codes, and ordinances prior to drafting.

Or one could use they/them as a gender-neutral singular pronoun:

> The architect will want to be conversant with local zoning requirements, codes, and ordinances even before they begin drafting.

Most contemporary public writers have a keen understanding of the ways language has been used in the past as an instrument for hegemony, assimilation, and dominion, though too many fail to comprehend how the continued use of gender-exclusionary terms risks perpetuating that baked-in bias. Our elementary school teachers may have taught us to prefer "humankind" to "mankind," for example, and "salesperson" to "salesman," but the patriarchal bigotry hard-wired into the lexicon extends far beyond such common culprits. Indeed, in its adoption of nonbinary language Berkeley identifies a long list of commonly found gender-biased terms while prescribing more inclusive alternatives:

"Bondsman" becomes "Bonds-person"
"Brother" becomes "Sibling"
"Chairman" becomes "Chair," "chairperson"
"Craftsmen" becomes "Craftspeople," "artisans"
"Fireman," becomes "Firewoman," "Firemen,"
"Firewomen" becomes "Firefighter," "firefighters"
"Fraternal" becomes "Social"
"Heirs" become "Beneficiaries"
"Journeyman" becomes "Journey"
'Maiden" becomes "Family"
"Male" and "female" become "People of different genders"
"Manhole" becomes "Maintenance hole"
"Manmade" becomes "Human-made"
"Artificial" becomes "manufactured"
"Machine made" becomes "synthetic"
"Manpower" becomes "Human effort"
"Manpower" becomes "Workforce"
"Master" becomes "Captain," "Skipper," "Pilot," "Safe-
  ty Officer,"
"Men and women" become "People"
"Men or women" "A single gender"
"Ombudsman" "Ombuds," "Investigating Official"
"Patrolmen" "Patrol," "Guards"
"Policeman," "Policewoman," become "Police Officer"
"Pregnant" (woman, women) becomes "Pregnant employees"
"Repairman" becomes "Repairer"
"Salesman" becomes "Salesperson" or "Salespeople"
"Sister" becomes "Sibling"
"Sorority," "Fraternity" become "Collegiate Greek sys-
  tem residence"
"Sportsman" become "Hunters"

CENSORSHIP VERSUS SENSITIVITY

Some writers feel that Berkeley's ordinance crosses the line from sensitivity to outright censorship, arguing that they should be able to use words such as "fraternal," "heirs" and "manhole" whenever they choose. In implementing its new policy, Berkeley isn't attempting to legislate what language can be used by the general public, but is instead setting standards for gender-neutral terminology in city codes, ordinances, and publications. Even writers who feel passionately about freedom of speech must recognize that every client or publisher maintains its own lists of unacceptable speech. Several years ago, for example, the list of banned or filtered words on a popular gaming system was leaked by free-speech advocates. Users, they claimed, could not name their characters "pimp," for example, or "Hitler" or, curiously, "badwords," or the word "censor" itself.[3] Most of the banned words on the list, gaming websites reported, referenced drugs, slurs, and sexual terms or dealt with controversial topics like anorexia.

Public writers must also be mindful of the growing list of microaggressions, defined in part "as slights, snubs, or insults, whether intentional or unintentional, that communicate hostile, derogatory, or negative messages to target persons based solely upon their marginalized group membership." Microaggressions can include, for example, references to America as a "melting pot," which can appear to encode assimilationist demands. Even intended compliments, including ascriptions of intelligence based solely on race or gender, can fall under the category of unacceptable speech.

INCLUSIVE WORDINGS IN THE WORKPLACE

Job ads serve as a litmus test for inclusivity or exclusivity. Highly crafted ads offer a built-in feedback loop, making it possible to track how certain words and phrases help shape a job pool, and, via experimental design, to suss out the words and phrases that net a more diverse candidate pool.

Corporate giant BBVA recently published its own recommendations for gender-inclusive language, suggestions that included avoiding words said to convey gender stereotypes, such as "compete" or "dominant," that may deter female candidates.[4] Better, they advised, to use words

3. Lauren Keating, "These Are the Words Nintendo Censors from Appearing on the 3DS," *Tech Times*, February 17, 2016, https://www.techtimes.com/articles/134442/20160217/words-nintendo-censors-appearing-3ds.htm.
4. Cristobal Baeza, "An inclusive workplace begins with the wording of job ads," *BBVA*, March 7, 2019, https://www.bbva.com/en/an-inclusive-workplace-begins-with-the-wording-of-job-ads/.

like "motivation" or "tireless" as more inclusive synonyms. They cite research conducted by Textio, a platform that predicts the type of response job ads will get based on their wording. Textio finds that ads that use the second-person pronoun "you," the second person-plural "us," and the first-person plural "we" fill faster. Phrases such as "you love finding the best solution to a problem" are more effective at attracting candidates, they claim, than impersonal, third-person references like "the ideal candidate." Textio's findings track closely with best practices for inclusivity-minded public writers. Both job ads and public writing seek to create a wider tent, to communicate truthfully and transparently, speaking cogently and coherently to wider audiences in a language that helps them feel included and valued.

A more detailed study by academics Daniel Gaucher, Justin Friesen, and Aaron C. Kay returns concrete data on the way workplace-related words include and exclude. The researchers gender-coded over four thousand job-ad and workplace-related words. Their experiment proposes to test something called social dominance theory, a tenant of social psychology that asserts that institutional-level mechanisms reinforce and perpetuate existing group-based inequalities. Gaucher, Friesen, and Kay hypothesize that language itself serves to maintain inequalities in workplace environments. When job advertisements are constructed to include more masculine than feminine wordings, the researchers discover, participants perceive more men within those occupations, and women find the jobs less appealing. Their study confirms that "perceptions of belongingness (but not perceived skills) mediate the effect of gendered wording on job appeal."[5]

Here is a list of the words the research team codes as highly masculine and highly feminine respectively, with an asterisk used to denote a truncation:

---

5. Danielle Gaucher, Justin Friesen, and Aaron C. Kay, "Evidence That Gendered Wording in Job Advertisements Exists and Sustains Gender Inequality," *Journal of Personality and Social Psychology* (March 7, 2011): 17–20.

Masculine Words	Feminine words
Active	Affectionate
Adventurous	Child*
Aggress*	Cheer*
Ambitio*	Commit*
Analy*	Communal
Assert*	Compassion
Athlet*	Connect
Autonom*	Considerate
Boast*	Cooperat*
Challeng*	Depend*
Compet*	Emotiona*
Confident	Empath*
Courag*	Feminine
Decide	Flatterable
Decisive	Gentle
Decision*	Honest
Determin*	Interpersonal
Dominant	Interdependen*
Domina*	Interpersona*
Force*	Kind
Greedy	Kinship
Headstrong	Loyal*
Hierarch*	Modesty
Hostil*	Nag
Impulsive	Nurtur*
Independen*	Pleasant*
Individual*	Polite
Intellect*	Quiet*
Lead*	Respon*
Logic	Sensitiv*
Masculine	Submissive
Objective	Support*
Opinion	Sympath*
Outspoken	Tender*
Persist	Together*
Principle*	Trust*
Reckless	Understand*
Stubborn	Warm*
Superior	Whin*
Self-confiden*	Yield*
Self-sufficien*	
Self-relian*	

The results of this survey and others strongly suggest what writers, rhetoricians, marketers, and advertisers have long known—certain words strongly attract certain groups while strongly repelling others. If public intellectuals hope to reach a large and diverse audience they must be careful to avoid words that needlessly exclude, alienate, or isolate.

However, there is a flipside to this same point, and one that professional writers do well to consider. If the results of the study hold, it stands to reason that those hoping to attract a narrower subset, or specific demographic, might in some cases purposefully choose highly gendered words and phrases. Consider recently defunct *ESPN the Magazine* with an annual circulation estimated at two million readers, eighty-two percent of whom are men. One would assume that a highly masculine word such as "dominant," "dominating," or "dominated" would magnetize rather than alienate the publication's target audience.

A United Nations of Gender Neutrality

In a push for inclusivity the United Nations published its own guidelines for gender-neutral language across its six official languages—Arabic, Chinese, English, French, Russian and Spanish. The English language, the organization points out, has relatively few gender markers beyond its telltale pronouns and possessives (he, she, her and his); and some nouns and forms of address. Most English nouns do not have grammatical gender forms, though the authors of the UN guidelines point out the long-standing difference between what they call "grammatical gender" and "gender as a social construct," which they describe as "the roles, behaviors, activities and attributes that a given society at a certain time considers appropriate for men or women."

By what methods does the UN recommend writers and speakers achieve greater gender neutrality and inclusivity? Unlike the city of Berkeley, they suggest pairing—the use of both feminine and masculine forms in tandem (he or she; her or his). Pairing, they advise, works best when the writer/speaker wants to "explicitly make both women and men visible."[6] Because pairing can become tedious in long-form pieces, they recommend using the strategy in moderation. It may be

---

6. United Nations, "Guidelines for Gender-inclusive Language in English," accessed October 15, 2019, https://www.un.org/en/gender-inclusive-language/guidelines.shtml.

more appropriate, they say, to alternate masculine and feminine forms by paragraph or section, rather than by sentence or phrase, as in the following example:

> When a staff member accepts an offer of employment, *he or she* must be able to assume that the offer is duly authorized. To qualify for payment of the mobility incentive, *she or he* must have five years' prior continuous service on a fixed-term or continuing appointment.

Writers and speakers seeking greater gender inclusivity can sometimes achieve the same effect by removing extraneous or superfluous pronouns. Compare:

> If a complainant is not satisfied with the board's decision, he can ask for a rehearing.
> A complainant who is not satisfied with the board's decision can ask for a rehearing.

In the second iteration, the default masculine pronoun has been deleted, since the gender of the complainant is presumably irrelevant to the complaint. Writers can also purposefully use the passive voice to eliminate gratuitous gender pronouns. For instance, compare:

> The author of a communication must have direct and reliable evidence of the situation he is describing.

> The author of a communication must have direct and reliable evidence of the situation being described.

Finally, in addition to the use of "they" as a gender-neutral singular pronoun, the UN recommends writers and speakers consider the relative pronoun "one." In North America "one" can sometimes feel stilted or stuffy, though it is more inclusive. Compare:

> A staff member in Antarctica earns less than he would in New York.

> A staff member in Antarctica earns less than one in New York.

ACHIEVING REAL CONCILIATION

Public writers hoping to persuade readers via an appeal to ethos often face a skeptical if not openly dubious audience. On the positive side, writing to a resistant audience tends to sharpen the writer's skills, demanding that the public intellectual use their full repertoire, including what rhetoricians call "conciliatory arguments." At some point in any given argument it's incumbent upon the arguer to show that they understand the opposing viewpoint.

Sadly, few politicians, orators, debaters, polemicists, or public intellectuals really invest in hearing the other side. With most of their intellectual resources deployed to win the battle, they can't afford to give the opposing side much sympathetic thought. If they do hear the other side, they show weakness, and if they show weakness, they worry they may lose the edge they have on their opponent. Too often public discourse devolves into an attempt not to hear the other side, but to degrade, disparage, or defame it. The result is often that the arguer-persuader falls victim to the most common logical fallacy—an attack on the character, motive, or other attribute of the person or persons making the case.

Real conciliatory argument, by contrast, builds ethos by endeavoring to understand the other side. In a pro forma college essay, a conciliatory argument might be as simple as a phrase, for example:

> While climate change skeptics eagerly cite the cooling of the North Atlantic as evidence for claims of climate hype, rising temperatures across the globe make climate change a settled matter.

Can you spot the conciliation in the opening subordinate clause? Here the writer concedes that there is at least one significant climatological phenomenon—better known as the Atlantic Multidecadal Oscillation—that appears to contradict the theory of rising sea-levels caused by Arctic melting and a hotter planet overall. In the second half of the sentence the writer returns to their core claim, however—that climate change should be considered fact rather than theory. This level of conciliation is the minimum expected of a thoughtful writer on most issues, but it's possible to give even more time to minority or opposing views. Briefly propping the opposing side's argument up only to tear it down at our convenience enacts another logical fallacy, the straw man.

The public writer who succumbs to the straw man fallacy presents a slight or superficial representation of the opposition that's easy to knock down. The arguer gives the impression of decisively refuting an opponent's argument, while actually refuting an argument that's less complete, or substantially different, than the one the opponent might have raised themselves.

Real conciliation, like real compromise, can make us feel vulnerable, but it often opens the door to new insight, mutuality, and respect. Respect, in turn, yields unexpected commonalities and shared solutions. While it might be a mistake for politicians on a crowded debate stage to spend valuable seconds agreeing with their ideological antithesis, public writers determined to find common cause on difficult issues like global warming will find real conciliation worth their time. On a broader level, genuine conciliation is born of true tolerance for the views of those on the opposite side, an artifact not just of our ethos but of our essential humanity. Among writers, adages such as "respect your reader," and "don't talk down to your reader," border on cliché, and yet for most authors embodying chestnuts like these proves a perennial challenge. In business, a company that fails to respect its customers cannot fully have their best interests at heart; they may turn a tidy profit for a month, or a year, but eventually their insincerity will be discovered and the business will suffer. Similarly, a lover that fails to respect their partner is likely to treat them poorly, cheaply, or not at all. Public writing is both relational and transactional, so when a writer fails to respect their audience, ethos inevitably suffers. The reader, not the writer, is the ultimate judge of ethos, so the writer who has offended finds themselves in the court of public opinion awaiting an uncertain verdict.

A classic example of failing to respect the audience is the infamously awful email believed to have been leaked by one of gameshow host Steve Harvey's former staffers. In the email, Harvey shows little respect for the very people who help make his TV show possible, constituting an epic failure of ethos from which its host never fully recovers. In the excerpt that follows, a few moments of superficial conciliation and nicety bubble up in the pro forma salutation "Good morning," and "Welcome back," as well as in the obligatory "Thank you, all," at the end, but everything in between smacks of bitterness or outright disdain. Here's the text:

Good morning, everyone. Welcome back.

I'd like you all to review and adhere to the following notes and rules for Season 5 of my talk show.

There will be no meetings in my dressing room. No stopping by or popping in. NO ONE.

Do not come to my dressing room unless invited.

Do not open my dressing room door. IF YOU OPEN MY DOOR, EXPECT TO BE REMOVED.

My security team will stop everyone from standing at my door who have the intent to see or speak to me.

I want all the ambushing to stop now. That includes TV staff.

You must schedule an appointment.

I have been taken advantage of by my lenient policy in the past. This ends now. NO MORE.

Do not approach me while I'm in the makeup chair unless I ask to speak with you directly. Either knock or use the doorbell.

I am seeking more free time for me throughout the day.

Do not wait in any hallway to speak to me. I hate being ambushed. Please make an appointment.

I promise you I will not entertain you in the hallway, and do not attempt to walk with me.

If you're reading this, yes, I mean you.

Everyone, do not take offense to the new way of doing business. It is for the good of my personal life and enjoyment.[7]

Thank you all,

Steve Harvey

As in most writing that fails the respect-thy-audience test, Harvey's writing is redundant (in most of the paragraphs the first of the two sentences would do), wordy, and defensive, casting one hundred percent of the blame on others. At one point Harvey acknowledges his role in the situation he has come to resent, but he chalks his culpability up

7. Chris Gardner, "An Executive Coach Rewrites Steve Harvey's Shocking Staff Memo," *The Hollywood Reporter*, May 11, 2017, https://www.hollywoodreporter.com/rambling-reporter/an-executive-coach-rewrites-steve-harveys-shocking-staff-memo-1002966.

to his own generosity of spirit—a classic move of self-aggrandizement that job interviewees often turn to when faced with the "Describe one of your weaknesses" question, to which they reply "I'm generous to a fault." In an email of just over two hundred words, Harvey uses the word "my" no less than nine times, a reminder, by repetition, of the writer's self-centeredness.

In the memo's aftermath Chelsea C. Hayes, who trains millennials and executives in workplace conduct, attempted a rewrite that might have kept Harvey's ethos intact. Hayes works for The Coaching Factory, an executive coaching company whose homepage states, "We believe corporate training is something that should be enjoyed, not endured. Our training experiences blend storytelling, games, teamwork, movies, and most importantly, clear takeaways to provide a training experience that is just as fun as it is fruitful." Here's Hayes's attempt at a public writing-styled makeover of Harvey's mean-spirited memo:

> Good morning team, welcome back!
>
> I cannot thank you enough for making Season 4 of the 'Steve Harvey' Show one of the best experiences of my life. Your hard work is what makes it happen.
>
> I've been experiencing some challenges around finding time to eat, prepare, and check in with my family when we're not shooting. This has become increasingly difficult and exhausting for me. For Season 5, please allow my dressing room to be a safe space where I can be alone so I can be sure to bring my absolute A game to each and every one of you.
>
> If any of you have ideas on a structured system we can implement outside of my dressing room for more touch points, please send those ideas to ABC (any representative you choose) by ABC (any date you choose).
>
> I can't wait for this new season, thank you for all that you do!
>
> Steve Harvey

Clearly, Harvey needs some executive coaching from someone with public writing chops. Still, Hayes's revision leaves something to be desired, with its heavy concentration of corporate-speak. Some of the revised memo's corporate clichés—phrases such as "safe space," "structured system we can implement," "bring my . . . A-game"—still feel a smidge insincere and euphemistic.

In the 1970s humorist and *Saturday Night Live* writer Don Novello challenged the officious and often insincere ethos of corporate America. Writing under his *nom de plume* Lazlo Toth, Novello pursues one of the most fundamental civic acts, commencing a letter-writing campaign to CEOs, politicians, and other public figures. He willingly plays the fool, aiming to bring corporate bigwigs and buffoons down to size (a gesture the Greeks called *bathos* . . . quite literally lowering the high-and-mighty by bringing them down to earth) by provoking comical corporate and bureaucratic responses to his willfully inane missives. In one such letter, Novello writes to the Golden Seal company, maker of Mr. Bubble bubble bath, expressing his confusion over the instructions on the box urging users to "keep dry," How can he use the bubble bath if he's forced to keep it dry?

Novello's dry wit as an epistolary writer is comical enough on its own, but the letter he receives in reply is humorous only if one appreciates farce. After several earnest sentences reiterating its product instructions, the Golden Seal consumer relations director takes a different tact with the incorrigible Novello:

> Our other products are listed above in our letterhead. We are enclosing an educational bulletin based on our "SNOWY" BLEACH which we would appreciate your giving to your mother. Perhaps you already use "SNOWY" in your home. "SNOWY" is the safe oxygen-type bleach for all washable fabrics and colorfast dyes. When regular laundry such as sheets, towels, underwear and linens are washed with "SNOWY" from the very beginning, and in each wash load, these items will have stronger fiber strength, longer life and better appearance than when harsh chlorine bleaches are used. Thank you again for writing to us. Yours very truly, M. Hershey[8]

Novello's response is a masterpiece of corporate satire, as his alter ego rightfully bristles at the letter's many presumptions, including the gender stereotype that men don't do laundry and that he should pass the bleach coupons on to his mother. (Does it also assume the Novello character is an adult man living with his mother?) The indignation

8. Don Novello, *The Lazlo Letters* (Workman Publishing, 1992) http://www. sullivansfarms.net/s1dneycom/lazlo/.

in Novello's reply is exaggerated for comic effect in classic hyperbolic fashion, but the nature of the offense about which he complains—companies that insult rather than honor the intelligence of their customers—is a serious one.

> To: M. Hershey, Consumer Relations Director, Gold Seal Company
>
> Dear M. Hershey,
>
> I was being nice to tell you about the error you have on your box and you send me coupons and tell me to give an additional bulletin about stains to my Mother. To begin with, I wouldn't give your lousy educational bulletin #22 to nobody! Everybody I know knows more about stains and that stuff than your fancy company will ever know! Why you don't even know how to thank someone when they offer you an intelligent suggestion! And then you have the nerve to try and give me some pitch about your BLEACH! I was writing about MR. BUBBLE, I don't care about BLEACH! What does BLEACH have to do with it? Come on! And how come the only words in capitals are your SNOWY BLEACH and MR. BUBBLE while my Mother doesn't even get a capital for her M! This is a warning that I'm thinking of moving on to another bubble bath. Stand by our President! With a right to be angry, Lazlo Toth.

Editor Constance Hale provides yet another example of failed corporate ethos, quoting a letter from the US Postal Service to a customer who, like Don Novello's Lazlo Toth, has the right to be upset, not only at their damaged package, but at the willful obfuscation and double-speak with which a government entity responds. The heart of the letter reads:

> Due to the fact that the post office handles millions of pieces daily, it is imperative that mechanical methods be used. Heavy volume and modern production methods do not permit personal attention to individual pieces of mail.
>
> Most problems occur when contents become separated from poorly prepared envelopers or containers. This causes damage to that piece as well as any properly prepared mail

> that may follow it. No matter how careful we are, mail will occasionally be damaged.
>
> Whatever the circumstances, please accept our apologies for this most unfortunate incident?[9]

Hale presents this letter as one of many examples of pleonastic (wordy) corporate writing, but its liabilities go well beyond its bureaucratese to include the use of the passive to avoid responsibility ("mail will occasionally be damaged," it confesses, without bothering to tell us by whom or by what), the use of polysyllabic, non-concrete, mostly Latinate words and phrases, and, worst of all, the indirect passive-aggressive blaming of the very customer whose mail was damaged in the first place. Reading between the lines it's clear that the plant manager at the postal facility in question has looked into the matter and found that the damaged package about which the customer writes to complain has been "poorly prepared," risking damage to others' mail and, potentially, to the facility itself. Not only does the plant manager fail to truly empathize with the complainant, they tacitly shame them, resulting in a failure in ethos that likely leaves the aggrieved postal customer feeling dismissed, disparaged, and angrier than ever.

A Bridge too Far

While classical rhetoricians believed ethos to be essential for winning arguments, writers since have learned there's danger in writing to be liked. Ever since E. B. White and William Strunk warned scribes not to affect a "breezy style" in their 1959 classic *The Elements of Style*, public writers have been trying to forge a connection with everyday readers without resorting to outright solicitousness. "The breezy style is often the work of an egocentric," Strunk and White maintain, "the person who imagines that everything that pops into his head is of general interest and that uninhibited prose creates high spirits and carries the day."

In our desire to please and to ingratiate ourselves we've all been the breezy scribbler at some point in our lives, wanting desperately for our words or ideas to be accepted or to come off sounding cool. Social media has fueled the move toward overly informal writing, with

---

9. Constance Hale, *Sin and Syntax: How to Craft Wickedly Effective Prose* (New York: Broadway Books, 1999), 162.

tweets, hashtags, and Instagram posts designed to let the writer be their most authentic, least guarded, self. The dangers of wanting too much to be hip or au currant are very real for public writers, in particular, whose livelihoods depend on establishing rapport with everyday readers. But surely speaking to lay readers means honoring their intelligence more than it does feigning an overly chatty or chummy style.

Examples of breezy, flippant writing are increasingly common in newsfeed culture. Though many of the respected journals, magazines, and newspapers where public intellectuals place their work try to hold the line, a breezy informality increasingly pervades online news sites whose traffic is driven by newsfeeds. Consider the following paragraph from Charles Fishman's article "Neil Armstrong and Buzz Aldrin were lost on the Moon. Really":

> Oh, Mission Control never lost radio contact with them. But NASA was never able to figure out where, exactly, on the Moon they had set down, while they were on the moon. And NASA sure did try.[10]

In his *New York Times* best-selling book *One Giant Leap: The Impossible Mission that Flew Us to the Moon* Fishman avoids loosey-goosey language like this, but in making the leap from the printed page to the newsfeed he appears to pander to his audience, deploying an "Oh, and by the way" style that sounds overly informal.

Another recent example comes from Alden Wicker writing for the respected news and culture site *Vox*. Wicker's challenge in the article is to explain the science behind the new line of "washless clothing," some of which, its manufacturers claim, can be worn for up to one hundred days without laundering. The writer relies heavily on interview quotes from Rachel McQueen, an associate professor in the Department of Human Ecology at the University of Alberta, to explain how sweat interacts with bacteria to produce body odor. Wicker quips that McQueen, "has smelled a lot of dirty T-shirts" before adding:

> Natural fibers, including cotton, merino wool, and rayon made from bamboo, trees, and—yeah, sure—seaweed, are hydrophilic, meaning they love water. That's why cotton gets so sopping wet when you work out.[11]

10. Charles Fishman, "Apollo 11 really landed on the Moon—and here's how you can be sure (sorry, conspiracy nuts)."
11. Alden Wicker, "Clothing You Don't Have to Wash," *Vox*, July 15, 2019,

It's the "yeah, sure," and breezy clauses appearing elsewhere in the piece such as "one day you're pulling a supposedly clean workout tank from your drawer and wrinkling your nose" that arguably push this researched, albeit odiferous, piece of public writing over the line from "just right" to "too much." For me, the author's mixing and mingling of McQueen's hard science with his own sometimes snarky style undermines his ethos on a topic of significance to consumers, some of whom are paying close to $100 per shirt for high-tech textiles. Wicker's perfectly welcome to mix tone, diction, and register in an article written by and about the senses, but there's a way of writing vividly and viscerally without sounding so off-the-cuff. In the passage below he nearly pulls it off, though note how the chatty asides and editorial comments detract from otherwise high-quality public writing:

> Sweat itself is odor-free (unless you've just eaten a lot of garlic) but as soon as it meets our body's bacteria—which varies from person to person—it's metabolized into volatile, gaseous compounds that float to our noses.

Wrapping Up

Ethos, inclusivity, and real conciliation are markers of successful public writing that aims to be read by the widest possible audience. While crafty or cunning writers can fake such ineffable qualities, sensitive readers can sniff out efforts that seem obligatory, pro forma, or ingenuine. As the infamous Steve Harvey email makes painfully clear, communications that fail to respect, include, and empathize with the reader often feature writing that is not only impolite and uncivil, but also ineffective, redundant, and insulting.

In the end, even the post post-modern public writer wary of universal truths can do worse than be a good person writing well. Enacting our role as citizens requires us to consider the golden rule, conveying, whenever possible, tolerance, community-mindedness, inclusivity, and openness to others' ideas and experiences.

---

https://www.vox.com/the-goods/2019/7/15/20686239/clothing-wash-less-environment.

11 Navigating the Politics of Public Writing

These days the public writer's work invariably puts them square-ly in the realm of politics. Public intellectuals take pride in putting themselves and their ideas into circulation, and in an ideology-driven age audiences are eager to read between the lines to determine whether the writer belongs to their preferred camp. Of course, it's not just editorial pages and blogs that are decidedly political these days but also board rooms, break rooms, pressrooms, and labs. As novelist Kate Zembrano points out in *Believer* magazine: "Naming is a political act . . . writing [itself] is a political act."

Most writers would agree with Zembrano's basic premise: that put-ting pen to paper, or finger to keyboard, amounts to a rejection of the status quo. But Zembrano's second point, that naming itself is po-litical, might raise eyebrows. If even the words we choose are steeped in politics, how do writers hoping to connect with a broader public navigate such a charged landscape? If we choose loaded language, our words are likely to act like a powerful magnet, strongly attracting or repulsing readers. On the other hand, if we sidestep difficult issues with bland or lukewarm euphemism, our sentiments are likely to be read for what they are: a naïve denial of the essentially political nature of discourse or, alternately, as an act of cowardly avoidance.

PARTISAN DIVIDES AND *THE BIG SORT*

Just what to do with one's own deeply held political beliefs is one of the questions I get most often. Honestly, it's a difficult question to answer, though I recommend that disciplined writers craft, where appropriate, the kind of fair-minded, common-sense appeals that have historically distinguished American electorates. Of course, if you're George Will or Ann Coulter on the right or E. J. Dion or Mark Brooks on the left, your living depends on the artful and timely whipping up of political fighting words. But if you're the sort of writer who is tasked with conveying information or research, or one who is seeking understanding from a wide cross-section of readers, it's best to prevent your personal politics from completely hijacking your message.

When public writers lead with their politics, they effectively narrow their audience, especially in a world increasingly unwilling to hear the other side. In his best-selling book *The Big Sort: Why the Clustering of Like-Minded America Is Tearing Us Apart*, journalist and public writer Bill Bishop points out that as a rule America's Democrats and Republicans no longer live next to one another, shop at the same stores, or buy the same products, let alone read the same books and newspapers. For this reason and for others, when we meet a stranger on an airplane we generally do not lead with our affiliations. We don't say, "Say, I'm a bleeding-heart liberal, how about you?" Instead, in seeking more fundamental connections we acknowledge that we first and foremost share a bond of humanity and shared circumstance, and our instinct is to let the conversation explore how that bond might be better built rather than sacrificed to partisan bickering.

Conjuring identity politics right out of the gate may create opportunities for certain kinds of writers, but just as often an in-your-face political affiliation damages the public writer's ability to speak to all sides of an issue with credibility. Suppose, for example, that for years you've worked diligently to help a conservative organization find its voice and its brand and are now applying for a job helping a laboratory disseminate its anti-global warming messaging. It's nice to think that your skill as a wordsmith would be the number one criterion for the hire, but, realistically, the politics of your previous position are likely to red-flag your application. Of course, such discrimination is blatantly unfair. After all, when athletes and performers are hired it's not usually because of their politics, but about whether they can help the team win and, in so doing, revitalize a community. Yet, the wider world struggles to view even public writers, let alone deadline journalists, as the fair-minded professionals most seek to be.

Politics and ideology affect writers and their writing in ways both visible and invisible, ranging from the selection of the words we use, and don't use, to the topics to which we are drawn as well as those we seek to avoid. For example, how many deeply conservative writers, if left to their own devices, would choose to write about new technology limiting carbon emissions? To be fair, how many liberal writers would decide, if given a choice, to tackle the alleged liberal bias of Silicon Valley? At root, the art of public writing seeks to further public discourse and the marketplace of ideas—getting clear, well-reasoned ideas out to readers empowered to join a broader discussion. So the writer intent on ideological inclusivity—creating the broadest possible tent—learns to choose their words carefully and respectfully, with parity and small "d" democratic pluralism in mind.

POLITICALLY-CHARGED CONNOTATIONS

Search online for the term *illegal immigrant*, for instance, and prominent among the results is likely to be Center for Immigration Studies or (CIS), an entity that describes itself as "an independent, non-partisan, non-profit research organization" that is "devoted exclusively to research and policy analysis of the economic, social, demographic, fiscal, and other impacts of immigration on the United States." That's language well-crafted to convey neutrality, though it belies the conservative moorings of a nonprofit the *Journal of Philanthropy* pegged as a "[Donald] Trump favorite." A close read of CIS's pre-selected topics display its willingness to conjure conservative parlance, from "chain migration" to "migrant caravans" to "welfare use." Increasingly, those on opposite sides of the political divide choose radically different words even when referring to the same phenomenon.

Fair-minded writers seeking nonpartisan language are more likely than ever to find themselves flummoxed by nomenclatures that are seemingly sanctioned one day, and verboten the next. Best practice suggests that you refer to the style guides of the publications you respect for direction on how to handle politically sensitive language. For example, the Associated Press opted to stop using the term *illegal immigrant* altogether, causing the *Seattle Times*, the *Los Angeles Times*, and the *Denver Post* to follow suit. AP Senior Vice President and Executive Editor Kathleen Carroll explained, "The [AP] Stylebook no longer sanctions the term *illegal immigrant* or the use of *illegal* to describe a person. Instead, it advises users that *illegal* should describe only an action, such as living in or immigrating to a country illegally."[1] Meanwhile, *The New York Times* urges caution. "Without taking sides or

---

1. Paul Colford, "'Illegal immigrant' no more," *The Definite Source*, Associated Press Blog, April 2, 2013, https://blog.ap.org/announcements/illegal-immigrant-no-more.

resorting to euphemism," *The Times* recommends that its writers "consider alternatives when appropriate to explain the specific circumstances of the person in question or to focus on actions: *who crossed the border illegally; who overstayed a visa; who is not authorized to work in this country.*"[2]

The discord between these two giants of journalistic style illustrates how fraught usage can be for the public writer, and how inseparably interwoven with politics. Though the Associated Press and the *New York Times* disagree about the permissibility of certain terms, they agree that caution is indicated where connotations are concerned. The lesson for public engagement-seeking writers is clear: when in doubt, choose the most accurate term available, and consult the style guide for the organization for which you are preparing your copy, as they will have the final say when usage questions arise. A single word, if carelessly used, can appear to readers to encode an entire political worldview. Whether you refer to government programs as "entitlement programs" instead of "Social Security" or "welfare" instead of "government assistance" signifies much.

A public writer working in a politically charged landscape learns to respect connotation—the penumbra of associated meanings surrounding any given term. The difference between the words *house* and *home* nicely illustrates the difference between denotation and connotation. When you read the word *house*, what do you picture? Perhaps the physical structure: a box with rectangular window cut-outs and a sloped roof of the sort many illustrate as kids? By contrast, the word *home* conveys a constellation of layered, subjective, and often emotional associations. The denotative meaning of the two words may be somewhat synonymous, but their connotations are as varied as readers themselves.

Higher education is full of examples of the power of connotation to shape experience. For years, many faculty members not on the traditional tenure track were referred to by the blanket term *adjunct*, a word whose dictionary, denotative definition suggests something supplementary or inessential. If you've ever been an adjunct, you've surely felt this apartness. To add insult to injury, adjuncts were often referred to

---

2. Stephen Hiltner, "Illegal, Undocumented, Unauthorized: The Terms of Immigration Reporting," *New York Times*, March 10, 2017, https://www.nytimes.com/2017/03/10/insider/illegal-undocumented-unauthorized-the-terms-of-immigration-reporting.html.

informally by administrators and department chairs as "part-timers," a term capable of conjuring someone wearing shorts and flip-flops, coming and going as they please with nary a care in the world, while the reality for adjuncts is often just the opposite. Ironically, it's often the employer's commitment to the "part-timer" that is noncommittal, fickle, or inconstant. Thankfully colleges and universities have begun to favor terms, such as *per-course hires,* with fewer baked-in negative connotations. The gain may be marginal, but this newer appellation is at least more precise, and it represents an evolution toward greater sensitivity to the plight of contingent faculty. One thing is certain: each time we as public writers choose to use a phrase or word, we give it new life, or, conversely, when we decline to use it, we ensure its downgrading and gradual obsolescence. In this way, public intellectuals shape public discourse for generations to come.

For a follow-up example, let's return for a moment to the debate over the use of the term *illegal immigrant.* For past president of the National Association of Hispanic Journalists Hugo Balta, the term wrongly implies guilt without a fair trial or hearing. He points out that even murderers are not considered illegal; they are "legal persons who committed an illegal act."[3] Balta urges fellow writers to use "undocumented immigrant" or "undocumented worker," on the grounds not just that such terms are more accurate, but that they better and more fairly connote a hardworking people seeking economic justice. Humans are not illegal, he reminds us, even if their actions may be.

In his critique of the *illegal immigrant* label, Balta offers a master class in the use of connotative language, describing the term's use as "dehumanizing, derogatory, and destructive." The words he chooses form a powerful alliterative triad, one that combines denotative precision with connotative force. Balta has already argued that humans cannot be illegal, hence his use of *dehumanizing* is spot-on in both the literal and figurative sense. As a word *dehumanizing* pings a reader's innate sense of injustice; who among us can argue that dehumanized is an acceptable condition in which to exist?

---

3. Hugo Balta, "Stop using the term 'illegal immigrants,' *Seattle Times,* May 20, 2013, https://www.seattletimes.com/opinion/guest-stop-using-the-term-lsquoillegal-immigrantsrsquo/.

"Off" Brands, Rebrands, and Bad Marketing

Brand names, mission statements, and job ads offer additional case studies in how connotation can reinforce or undermine the work of writers, marketers, and advertisers. Sometimes manufacturers get the all-important act of naming all wrong, resulting in failed launches and damaged credibility. For example, in Spanish *No Va* means "no go," which meant big trouble for Chevy when it first introduced the Chevy Nova in Mexico years ago. Another dubiously named car that failed to launch made *USA Today's* top twenty-five greatest product flops of all-time, the Ford Edsel, a curiously old-fashioned-sounding name for a vehicle billed as a "car of the future" in 1957. Ford flooded dealer lots with the new release on what it unfortunately resorted to calling "E-Day." With such an ignominious launch, it's no surprise that the car turned out to be a flop. Indeed, Ford stopped production two years later with losses totaling more than $300 million.

Words bristle with ideological or political connotation. Consider the political rebranding of French Fries as "Freedom Fries" by the US House of Representatives in 2003 in response to France's refusal to support the proposed US invasion of Iraq. Republican Chairman of the Committee on House Administration, Bob Ney, suggested the renaming to help Congresspersons feel patriotic when placing their lunch order in the congressional cafeteria in that war-sensitive time. Ney recognized naming as a political act and used it to his advantage. Rather than refuse to eat "French fries" or "French-fried potatoes," he simply renamed them, assimilating them into patriotic American culture in the process.

Of course, France and other European nations have waged cultural war against America's my-way-or-the-highway linguistic unilateralism for centuries, resisting many of the Americanisms that arrive, unbidden, on their shores. Many non-American writers agree with the thesis expressed by Hephzibah Anderson's BBC piece "How Americanisms Are Killing the English Language." In it, Anderson laments:

> Despite having been born, raised and educated on British shores, it seems my mother tongue has been irreparably corrupted by the linguistic equivalent of the grey squirrel. And I'm not alone. Whether you're a lover or a loather of phrases

like "Can I get a decaf soy latte to go?" chances are your vocabulary has been similarly colonised.[4]

Anderson presents Americans as the aggressors in a pitched political
battle to establish a lingua franca. In using the word "colonized," she
strongly connotes that America's alleged linguistic imperialism represents an insidious power-grab, an attempt to make the world in its
own image by naming it in its preferred language. If that's true, it is
perhaps doubly important that writers writing in English wield their
language mindfully and with an appreciation for its use as an agent of
oppression.

Language used as an instrument of political and cultural hegemony
doesn't just threaten nations oceans away, it also has geodemographic
implications for many diverse cultures within the US. A case in point
may be Lehigh University's recent attempts to alter the boilerplate language of its job ads, specifically those portions having to do with its
location. In tackling the revisions, the university working group hoped
to emphasize something it perhaps euphemistically called "positive geography," namely Lehigh's proximity to New York City and Philadelphia.[5] The committee determined that New York and Philadelphia
were more positive places to feature in promotional materials than the
more local, more descriptive reference to the university's location—
the Lehigh Valley—used previously. Why the big outlay of time and
money to make such a seemingly incidental change? Presumably the
more geographically accurate "Lehigh Valley" failed to ping as many
positives in focus groups, though for many years it had been preferred
as an alternative with fewer negative associations than the Great Appalachian Valley or the area's other appellation—Pennsylvania Dutch
Country—the latter a term that connotes religious conservatism for
some. In essence, Lehigh renamed and reframed itself not in relation
to nearby cities such as Bethlehem, Pennsylvania, known for Rust Belt
working-class factories, but by association with two increasingly high-
tech cosmopolitan areas. Lehigh's choice illustrates the role language
plays in the malleability and plasticity of identity. One imagines that

---

4. Hephzibah Anderson, "Americanism are killing the English language,"
BBC.com, September 6, 2017, http://www.bbc.com/culture/story/20170904-
how-americanisms-are-killing-the-english-language.
5. Lehigh University, "University Job Ad Language Primer," August 2013, 3.
https://advance.cc.lehigh.edu/sites/advance.cc.lehigh.edu/files/JobAdPrimer-
8-8-13-FINAL_0.pdf.

the city burghers of Bethlehem, Pennsylvania, would have preferred Lehigh to market itself as "Bethlehem's University" rather than to align itself so publicly with metropolitan areas an hour's drive away.

Of course, the communication experts who helped Lehigh repackage its geographic identity to better signify to an audience of urban and suburban parents and their children are public writers themselves, engaged in a quintessential act of outreach, translation, and explication, no more and no less than the able wordsmiths who aided Congressman Ney in his personal crusade to turn french fries into freedom fries. Both offer case studies of the pressures truly independent-minded public writers are under to use the words others would prefer they use—or to use the words they feel are least coopted by political and ideological forces. While the highly partisan nature of the coinage ensured that freedom fries lacked the legs to supplant french fries forever, cases like Lehigh's present public writers with a lasting dilemma. The next time a higher education commentator or other public intellectual writes about the "Hidden Ivy" university in Pennsylvania, will they parrot Lehigh's preferred metropolitan-biased language, referring to the institution as "a university an hour away from New York City and Philadelphia"? Or will they instead invoke the more geographically accurate, but connotatively problematic, "university located in the Lehigh Valley near Bethlehem, Pennsylvania"?

PARSING THE POLITICS OF POTENTIAL PUBLICATION VENUES

Most public writers come to realize not only that their subject matter has political ramifications, but also that the venues to which they submit their work hold unadvertised or unacknowledged political preferences. Most newspapers, magazines, and even academic journals evidence editorial bias. Because they cannot be all things to all people their selectivity lends their publication its distinctive flavor. For better and for worse, editorial identities are built by encouraging certain topics, experiences, ideologies, and approaches, while discouraging or actively suppressing others. The savvy public writer understands this doubled-edged sword, without necessarily being complicit in its perpetuation.

I now see how woefully (and in other ways wonderfully) naïve I was early in my career as a public writer, sending off work with little if any research into my would-be publisher's political or ideological lean-ings. An egalitarian streak runs deep in most practicing writers, and the egalitarian in me assumed that if the piece under consideration was well-written it would be judged on its own merits. I don't mean to sound cynical when I tell you that, looking back, I had a lot to learn. Two decades later it's become common knowledge that most publica-tions have a political bent. This newfound transparency is mostly a boon to emerging public writers eager to avoid the time-sink of sub-mitting to editors that refuse to give their work a fair hearing. Search-ing online for lists of conservative or liberal media may help make the public writer more efficient in their search for a simpatico venue, but such lists also do damage, in that they further reduce the media into self-reinforcing ideological camps. Perhaps it's time for a new genera-tion of public intellectuals to resist the de facto gag rule put on liberals attempting to write for conservative publications and vice versa, boldly attempting to change the system from within. In many ways, writers willing to send their work to, or accept occasional assignments from, outlets that don't share their politics are part of the solution, in the same way that Bill Bishop's *Big Sort* argues that we should all hope to be so lucky as to live in neighborhoods where our neighbors do not share our education level, income level, and political affiliations.

Wrapping Up

If the public intellectual's goal is to reach the widest possible audience, they must be mindful of the political ramifications of their words while giving careful consideration to reader demographics. To the ex-tent that a public writer serves as a translator, mediator, emissary, or advocate of the public interest, a politically neutral or ideologically pluralistic stance makes good sense, especially in cases where the aims are expository, didactic, or diplomatic rather than argumentative or persuasive. Learning to manage connotations, to reduce needless eu-phemisms, to brand and message with cultural awareness and sensitiv-ity, and to acknowledge a publication's biases and editorial preferences all stand to help the public writer reach the widest possible audience.

12 Writing Grants

E arly in my career I found myself serving on the committee that evaluated my colleagues' proposals for institutional grants. During the first several months of the academic year we would debate that year's call for proposals, revising and refining our guidelines with the goal of eliciting better funding proposals and evaluating them more transparently. After those preliminaries were over, we would spend the next four and a half months debating which of the hundred-plus requests would receive institutional funding. We were in the fortunate position to be able to fund the majority of applicants. Still we had to make some tough decisions, and tough decisions inevitably meant hurt feelings.

I like to think my most lasting contribution to the committee was my insistence that all applications include a paragraph of what amounts to public writing, wherein experts from across campus would be asked to frame their proposal for an audience of non-specialists in the kind of executive summary we came to call an abstract. Before the advent of the abstract requirement I recall one representative on our committee expressing deep frustration at their inability to comprehend the grants written by our colleagues in the sciences. I remember one meeting, in particular, where someone actually screamed, "I don't even know what I'm voting on here!" in a gesture of exasperation many a Washington DC politician buried in bureaucratic legalese can surely relate to.

On such occasions we would usually turn to the single scientist on the committee and ask, mafia-style, "Is this good?" They would say, "Yes" (if they in fact understood it, since the differences between, for example, ecology and astrophysics are vast), and we would move to the next grant awaiting our review in the never-ending slush pile. Dragging our heels wasn't an option, and contacting the applicant for clarification on what was missing or poorly worded in the app would have been both time-consuming and potentially unfair to those whose proposals we might turn down without providing a commensurate chance for clarification.

It was gratifying to be steeped in my colleagues' research, but it was teeth-gnashing, head-scratching, hair-pulling work that often followed me home at night. I was most troubled by the proposals on which I had, like some flummoxed senator, voted yes without fully understanding what I was voting for. The circumstance in which I and my colleagues found ourselves reminded me of the famous Sokal Hoax, wherein physics professor Alan Sokal submitted a bogus journal article to a leading North American journal of cultural studies. Sokal designed his prank to test if the journal would "publish an article liberally salted with nonsense if (a) it sounded good and (b) it flattered the editors' ideological preconceptions."

The answer, sadly, was yes.

At the time, the journal *Social Text* did not commission outside experts in the field to conduct peer review, so Sokal's bogus article, impressively yet impenetrably titled "Transgressing the Boundaries: Towards a Transformative Hermeneutics of Quantum Gravity" slipped into the pages undetected. Sokal owned up to the ruse in an article three weeks later in the journal *Lingua Franca*, initiating a firestorm of debate about the very issues we were grappling with on our grants committee: could someone in the humanities fairly and expertly comment on the scholarly merit of an article written in the physical sciences, and vice versa? In many ways our modest collective of interdisciplinary professors had gone the editors of the duly shamed *Social Text* one better; at least our applicants could claim their applications had been peer-reviewed. While others on the committee insisted that they could not and would not attempt to evaluate the quality of the applicant's scholarship if it fell outside their area of expertise, I argued that the committee's charge was precisely to evaluate the scholarship in the proposals; and if we couldn't because of opaque, esoteric, or obtuse writing, then that was on the applicant.

I lost as many battles as I won during my tenure reading grants, but I wouldn't trade the time spent on that worthy task, as it helped crystalize my views on the importance of crafting language comprehensible to those who don't share our field. Our committee did real work in wading through the many applications we received each year, and as we did, we rendered our judgements based on the set of criteria upon which most review panels eventually land. Rejected applicants usually failed because of a fundamental error not in the proposed timeline, budget, or means of dissemination, but in the formulation and framing of the all-important piece of the application: the grant narrative.

On occasions when we were compelled to send a rejection letter to one of our colleagues, the applicant had typically failed to:

1. Write the requested research proposal in a fashion that could be understood by readers outside the applicant's field.

2. Adequately address their research methodology.

3. Meaningfully discuss the significance of their research (the so-what factor) to the funding body, in this case the college or university.

Almost without exception, when the committee denied funding, it was because the applicant had failed to approach the task as a public writer writing to an audience of non-specialists.

GOOD ACADEMIC WRITING DOES NOT EQUAL GREAT GRANT WRITING

Good public writing and good grant writing are rhetorically analogous, as both seek to engage larger audiences and wider constituencies, mobilizing action and understanding where before there may only have been inaction or ignorance. In many other ways, however, strictly academic writing serves as the antithesis of good public writing and good grant writing. For the same reasons that purely academic writing often fails to cast as wide a net as public writing, or create as broad and inclusive a tent, it often fails in its quest to earn funding for the causes we believe in. In his article "Why Academics Have a Hard Time Writing good Grant Proposals," Robert Porter, Program Development Manager in the Research Division at Virginia Tech University, offers a handy chart delineating the key differences:

Academic Writing	Grant Writing
scholarly pursuit	sponsor goals
individual passion	service attitude
past oriented	future oriented
work that has been done before	work that should be done
theme-centered	project centered
theory and thesis	objectives and activities
expository rhetoric	persuasive rhetoric
explaining to reader	"selling" the reader
impersonal tone	personal tone
objective, dispassionate	conveys excitement
individualistic	team-focused
primarily a solo activity	feedback needed
few length constraints	strict length constraints
verbosity rewarded	brevity rewarded
specialized terminology	accessible language
insider jargon	easily understood

"All too often, the core problem in a failed proposal lies in the writing itself," Porter observes, "which bears too many characteristics of academic prose."[1] He recalls how a puzzled professor once hand-carried to the grants office the critiques he had received from reviewers of a proposal that never received funding. "One of them," Porter recalls, "included this killer remark: 'Reads like a journal article.'"

In helping faculty members write grants and reports at Virginia Tech, Porter has noticed a disconnect between the obsessive and often idiosyncratic devotion faculty members bring to their individual research agendas and the larger institutional or corporate goals of those holding the purse strings. "With the exception of a few career development programs, funding agencies have little interest in advancing the careers of ambitious academics," he opines. "Sponsors will, however, fund projects that have a good chance of achieving their goals. This is why seasoned grant writers devote a good deal of time parsing grant program announcements, highlighting passages that express what the sponsors want to accomplish, and what kind of projects they will pay for." To illustrate the point, Porter recounts the story of one of his university's most successful grant writers, who once told him, "My epiphany came when I realized that grant programs do not exist to make me successful, but rather my job is to make those programs successful."

---

1. Porter "Why Academics Have a Hard Time," 1.

Porter draws a bright contrast between the "past-oriented" bent of academic writing and the "future-oriented" outlook of successful grant writers who use solid public writing techniques. In academic writing, he notes, the researcher very often synthesizes work already done: "Literature has been reviewed, an issue examined, a thesis presented, a discovery made, a conclusion drawn." By contrast, grant writers describe the important work they have yet to do, but will do, if funded. Another key distinction exists between the theme-centered world of the scholar and the action-oriented inclination of the investigator who successfully secures a grant. He maintains that scholarly writers habitually "dwell on theme, thesis, and theory," because the essays and books they produce "draw us into the realm of ideas." Grant writers, on the other hand, "draw us into a world of action," identifying a problem before describing how they would propose to solve it. Review panels have money to give, but little time or patience for academic pontification. Writers must "use language strong enough to win their [reviewer's] reluctant support" in what amounts to "an elegant sales pitch." He notes:

> Grant reviewers are impatient readers. Busy people with limited time, they look for any excuse to stop reading. They are quickly annoyed if they must struggle to understand the writer or learn what the project is all about. Worse, if the proposal does not intrigue them by the very first page, they will not read any further (unless they must submit a written critique, in which case they immediately start looking for reasons to justify why the proposal should not be funded). When asked to describe the characteristics of good grant writing, senior reviewers put qualities such as "clear" and "concise" at the top of the list. Brevity is not only the soul of wit; it is the essence of grantsmanship.

GRANTS GONE WRONG

Many granting agencies make successful grant applications available as models, and such templates are indeed helpful, though in many instances their exceptional polish makes them only marginally useful to first-time applicants. The grantors hope that by making such models accessible applicants will simply imitate their way to grant writing greatness. Unfortunately, that's a bit like a partner putting a picture of a magazine model in front of us and saying, "Look like that, please." Maybe it's just me, but I've always found failed, in-progress, or revise-and-resubmit examples more instructive. In that spirit arrives the not-so-perfect grant narrative below. While it tries to do a number of good things, it trips over its shoelaces more than a little:

Funding Proposal: Human-Animal Conflicts in Kenya

You're walking through the forest in northern India. You're all alone, except for your goats. You just want to get your goats to market so you can sell them and get food for your family. You have seven children and they are hungry. All of a sudden a tiger leaps out at you. You try to defend the goats but it's too late, the tiger has eaten one of your goats and killed two others. That means less food for you and your family this week.

Many people have been living this story all over the world. Human-wildlife conflict is rampant and a critical part of the everyday lives of millions of people living in developing countries (Smith et al. 1999, 2000a, 2000b). This proposal is focused on human-wildlife conflict having grown up in Kenya. This research will be studying human-wildlife conflict in the savannas of Africa between humans and Lions (*Panthera leo*) and Leopards (*Panthera pardus*).

As the ecologists S. Smith and A.T. Smith and anthropologist J. Smith have related in numerous publications over the last decade and a quarter, cattle (*Bos primigenius*) in Kenya often fall prey to lions (*Panthera leo*) and Leopards (*Panthera pardus*) (Smith et al. 1999, 2000a, 2000b, 2002, 2003, 2004a, 2004b, 2004c, 2005). This has been a problem because people rely on cattle (*Bos primigenius*) for their livelihoods (Smith et al. 1999, 2000b, 2002, 2003, 2004c, 2005). The cattle (*Bos primigenius*) that have been killed by wildlife can no longer be sold and so cease to have value (Smith et al. 1999, 2000a, 2000b). This is unfortunate because the majority of people (*Homo sapien sapien*) living in this region are living on only about $15 a week (Smith et al. 2004c, 2005) and a single head of cattle represents a $300 investment (Smith et al. 1999, 2000a, 2000b, 2002).

This proposal proposes a survey of people who live in this area to see how their lives are affected by wildlife.

This proposed research will conduct surveys in villages at [0°22'41.35" S, 36°42'04.22" E], [0°22'41.37" S, 36°42'04.23" E], [0°22'41.42" S, 36°42'04.52" E], [0°22'41.12" S, 36°42'04.97" E], [0°22'41.40" S, 36°42'04.56" E]. I would be speaking Swahili so the surveys would be in the local language and so will be more robust (Smith et al. 1999, 2000a, 2000c).

This project will make a major contribution to this literature because despite the several publications by Smith et al. (Smith et al. 1999, 2000a, 2000b, 2002, 2003, 2004a, 2004b, 2004c, 2005) This research's surveys will be a good additional look at the livelihoods of these pastoralists. This work will have significant broader impacts because there are pastoralists all over the world suffering due to human-wildlife impacts (Scott et al. 2004). Bringing attention to their concerns may have a significant impact on their livelihoods.[2]

Let's begin by inventorying what this narrative does well. It's written in a plainspoken if not somewhat plodding manner. It undertakes a review of literature that addresses the work of scholars working in a similar vein. It could potentially make a contribution to the fields of ecology and human ecology, as its findings promise to help Kenyan pastoralists suffering economic hardship from human-wildlife impacts.

What's not to like? Well, lots of things, actually. While that opening paragraph represents a good college try at engaging a broader audience, the hypothetical narrative it proffers feels contrived and a bit goofy, and especially so given the dubious usage of the second-person "you." The second-person can be highly effective when the reader is likely to read themselves into the narrative, but that is clearly not the case here. Not too many of the "yous" who read the writer's appeal will find themselves walking goats through the woods of northern India anytime soon, as the opening vignette asks us to imagine. Then there's the misdirection of the opening setting, which puts us in India rather than the location of the proposed study: sub-Saharan Africa. While to its credit the narrative opener attempts to invoke a few of the precepts of effective public writing, it feels like a token attempt, as, by the time we each the applicant's second paragraph, the tone

2. Colin Donihue, "How to write a bad research proposal," October 12, 2012, accessed October 15, 2019, https://colindonihue.com/2012/10/10/how-to-write-a-bad-research-proposal/.

has shifted abruptly, leaving even the modest virtues of that engaging narrative to feel contrived and gimmicky in retrospect. The body of the grant narrative suffers from an overreliance on, and overcitation of, Smith, such that it feels like Smith must be the only other scholar in the world, excluding our earnest applicant, working on the issue of human-wildlife encounters. Moreover, the repeated mention of Smith and the italicized genus and species (*Panthera leo, Panthera pardus,* etc.) of every mammal mentioned, including, as a last straw, the mention of *Homo sapien sapien,* further annoys. The tone-deafness of the grant may cause a reviewer to question the applicant's audience awareness, which in turn may cause them to wonder whether the requestor knows much about the body to which they have applied for funds. (For example, if the reviewers were ecologists or biologists themselves, they surely would know the genus and species of the mammals mentioned.) The grant writer seems to have a poor instinct for when to be specific. For example, the narrative lacks a robust discussion of the investigator's methods and methodologies, but on less important matters, such as the exact GPS coordinates of the communities to be surveyed, the applicant provides excessive detail. Finally, the applicant makes no mention of the research ethics and cultural sensitivities involved in surveying a pastoral people in a foreign culture, or whether the grant writer, as primary investigator, has secured approval from a research ethics board to conduct their proposed research. Clearly, our well-meaning applicant loses the forest for the trees in justifying their proposed ecological investigation, so much so that at times the grant narrative serves as a model of what *not* to do.

In fact, NSF Postdoctoral Fellow at Washington University and science blogger Colin Donihue drafts this flawed narrative of an overzealous, oversolicitous ecologist to exemplify the many grant writing errors and omissions that crop up in science research proposals. If you want your grant to be gleefully rejected, Donihue recommends the following sure-to-miss techniques:

- Fill your proposal with technical language (It makes you seem smarter).

- Make sure your proposal's argument is exceedingly complicated (Only smart people should be able to follow your logic after all!).

- Delight in irrelevant examples.

- Never provide any kind of synthesis (It should be self-evident, right?).

- Be overly vague or overly specific or both, overly.

- Clearly imagine your audience, then write your proposal for someone else.

- Never contextualize your research.

- Make sure your title either grabs the reader's attention (Exclamation points help) or summarizes the entire project.

- Use third-person perspective in detailing your research so as not to appear self-centered with all those "I"s (Or use the second person to really grab the reader's attention!).

- Cite a lot (I'm standing on the shoulders of [an army of] giants!) or not at all (Who needs giants anyway?).

- Don't define A.C.R.O.N.Y.M.S.

- Propose research with serious moral/ethical concerns (Science ain't for sissies!).

- Propose research that cannot feasibly be accomplished (Because you might be the one who can finally do it).

- Don't proofread (If stats can have margins of error so can your spelling).

The Beauty of Bad Examples

Each year the Finger Lakes Community Arts Grants (FLCAG) in New York offers a series of arts grants. Like many modest-sized granting agencies FLCAG attempts to streamline its application process, both to encourage artists—most of whom would rather be making their art—to apply and to make the review process easier on themselves. Their requirements are best regarded as bare bones, as they ask the applicant to address the following in no more than a couple of pages:

- Write a clear, concise, detailed description of the project.

- Name artistic personnel. Speak about the qualifications or experience of your proposed artistic personnel. Note that you will also be attaching a resume. The caliber of the artistic personnel is a major consideration for the panel.

- Describe or name the administrators of the project and their qualification to administer.

- Describe the size and type of audience that will be served by project. Comment on community interest in your proposed project and community benefit.

- Speak about the need for these funds.[3]

Despite the simplicity of its guidelines, FLCAG receives a number of proposals that fail to address their bullet points, to such a degree, in fact, that they now post examples of poorly conceived or incomplete grants alongside exemplars of funded projects. Here is an example of a grant narrative that still needs a little work. (Note: FLCAG adapted the faulty narrative below from Community Arts Partnership):

> Johnstown is a town that lost its industrial base twenty years ago, and suffered serious economic decline from which is never fully recoverd. Not only has the town seen a loss of shops and municipal services, it has also lost population. In the 1970 census, Johnstown was listed as having over 30,000 people living within its town limits. Today, we have fewer than 22,000 people.
>
> We have been presenting an important chamber music series in Johnstown since 1991, and regularly receive very positive press reviews for our efforts. Our exciting concerts are presented in the town's high school auditorium and are sometimes attended by over 50 people. Our ten musicians are drawn from the faculty of the local junior college, which was founded in 1982 and has several professional and technical degree programs. We perform a varity of music, from chamber to the moderns, and vary the ensemble to include trios, quartets and the full chamber orchestra.
>
> We are proud of our ability to publicize our concerts widely, including newspaper ad, local radio spots and a mailer to our membership. We hope the panel recognizes our significant accomplishments in this relatively poor community, and fully supports our request this year.

---

3. Finger Lakes Community Arts Grants, *Writing an Effective Application*, 2016, 4, accessed October 15, 2019, http://flcag.org/wp-content/uploads/2015/07/Writing-An-Effective-DEC-Grant-Application.pages.pdf.

Unfortunately, the review panel finds the requested "Detail Statement" less than detailed. The application contains other errors and omissions that ultimately sink its chances, including an inexact budget and a missing "Summary Statement." Still, the narrative itself proves to be the biggest stumbling block. The committee wonders what the first paragraph—detailing the community's declining demographics—has to do with the funding request; the applicant doesn't connect the dots. By the second paragraph panelists are confused: to whom does the "we" refer? The first-person plural pronoun feels inclusive, but it's not clear whom, exactly, it's including. Who will assume leadership for the proposed concert series? The narrative's inexact language, and specifically the places where it appears to hedge, also raise doubts. That's especially true of the curious statement: "Our exciting concerts are presented in the town's high school auditorium and are sometimes attended by over 50 people." The sentence begs a question—how many people attend the less popular concerts? Most funding bodies seek assurances that they're getting the biggest possible bang for their buck, and the applicant's indeterminate estimate of audience size gives them pause. Last but not least, the narrative's spelling mistakes and other typos solidify the committee's decision. Regrettably, this otherwise worthwhile concert series won't receive funding.

FLCAG decides to take its lemons (poorly written or incompletely conceived proposals) and make lemonade, publishing specific tips for crafting more compelling project narratives. Some of the committee's recommendations (for example, "do your math carefully . . . over 20 percent of applications contain an incorrect computation; make sure your budget narrative and itemized budget align") border on the self-evident. But other pieces of advice offer public scholars useful tips for effective grant writing, including the need to clearly state the connections between research objectives, research questions, hypotheses, methodologies, and outcomes. The review panel's advice on writing a strong narrative especially resonates:

> For the project narrative, pre-empt and/or answer all of the reviewers' questions. Don't leave them wondering about anything. For example, if you propose to conduct unstructured interviews with open-ended questions, be sure you've explained why this methodology is best suited to the specific research questions in your proposal. Or, if you're using item response theory rather than classical test theory to verify the

validity of your survey instrument, explain the advantages of
this innovative methodology. Or, if you need to travel to Valdez, Alaska to access historical archives at the Valdez Museum, make it clear what documents you hope to find and why
they are relevant to your historical novel on the '98ers in the
Alaskan Gold Rush.

Note that the tips given by the arts nonprofit apply to the ecologist
writing his narrative for the proposed study of human-animal interac-
tions in Kenya. Like many grant reviewers, FLCAG places a premium
on the clarity and completeness of applications, a quality they suggest
can be achieved in these relatively simple steps:

- Read the application, guidelines, and instructions carefully.

- Answer each question and do not leave anything blank.

- Correct spelling, math, and a neat presentation count.

- Be clear and concise. Avoid technical jargon.

- Do not assume the panel is familiar with your organization
  or your work.

- Be clear about funding needs.

- Take advantage of the draft review.

The group's last suggestion is an especially important one for writers
new to the application process, and one whose value is consistently
overlooked. Too often busy professionals who don't write and edit
grants for a living end up putting together funding proposals at the
last minute, on top of their regular work duties. Grant agencies know
this, and often seek to grow good grants in advance by offering to
consult with potential applicants on their drafts. For the same reasons
that teachers are flattered and impressed when students seek their help
in advance of a deadline, grant coordinators appreciate applicants willing to be guided. If the grants coordinator works with you, they may
be more likely to recognize your proposal, and advocate for it, when it
comes up for review.

GRANTS, REVISED AND REVISITED

The folks at FLCAG kindly provide an example of a well-written version of the same grant, one that would leave the panelists with few

if any questions and would likely rank the application high on the list of projects to receive funding. In the revised proposal that follows, it's much more clear who the applicant is, how much they need, and what they would do with the funds if awarded (compensate the performers and use any leftover monies for marketing and publicity). The new-and-improved version also includes a short abstract under the heading "Summary Statement," allowing a busy reviewer to ascertain at a glance the what, where, why, when, and how much. Note all the additional niceties in the revamped funding proposal that follows:

SUMMARY STATEMENT

The Johnstown Performing Arts Group requests $1,400 to fund artistic fees and increased publicity costs for three chamber music concerts for the Johnstown community.

DETAIL STATEMENT

The Johnstown Performing Arts Group has been presenting chamber music concerts in Johnstown since 1991. The board of directors is made up of five of the musicians that regularly perform with the group. All of our musicians are drawn from the music faculty of the local junior college (See attachment for a brief paragraph about each musician). We perform a variety of music, from the classics to the moderns, and vary the ensemble to include trios, quartets, and the full chamber group. The board meets 8 times a year and performs all tasks associated with the logistics of the concerts. Currently, the chamber music series is the only classical music presented in the town of Johnstown

In 2013 we will present three concerts: The first will be on Sunday, February 9th and will feature a chamber music quartet playing Mozart and Bach. The musicians will be available to the public after the concert to chat and answer questions. The second concert will be in May and will feature the full chamber group (eight musicians). The last concert will be in October and will feature a trio. Each concert will be on a Sunday and will start at 2 p.m. All will be held at the High School auditorium. Exact dates and programs for the second and third concert will be confirmed by February.

We charge $3 for performances but do not turn anyone away if they can't pay.

Attendance at these concerts has not been wonderful, although we have an enthusiastic core of followers. We would like to increase attendance from an average audience size of 25 to 75. We would like part of the grant funds to help with the cost of publicity so that we can get the word out to the public. We currently send out a mailer to our membership (150 people) and utilize whatever free publicity the local newspapers offer. This year we would like to print and distribute posters, send out an additional 500 postcards, send an e-blast using the college's listserv and pay for three print ads in the Johnstown paper (one before each concert.)

Good (and Great) Grant Writing

Though there is a push by some, particularly in the sciences, for more confidentiality in the sharing of government-funded research, most taxpayer-funded granting agencies make successful applications available in full or in part to the broader public—an example of the wider dissemination the public writer endorses as a matter of creed.

The National Endowment for the Humanities (NEH) helpfully archives examples of successful grants, including a recent narrative written by Patrick Manning at the University of Pittsburgh and Ruth Mostern at the University of California, Merced. In it, Manning and Mostern request funding for a World-Historical Gazetteer through the University of Pittsburgh as a Digital Humanities Start-Up Grant.

As early as their narrative's first paragraph, we understand the aim and scope of the project and appreciate the modesty of their request for dollars. Importantly, Manning and Mostern have not asked for complete funding for the creation of their digital gazetteer, but simply start-up funds to develop content, standards, and services, funds to get the ball (or, in this case, the atlas) rolling. Their narrative reads:

> Digital historical gazetteers—databases of place names that include information about location, other attributes, and changes over time—are the foundation of spatial humanities reference and infrastructure. This Level I startup proposal seeks funding for a project to develop **content**, **standards** and **services** for a world historical gazetteer to

serve as an authoritative resource for named places and administrative systems from 1500 CE to the present day. As a starting point, the gazetteer will include all historical place entities from the WikiData project and from GeoNames, and will be augmented by any new historical places submitted by CHIA partners. Our aim is to create a spatial entity reference system that is global in scope and is implemented as an open, freely accessible web service to support ongoing research by historians and social scientists.

Enhancing the humanities through innovation. Creating a world-historical gazetteer builds on the previous and current comprehensive work in gazetteers, notably that of the Pelagios 3 project (led by Leif lsaksen—this project focuses on the world before 1500) and the PastPlace project (led by Humphrey Southall). The world-historical gazetteer, which may well take the form of a distributed model rather than a single gazetteer, takes the further step of addressing a fuller range of problems. Places are described in a typology by a range of attributes. At one pole are places defined by location and boundaries with clear times of existence; at another pole are places with names but no precise location or limits on their time frame. In both cases, administrative units are distinct from places defined by communities, or places as un-ty ped entities. For world-historical datasets, which are to include data for the whole world despite the vary in g degrees of certainty, there is a need for gazetteers that flexibly include a wide range of spatial attributes; in addition , a gazetteer system will require description of exceptional cases.

The system will be integrated with the world-historical data archive that is under development by the Center for Historical Information and Analysis (CHIA), so it will permit spatially aware analysis of historical quantitative social statistics. It will also be designed as a free-standing work of reference, infrastructure, and standards specifications for any project or user in the spatial humanities. The contents, in addition to being accessible from an open application programming interface (API), will be exposed in standard resource description framework (RDF) format to support linked open data. At present, no single gazetteer database or system of gazetteer services allows for historical named-entity query, visualization, and management at the world historical scale. While much development in this domain has occurred over the last twenty years, there are no consensus-based, community standards for design or services, let alone accessible global content. The purpose of this grant is to rectify those problems and to begin developing the needed content.

We seek start-up funding to inaugurate this project by completing two essential, integrated first-step activities. The first is a two-day working meeting . . . . This will be held at the University of Pittsburgh in conjunction with the annual CHIA meeting. We are proposing a meeting because there are a number of promising historical and thematic gazetteer projects and linked open-data gazetteer projects presently underway—inside and outside of academia, and inside and outside the humanities—but the developers and scholars involved with them are only in loose communication. Moreover, many tasks necessary to global historical gazetteer development are not within the purview of any of them. The working meeting will include representatives from all of the major projects. It will ensure that subsequent CHIA world-historical gazetteer development is aligned with best standards and best practices that it builds on related efforts rather than duplicating them, and that it enriches and coheres the vibrant intellectual community around historical and humanistic place-name entity scholarship and development. The meeting will inventory and analyze existing regional historical gazetteer content development projects and gazetteer infrastructure and standards projects; it will reach firm decisions about subsequent steps. For the workshop agenda, see Appendix A.

In addition to the meeting, we are funding a Pitt history graduate student, Matt Drwenski, to support four small development tasks. He will assist in building gazetteer capacity into the CHIA information system (**services**). He will also assist in providing a working implementation of a historical place name API that includes temporal queries and a draft proposal for a temporal gazetteer schema for interoperability between gazetteer services (**standards**). Finally, he will assist in building a testbed of global scope. This involves two tasks. One is to ingest and standardize the 1.4 million entries in English language Wikipedia with geographical coordinates according to the requirements of this proposal. The other is to identify gaps in coverage, supplementing the Wikipedia testbed as needed by names harvested from print historical atlases. These development activities will allow us to complete the highest priority development tasks pertaining to the global historical gazetteer, and they will ensure that the working meeting focuses on results rather than abstract discussion.

This grant would solve urgent development bottlenecks for historical quantitative social science repository development, and it would permit several activities of fundamental significance for the spatial humanities: 1) minimize duplication of effort while raising awareness of best practices throughout the historical spatial-entity research community, 2) identify specific global times and places for which historical spatial entity data is poorly or unevenly documented and develop strategies to fill those gaps, 3) solve the technical and semantic problems associated with multiple attributions for historical spatial entities, which result in many kinds of overlapping, inconsistent and fluid kinds of data being associated with the "same" place.[4]

In fewer than one thousand words, Manning and Mostern answer most of our questions. Though some disciplinary jargon (i.e., "Wikipedia testbed" and "spatial entity research community") impedes our understanding, the grant writers take pains that the first 750 words of the approximately 1000-word narrative remains jargon-free. If the reviewer has made it this far into the narrative, they are likely ready for the specialist's vocabulary, and eager for Mostern and Manning

---

4. National Endowment for the Humanities, "Narrative of a Successful Grant Application," accessed October 15, 2019, https://www.neh.gov/sites/default/files/inline-files/university_of_pittsburgh_work_toward_the_creation_of_a_world_historical_gazetteer.pdf.

to wield the language of their disciplines. The writers organize their narrative logically, moving organically toward a conclusion that states the contribution their research promises to make. Helpfully, the writers have bolded key conceptual and categorical terms from the NEH guidelines (words like *contents, standards,* and *services*) to visually identify that they have read the guidelines carefully and incorporated the requested language. The prose bristles with intellectual energy and precise thinking. Indeed, much of the language drafted for the narrative could be used on a project website. The language bespeaks crisp professionalism without being cold, remote, or removed.

WRITING FUNDING REQUESTS WITH HEART

While many grants strive for a dispassionate description of need, some remarkable proposals risk an appeal to pathos as well as to logos, such as this successful NEH Challenge Grant written by the Queens Community College in cooperation with the Kupferbeg Holocaust Resource Center and Archives in New York City. The overview of the project reads almost lyrically:

> Memory and history, justice and responsibility, despair and hope, are enduring interrelated themes of humanistic inquiry, which the often horrific events of the twentieth century have cast in an unforeseen light. In a twenty-first century America, scholars and educators have a duty to bring these events and their significance to life for an increasingly diverse and globally interconnected population.... Ellie Wiesel, his preface to the new translation of *Night*, writes that "for the survivor who chooses to testify, it is clear: his duty is to bear witness for the dead and for the living. He has no right to deprive future generations of a past that belongs to our collective memory. To forget would be only dangerous but offensive; to forget the dead would be akin to killing them a second time." The KHRCA was born as a "grass-roots" recognition of this truth. It grew organically out of a community of Holocaust survivors who came together to offer one another moral and emotional support, but who also shared a common vision of the pedagogical potential their narratives carried to broaden the perspective of future generations. With the aid and support of QCC faculty and administrators, they came together to

preserve memory and awaken the conscience of the young. As explained by Ethel Katz, a survivor and resident of Queens whose testimony is featured in the KHRCA permanent exhibit, "If you listen to your conscience…you will respect the humanity of your fellow man."

In the past decade, that early vision for the KHRCA has taken flesh, with a full-time professional staff, a new building, an endowment fundraising campaign, a permanent exhibit, historical exhibits on a variety of topics relating to the Holocaust and other genocides, a hate crimes program that situates the Holocaust and its lesson within a spectrum of violence and prejudice, and an internship program that regularly brings community college students in contact with the remaining community of survivors. Yet these Holocaust survivors, whose engagement with KHRCA and with QCC students has been one of our most valuable educational resources to date, are not very advanced in age, and dwindling. Ensuring that those who died are not killed a second timed demands timely action to create new connections and resources that will endure in perpetuity.

It is imperative that we develop a durable and replicable model for Holocaust education that establishes the curricular relevance of Holocaust and Genocide Studies to humanistic learning for future generations to come. Through this Challenge grant we will do so by enabling systematic research and curricular development by our own faculty, by bringing first-rate scholars to our campus, and by refreshing and renewing humanistic inquiry in each new year and generation.[5]

This is elegant writing on a subject—the need for intergenerational memorialization and memory—that warrants poetic prose. The beauty of its language is far from superficial, as its call-to-action moves skillfully between asking for necessary funds (deploying phrases such as "It is imperative" and "demands timely action") and high-minded appeal to social justice and common cause. No reasonable review panel would want to be associated with the consequences of inaction that, the narrative strongly implies, would be akin to killing brave survivors a second

---

5. National Endowment for the Humanities, "Narrative of a Successful Grant Application," accessed October 15, 2019, ch_cuny_rf_qcc_ogc_redacted_2-2015.pdf.

time. In the end, the narrative's willingness to appeal to feeling as well as logic, to evoke real-life characters (Wiesel, Ethel Katz, and other survivors), and to make a big Ask recommend this grant as a model of effective public writing.

It makes sense that humanities narratives would speak plaintively and persuasively to concepts such as witness, testimony, and cultural grieving, but effective science grant applications can be stirring in more subtle ways. An example comes in the Public Health Relevant statement in a successful National Institutes of Health (NIH) grant awarded to the ICAHN School of Medicine at Mount Sinai for a project to help the school of medicine mount a training program in cancer biology. On the surface, such a funding request seems pedestrian enough, yet the required Public Health Relevance Statement eschews jargon to drive home the point that doctors need the best training to win the battle against cancer:

> Translational research is also directed at improving diagnosis and therapies for this terrible disease, and our training faculty have made discoveries that have led to new cancer therapies. Both pre- and postdoctoral trainees participate in rigorous didactic as well as state-of-the-art laboratory and/or computational research training with the earliest cadre having now established academic careers in cancer research.[6]

The inclusion of the single phrase "this terrible disease" within an otherwise stoical scientific request hints at the pathos just beneath the surface. Ultimately the proposal is awarded over a half million dollars, administered via the National Cancer Institute, to better provision cancer doctors to fight this good fight.

WRAPPING UP

Grant writing presents a potentially lucrative outlet for dedicated public writers, whether they work as a paid grant writer, grants coordinator, or individual applicant. As public intellectuals we could do far worse than convey our ideas to general readers using the same acces-

---

6. National Institutes of Health, "Project Information Help 5T32CA078207-19," accessed October 15, 2019, https://projectreporter.nih.gov/project_info_description.cfm?aid=9531264&icde=46751664&ddparam=&ddvalue=&ddsub=&cr=2&csb=default&cs=ASC&pball=.

sible and engaging language we might use to win over a review board. The challenge is very much the same. Public writing audiences, like the expert panelists that review our proposals, are often put off by the obtuse and equivocating language we use in our professions, and are impatient to know what we are proposing, what change we hope to beget with our knowledge, and how exactly we propose to create that change. They're compelled by narratives, by conceptual clarity, and by concise statements that speak to the urgency of the issue at hand. They want active, intellectually precise prose, and a clear and unambiguous statement of purpose and potential pay-off.

Many academics struggle with proposal writing not only because in the past they have been able to take their readers' attention for granted, but because they've grown well-practiced in abstract thinking. Only the most extreme critics of academe would attempt to change the intellectual's deliberative nature, but the epiphany had by the professor at Virginia Tech when he realized that successful grant writing is all about helping the grantor better achieve their mission should galvanize the servant heart in scholar-writers. If the public intellectual can approach public writing with the same service mindset they bring to the writing of effective grants, readers may be more willing to support their cause with their own hard-earned dollars and cents.

13 Analyzing News, Weighing Evidence

D ick Polman, who worked for many years as a national politics analyst for *The Philadelphia Inquirer*, captures the essence of evidence-based news analysis:

> I view "news analysis" as essentially synonymous with "explanatory journalism." In recent years, as the information revolution has exploded, there has been much debate over what the proper role of a newspaper should be. Citizens . . . often get the basic news not just from television and radio, but from the Internet. . . . Newspapers can provide a valuable service not just by laying out facts, but by trying to make some sense of what those facts mean in a larger context, perhaps with some historical perspective. Or, at the very least, a lot more nuance than can be found in a just-the-facts-ma'am format. That is what I often try to do. And I am a firm believer that analysis pieces should be labeled for the reader, to minimize confusion. I start from the premise that an analysis piece is not designed to render an opinion on what's right or wrong. That is the job of the editorial page writer. That is also typically the job of a columnist who has cultivated a consistent voice and point of view. I'm just trying to look at events and understand what they might mean. Sometimes I'm just trying to connect the dots between events in some way that may enlighten people. Clearly, however, I am rendering some judgments, and that does involve a certain amount of subjective thought.[1]

---

1. Dick Polman, "Writing a news Analysis," 2001, accessed October 15, 2019, https://1pdf.net/writing-a-news-analysis-wiley-home_585c111be12e89ab3f 000636.

WRITING EVIDENCE-BASED ANALYSIS

When the online news site *The Conversation* reached out to me as a potential contributor, I found their language puzzling. If they didn't want op-eds and personal commentaries written by academic experts, what, exactly, where they looking for? Eventually, I posed the question directly to the publication's editor and general manager, who in inviting me to write, replied that they were seeking evidence-based analysis and explanatory reporting. *The Conversation* authors were only allowed to write on a subject on which they had proven expertise, illustrating the inside-out perspective of informed public writing.

Remember the Mayan trophy skulls piece of evidence-based analysis we discussed earlier in this book, the one whose readership had grown exponentially as a result of its appearance in *The Conversation*? How did anthropology professor Gabriel Wrobel and his colleagues reach such a sizable audience on exactly the same topic they had published previously to a tiny audience in a little-read academic journal? Wrobel and company had transformed their existing anthropological research into a different genre entirely: evidence-based analysis.

By now the specific writerly techniques used to translate disciplinary knowledge to a broader public should be familiar to you. See if you can pick out some of the particular moves Wrobel makes as a public scholar in the short excerpt below:

> The defleshed and painted human skulls, meant to be worn around the neck as pendants, were buried with a warrior over a thousand years ago at Pacbitun, a Maya city. They likely represent gruesome symbols of military might: war trophies made from the heads of defeated foes.
>
> Flecks of red paint decorate one of the jaws. It's carved with glyphic writing that includes what my collaborator Christophe Helmke, an expert on Maya writing, believes is the first known instance of the Maya term for "trophy skull."
>
> What do these skulls—where they were found and who they were from—tell us about the end of a powerful political system that thrived for centuries, covering southeastern Mexico, all of Guatemala and Belize, and portions of Honduras and El Salvador? My colleagues and I are thinking about them as clues to understanding this tumultuous period.

An if-it-bleeds-it-leads headline, lots of supporting images and il-
lustrations, active verbs with subjects given agency, timely and relevant
questions, expert interpretation and analysis—no wonder this piece of
public writing was picked up by ten news outlets and two blogs. It conjures a compelling centuries old-mystery (why the all-powerful Mayan
civilization collapsed) while hinting at brutal skullduggery and societal upheaval as Mayans from the northern regions of Central America
returned home with trophy skulls harvested by brute force from those
in the embattled, imploding South. Wrobel concludes his evidence-
based analysis with a summary note reinforcing the story's strong so-
what factor: "These grisly artifacts lend an intriguing element to the
sweep of events that resulted in the end of one of the richest, most
sophisticated, scientifically advanced cultures of its time."

Evidence-based analysis and explanatory/expository writing offer
us wonderfully fluid and portable methods, as capable of explaining
why Mayans were bashing one another's skulls in as they are of explaining our need to explore future homes in distant solar systems.

The Real Stars of the Show

K2-18 b was discovered in 2015 as one of hundreds of "super-Earths"—
planets with a mass between Earth and Neptune—found by NASA's
Kepler spacecraft. Angelos Tsiaras and his team at the University College London didn't discover K2-18 b, but they did set out to determine
whether the planet could reasonably be declared habitable, relaying
their findings in a piece of public scholarship published under the title:
"How we detected water on a potentially habitable exoplanet for the
first time." Tsiaras begins his explanatory write-up with appropriate
context that reminds readers that K2-18 b is far from exceptional:

> With more than 4,000 exoplanets—planets orbiting stars
> other than our sun—discovered so far, it may seem like we
> are on the cusp of finding out whether we are alone in the uni-
> verse. Sadly though, we don't know much about these plan-
> ets—in most cases just their mass and their radius.
>
> Understanding whether a planet could host life requires
> a lot more information. At the moment, one extremely im-
> portant piece of information that is missing is the presence,
> composition and structure of their atmospheres. Signs of

atmospheric water, oxygen and methane would all be signs that a planet may support life.

Now we have for the first time managed to detect water vapor in the atmosphere of an exoplanet that is potentially habitable. Our results have been published in *Nature Astronomy*.

A planet's atmosphere plays a vital role in shaping the conditions inside it—or on its surface, if it has one. Its composition, stability and structure all provide important clues about what it is like to be there. Through atmospheric studies, we can therefore learn about the history of the planet, investigate its habitability and, ultimately, discover signs of life.

The primary method that we use when examining exoplanets is transit spectroscopy. This involves looking at starlight as a planet passes in front of its host star. As it transits, stellar light is filtered through the planet's atmosphere—with light being absorbed or deflected based on what compounds the atmosphere consists of.[2]

The article is considerably less visceral than "Two Trophy Skulls," though it checks off all the items on the list of effective science writing—research methodology, limitations of the study, key definitions, conclusions, ongoing research questions. As in many evidence-based pieces originating in the empirical sciences, the writer proceeds with caution, careful not to overstate the case or make exaggerated claims. The writing is more tentative, and less outwardly stylish (perhaps explaining why its Facebook shares amounted to a small fraction of the Mayan article). Yet, it's Online Attention Score of 3380 far exceeds the number earned by "Two Trophy Skulls." While the Mayan piece had been tweeted by only a handful of readers, the story on the potentially habitable exoplanet was tweeted 873 times across the world, including from places as remote as Rwanda, Nepal, and the Isle of Man. The sheer number of tweets is partially explained by the article's distribution in more than 450 outlets ranging from *Forbes* to the *Independent*. Overall, the exoplanet piece was accessed approximately 3500 times, ranking it in the 99th percentile (5th) of the 182,661 tracked articles of a similar age in all journals.

2. Angelos Tsiaras, "How we detected water on a potentially habitable exoplanet for the first time," *The Conversation*, September 11, 2019, https://theconversation.com/how-we-detected-water-on-a-potentially-habitable-exoplanet-for-the-first-time-123239.

The metrics reveal the intensity of interest in what may be the ultimate mystery of all—life—as well as the ultimate adventure story—the probability that humankind will ultimately be compelled to try its fortunes on new planets. The enhanced metrics also reflect the crucial synergy between public-facing academic outlets such as *The Conversation*, and more specialized academic journals such as *Nature Astronomy*. In such a relationship, the popular public scholarship site can generate traffic back to the original, overlooked journal article, and vice versa, augmenting the page views and/or download stats on both ends.

PUBLIC WRITING WITH ITS WIRES CROSSED

Not long ago, I pitched a piece in which I hoped to analyze a worrying trend in higher education. I supposed my primary audience would be the sort of folks who would read *Insid Higher Education*, but I also wanted to reach the parents and students most directly impacted by the issue I had chosen to tackle. I proposed to examine the early-alert systems used by over eighty percent of American colleges to flag students' academic difficulties and behavioral issues. As a professor, I wanted students (and parents) to realize a little-publicized fact: that faculty often serve as anonymous informants concerning student behaviors ranging from body odor, to listlessness, to changes in weight.

The opening paragraph of the draft read:

> "Early-alert them" has become the catch-all twenty-first century response for concerned faculty and staff members noticing unusual behaviors on campus. Once early-alerted a student or faculty member is "in the system," and a simple referral unlocks a series of interventions and support services designed to retain students and their all-important tuition dollars. In well over 80 percent of the colleges and universities surveyed by the Gardner Institute for Excellence in Undergraduate Education, October midterms and progress reports will produce a surfeit of early-alerts destined to be used by "Behavioral Intervention Teams." Studies show that even colleges and universities engaged in early-alerting have good reason to doubt their efficacy. For example, among respondents to the Gardner Institute survey, only 40 percent reported that "improved retention/graduation rates" resulted from the use

of an early-warning systems, and this from the very population of institutional practitioners tasked with implementing
the system in the first place.

The idea for the article had first come to me as an op-ed, but as
I drafted and developed it over a period of several months, I moved
toward the facts and studies indicative of evidence-based analysis, perhaps expecting resistance from the majority of academics who had already bought in to the early-alert doctrine. Ultimately, I developed the
piece as the kind of evidence-based analysis published by *The Conversation* and its ilk. The trouble was, I still had an *Inside Higher Ed*-styled
beginning.

After letting the piece lay fallow for a couple of months I could see
more clearly how the otherwise sound public writing techniques I had
used to prepare it for an *Inside Higher Ed* online readership of 1.2 million unique individuals would prove inadequate for an audience outside academe.[3] Over eighty-five percent of *Inside Higher Ed*'s readers
are academics, institutional or academic administrators, or senior executives—well-educated readers with advanced degrees. Meanwhile,
by comparison, *The Conversation* encourages its contributors to write
at a tenth-grade reading level—a standard target for publications such
as newspapers and news magazines that seek to reach the widest possible cross-section of concerned citizens.

In light of the reader demographics, let's take another look at
that opening paragraph, noticing the ways in which I got my wires
crossed—using *Inside Higher Ed* syntax and diction while pitching my
piece to *The Conversation*-styled outlet.

> "Early-alert them" has become the catch-all twenty-first cen-
> tury response for concerned faculty and staff members notic-
> ing unusual behaviors on campus.

For starters, that first sentence includes too many polysyllabic
and hyphenated words ("catch-all," "twenty-first century.") At twenty
words in length, it's a bit too long. Taken together, its length, syntax,
and polysyllabic diction put it more in the wheelhouse of those on
college and university payrolls than those (students and their parents)
paying tuition bills.

---

3. *Inside Higher Ed*, "Recruit with Insider Higher Ed," accessed October 14,
2019, https://www.insidehighered.com/content/recruiting-faq.

Regrettably, my second sentence isn't much better, likewise failing to hit the preferred tenth-grade reading level. It reads:

> Once early-alerted a student or faculty member is "in the system," a simple referral unlocks a series of interventions and support services designed to retain students and their all-important tuition dollars.

At thirty-one words, pleonasm, or wordiness, only deepens in this complex sentence. For all its decorum, the sentence also fails to provide examples of the far-ranging behaviors that cause students to be early-alerted. The rest of the overlong opening paragraph isn't much better, delving into a definitive study that might have been better saved for a later body paragraph.

Here's one way I might revise that cumbersome opener:

> "Early-alert them."

> That's what some college faculty and staff say whenever they see someone engage in odd behavior on campus.

This modest revision leads with the quote on its own line, in something akin to a journalistic "hook." This iteration attributes the quote, too, letting readers know that college faculty and staff are the ones mostly likely to invoke the phrase.

An even more provocative opener might risk the first-person, since as a professor I'm expected, despite what ethical and philosophical objections I may have, to issue early-alerts on students who display telltale signs such as weight gain or loss, listlessness, or extreme fatigue. With a bit more courage and chutzpah, I might lead with:

> I'm paid to spy on my students.

Of course, the picture is more complicated than that, thank goodness, since I'm also paid to teach my students, to mentor them, and to care for and about them and their well-being. Still, the substance of the more provocative lead (spelled "lede" in journalism) rings true; I'm also paid to notice things about students that fly beneath the radar, making me a "spy" in practice. Therein lies the issue I unpack in the rest of my evidence-based analysis.

DUELING NEWS ANALYSES

In 2009 Verlyn Klinkenborg published a piece of news analysis for the *New York Times* under the feel-good title "Good News from Iowa." The United States Department of Agriculture had just released the data from its once-every-five years Ag Census, and the results were surprising, documenting a small increase in the total number of farms overall in a country where agriculture was widely assumed to be dying. Klinkenborg's article offered exactly the kind of context that distinguishes news analysis written by astute public writers. And, importantly, the author was not just a random reporter assigned a story, but someone who had grown up in Iowa during years of farm prosperity, someone who, even after moving to New York, had continued writing a popular column for *The Times* called "The Rural Life." His analysis put the surfeit of new data in a useful perspective, invoking a historical lens:

> When I was born in 1952, there were 203,000 farms in Iowa, only 11,000 fewer than when my dad was born in 1926. By 2002, the number had dropped to about 90,000, with roughly the same acreage in production in a state with a population that had remained roughly the same. The national numbers followed the same track: fewer farms, bigger farms, less-diverse farms. To a lot of people, this looked like progress because the ideal of efficiency promulgated by the Department of Agriculture was bigger yields with fewer people.
>
> So it comes as a pleasant surprise to find in the 2007 Census of Agriculture that the number of farms in Iowa has risen to 92,856, a level last seen in 1992. Some 4,000 new small farms have been created since 2002. These are very small farms, 9 acres or less, and they are producing a much wider array of crops than the rest of Iowa, which specializes in corn and soybeans.[4]

Klinkenborg seemed determined to see the bright side of the data, and I wanted to agree with the writer's happy conclusion: "This is a genuine source of hope for American agriculture." But as a faculty member teaching place studies and demographics courses in addition

---

4. Veryln Klinkenborg, "Good News from Iowa," *New York Times*, February 9, 2009, https://www.nytimes.com/2009/02/10/opinion/10tue4.html.

to English, I knew better. So, after the next Ag Census was released to the accompaniment of overly optimistic rhetoric, I wrote my own piece of evidence-based analysis as a counterpoint to the erroneous idea given urban Americans that America's agricultural economy was booming. My piece, entitled "Portrait of a Midwestern Harvest," attempted to put the potentially misleading numbers in the Ag Census in a more concrete context, while also offering an ethnographic take on the *culture* in contemporary a*griculture*:

> Of all the small and subtle clues to farming's radically changed landscape perhaps the first and least obvious is the paucity of numbers. Folks from the Coasts sometimes lump Corn Belt citizens together as "a bunch of farmers," or "salt of the earth types," but in real terms farmers grow fewer by the year. According to the latest Agricultural Census only about 48,000 "principal operators" list farming as their primary occupation in the heart of the heartland: Iowa. If we crowded them all— at our peril of, course—into the University of Iowa's Kinnick Stadium on a single Big Ten football Saturday, more than 30 percent of the seats would still remain empty. The average age of principal operators (a whisker over 57 and aging) surprises, too, given the youthful face of small, sustainable, organic, specialized, and boutique agriculture. In rural Tennessee, where I first began my career as a writer-scholar on a rented tobacco farm, the numbers aren't much better. There just over 79,000 principal operators work their acres statewide, a number that would only half fill NASCAR's famous shrine to speed, the Bristol Motor Speedway in Bristol, Tennessee.
>
> Bear in mind that for many years the USDA has defined a farm "as any place that produced and sold, or normally would have sold, $1,000 or more of agricultural products during the Census year." If we live in a city, and have a rooftop garden or patio planted densely with a valuable crop grown for sale, we could be a farmer. Even if we only sold $150 this year due to weather, or insect plague, or, in theory, any "life event" that prevented us from realizing the full financial potential of our crop, we still may be a farmer on "points," according to the USDA system. Of course here it is important to note, according to Farm Policy Facts, that the 210,000 farmers nationally

with sales of more than $250,000 produce 80 percent of the country's food and fiber.

A farmer is a difficult thing to count precisely because he or she doesn't always care to be counted, perhaps explaining why the USDA is so keen to include just about any food- or fiber-producing operation in their once-every-five-years bean-counting. A visit to the department's website and you'll be exhorted to "Make Sure Your Farm or Ranch Counts!" Large or small, the bureaucracy notes, "your agricultural operation is important . . . . This includes retirement/lifestyle farms and ranches that grow a small amount of plants or crops or keep only a few animals, up to the largest of operations . . . . Land-owners that only have income from government programs are also counted as farms."

It's a difficult profession to isolate and pin down, too, for the jack-of-all-trades virtuosity it requires. In this postmodern age, and more and more, a farmer is as a farmer does. In Iowa, the heart of the heartland by any measure, nearly 40 percent of those listed as farm operators report working more than two hundred days each year off the farm. Of the 89,000 or so individual farms counted there, nearly 20 percent total less than 100 acres.

WRAPPING UP

Public intellectuals nimble enough to analyze the ever-shifting head-lines of the 24-7 news cycle will find evidence-based analysis and explanatory reporting a natural fit for their existing public writer's toolkit. The inside-out nature of much effective public writing sug-gests that we contribute our most useful analyses in subject areas that closely match our credentials, degrees, and expertise. While opinion writing and personal commentaries allow the public writer a wider tonal and emotive range, evidence-based analysis is highly valued by public writing venues that seek to move away from increasingly ubiq-uitous opinion to intellectual discourse grounded in fact.

Researchers, scholars, and other professionals uncomfortable with personalizing or embodying their research questions may find evidence-based analysis especially appealing. The public writer-cum-analyst focuses on reading between the lines, invoking the kind of deliberate close reading, careful exposition, and sometimes startling inferential thinking that serve as hallmarks of critical thinking. Effective evidence-based analysis helps busy readers sift through the muck of everyday news, with the analyst serving as an expert guide and teacher.

14 Publishing Opinion Pieces

While emerging authors sometimes overlook the op-ed as a publication opportunity, or simply discount it for fear they're not ready for such a big stage, most public writers who have been successful at their trade will eventually be asked by someone—editor, agent, publicist, colleague, or supervisor—to try their hand at this influential genre.

In fact, accomplished public writers frequently find themselves in demand as authors of op-eds or guest editorials. In many cases, the writer of the op-ed is required to take the gist of a book or study recently completed and boil it down to a 500- to 750-word argument that also presents solutions to the problems the author flags. Many of the skills we learned in the previous chapter on personal commentaries apply to opinion writing as well, as the two genres are kin to one another. However, the op-ed is emphatically less personal, and more timely, than the "My Turn" *Newsweek*-styled piece, mostly because the primary outlets for op-eds are major metropolitan newspapers that focus less on personal accounts and more on news and views related to the common good. In a digital age, opportunities to share personal, emotive, or affective stories with a wider public abound, while venues that publish thoughtful, well-reasoned viewpoints by those with real credentials seem to grow fewer with each passing year. My intent is not to disparage the important inroads made by personal commentary, but to offer a bright contrast between it and its cousin: the op-ed column.

When I work with aspiring columnists, I find that many have written a letter to the editor at some point in their lives. Letters to the editor are a great place to find our voice; in crafting them we learn to respond to someone else's well-reasoned argument with a well-thought-out argument of our own. Letters to the editor, however, are primarily reactionary. By comparison, undertaking an op-ed, viewpoints piece, or guest editorial asks us to initiate the conversation, writing something sufficiently compelling that it might inspire others to write their own letter in reply to our piece, thereby turning the civic wheel by which public debate and discourse are advanced.

A PERSONAL OPINION PRACTICE

My practice of writing op-eds for national newspapers heated up with the release of my book of popular history, *March of the Suffragettes*. By that time, I had already written a handful of influential op-eds for regional newspapers and popular news sites, so I was something less than a neophyte. Still, the thought of "going national" gave me pause. I had purposefully built a platform as a public writer heavily invested in the issues of concern to my home region—the environment, land-use, conservation—and part of me worried I would be seen as abandoning my roots for the bright lights of San Francisco or New York City. It was a silly worry, really, but where I come from people who "get too big for their britches" can be the object of intense ridicule. In fact, it took a direct request from the book's publicist to help me overcome my personal inertia and power through the Middle American hang-ups cautioning against notoriety or publicity.

Now I had a new concern. While I could hear the historical rhyme of my book's subject—Progressive Era social justice warrior and suffragette Rosalie Gardiner Jones—I understood that busy readers around the country could probably care less. It would be difficult to turn the famed leader of the votes-for-women marches of the 1910s into something newsworthy and contemporary more than one hundred years later. The book's publisher was located in San Francisco, and at the time of publication I was two thousand miles away in fly-over country. In this case, the geodemographic odds seemed stacked against me, though certainly my chops as a professor of writing for social change courses and an author of a recent biography on an equal rights revolutionary would help me, as would current events. My op-ed about the leader of the longest women's rights marches in American history would coincide with a major news item: the Women's March on Washington.

I understood that while that one-hundred-year-old activist had been the center of my book of popular history, she could not be the center of a contemporary op-ed penned in an era with its own pressing political and gender divisions. She could be a garnish, perhaps, but not the main meal. That was a hard pill for me to swallow, as it is for many writers of historical biographies who, by dint of their years of research on a single individual, turn into unabashed boosters of the historical protagonists whose cause they are determined to champion. Still, though it could not be dominated by her, my proposed column needed to stay true to its original impetus and inspiration: the daring activist who marched from New York to DC for gender equality. I also understood that I could not speak credibly from a woman's perspective just because I had spent years researching women's history as a public scholar and historian. In the end, I decided to write from a perspective I could own, titling my piece "Men Fear When Women March." The first draft I submitted read:

> On January 21ˢᵗ, the day after Donald Trump's planned inauguration, two hundred thousand women plan to march on Washington in support of the women's rights agenda threatened by the incoming administration.
>
> It wasn't until I published a book on the last such large-scale women's marches on inauguration week in Washington—those led by the inimitable "General" Rosalie Gardiner Jones and Inez Milholland in the winter of 1913—that I understood how rare such gatherings of American women have been in history.
>
> As a historian of the votes-for-women movement what interests me most about the coming March on Trump is not necessarily the way history rhymes, as Mark Twain put it, but how little seems to have changed in the palpable fear many men still feel when women don their marching boots. It's an abiding cultural if not biological anxiety that seems to emerge every time the issue of women in combat (read: militant women) bubbles up in public discourse, as it did this past year with the Obama administration's support of women registering for selective service.
>
> Why is it that when women put boots on the ground and march, military-style and en masse, that they tend to meet with ideological if not physical violence, as they did in 1913, when the inauguration march turned out to be as much about men's fears as about women's rights. Is it women's displays of physical and intellectual strength that men historically fear, or widespread women's community, solidarity, and mobilization?

In 1913 votes-for-women activists stormed Pennsylvania Avenue on the occasion of Woodrow Wilson's inauguration, hoping to serve notice to the president-elect. Then as now marchers came from across the country for a grand parade led by Milholland wearing a white cape and riding a white horse at the front of a woman's army. Milholland's forces included five mounted brigades, twenty-six floats, and between 8,000 and 10,000 marchers.

Back then what most unsettled American men was the militant metaphor of Jones's and Milholland's march. Jones dubbed herself a "general" while her right-hand woman, Ida Craft, described herself as a "colonel." The reporters following the march of "Rosalie's army" were widely known as "war correspondents." Though the votes-for-women processions were peaceful (Jones actually carried doves), so-called "militant" suffragists such as Alice Paul understood that great gains in civil rights seldom arrived without first confronting the powers-that-be with their deepest (and often darkest) fears.

Brigades of "troops" advancing up Pennsylvania Avenue by the tens of thousands will always get the attention of institutionalized power-holders. And if president-elect Donald Trump's past disparagement of women is at root an expression of some deep-seated fear of them, this latest march will surely succeed, as it did in 1913, in drawing out and identifying the latent sexism and bigotry in Washington DC.

In 1913 mostly male fear of a mobilized and marching women's army resulted in mob violence in Washington, and a public outcry that ended in an eleven-day Congressional inquiry whose results, in part, helped secure Congressional passage of the 19th Amendment six years later in 1919. And while the boots-on-the ground marchers of 2017 do not expect to be greeted with violence on the National Mall come January 21st, history tells us their exceptional solidarity should leave the Trump administration sobered if not shaken.

I was gratified to have written something that honored the original impetus—the historic figure of Rosalie Gardiner Jones—while nevertheless speaking to the contemporary moment. However, I made the mistake many public writers make when a piece is formally accepted for publication; I wrongly assumed acceptance meant "Nice work. It's a wrap!" Now the editors wanted to know if there had been other women's marches on Washington. If so, shouldn't we mention of them? The most significant change requested of my draft came in the ending. The opinion editor wrote, "As far as I can tell, there is fear the 2017 marchers will encounter violence. Can [you] rework the last paragraph? I don't want to sow fear, but I don't want to say there isn't fear when there is concern. Can you get this back to me tomorrow morning . . . reworked?"

Tomorrow?! I almost laughed, or cried, when I read the editor's message in the fleeting moments before a night class that would demand my attention until 10:30 p.m., followed by six hours of sleep, if I was lucky, and another full day of classes and meetings the following day, which was now my new deadline. And to be honest, I wasn't so sure I agreed with the claim that the newspaper didn't want to sow fear. The more I let the feedback sink in that night and the following morning, however, the more I realized the opinion editor was right. In effect, I had missed an important point about op-eds: the need for a call to action or a restatement of the problem or challenge ahead. While revising I reminded myself that readers expected me to do more than bemoan the current state of affairs or simply restate the problem; they expected me to go out on a limb and make a statement. After an afternoon of frenetic revision sandwiched fitfully in between classes and meetings, I submitted this proposed revision of the final paragraph:

> The boots-on-the ground marchers of 2017 do not expect to be greeted with violence on the National Mall come Saturday. Still, history reminds us that the activists of 1913 did not anticipate mob violence either. Saturday's marchers have the right to protection by law enforcement and to a peaceful and productive protest. They have the right to expect that the wrongs of the past will be righted.

Once I had the hang of taking what I knew, and was comfortable representing, and shaping it to meet the needs of a particular publication and its readership, I was able to place op-eds on Jones in more than a half dozen major newspapers around the nation in the weeks and months that followed. For the *Huffington Post* I wrote a piece entitled "In Praise of Political Kids Who Buck Their Parents Politics." The topic allowed me to write about something I truly believe in (a child's prerogative to decide their own politics for themselves) through the lens of a remarkable detail unearthed in my research: an ardent suffragist, Jones was the daughter of one of New York's most vehement anti-suffragists, or Antis for short. Most public writers go through a similar process of accommodation when finalizing the topic of their viewpoints piece, finding a middle ground between what they know and want to share, and what the reader is likely to find relevant to their own life at that precise cultural moment.

Years ago, a talented public writer enrolled in one of my workshops wanted to try their hand at writing op-eds. An émigré from the Philippines, they had spent years studying Filipino history and colonialism since coming to America. Previous research and writing on the subject certainly had made them an expert, but now, faced with just a 500- to 700-word canvas to fill, they needed to find a way to make their knowledge of, and experience with, American imperialism relevant to the issues of the day. After careful thought they landed on a topic that was a perfect blend of their personal experience as a Filipino émigré and expertise as a scholar of Philippines history now living in America and writing for American audiences. All these they successfully applied to a long-simmering controversy over the Bells of Balangiga, a spoil of war from the brutal Philippine-American War of 1899–1913 and a painful symbol of a genocide the writer felt America had never owned up to.

SETTING A SUBMISSION STRATEGY

Once the writer had the Bells of Balangiga piece written and edited, we discussed a submission strategy. Naturally, the writer wanted to begin with some of the best-circulated newspapers in the nation, the *New York Times* and the *Chicago Tribune*. So long as the newspapers to which they pitched covered international affairs, we saw no harm in starting at the top, though we understood that in so choosing extra time would need to be allocated for acceptance or rejection. Most major newspapers ask writers to give them approximately one to two weeks of exclusive review. So, if the writer pitched the *Times* and the *Tribune* in turn, and they each said no in a timely fashion, it would be at least two weeks before they would be free to submit their column to a third newspaper. We agreed that a logical third choice would be the *Tribune Eagle* in Wyoming. Since the bells, as the spoils of a long-ago war, were then kept at a former Air Force base in Cheyenne, this international topic also possessed local and regional relevance.

Where possible, it's a good idea to keep your intended venue in mind before you begin drafting your op-ed or column. Is your piece primarily of national/international, regional, state, or local interest? In many cases your answer might depend on context and approach. For example, if the writer submitted their op-ed to the top-circulating newspaper in their native Philippines, the *Manila Bulletin*, readers would no doubt find the Bells of Balangiga highly relevant if not, to a certain degree "old news," since the government there had been calling for the return of the bells for years and much ink had previously been spilled on the topic. By contrast, American readers might indeed find the controversy over the bells new and noteworthy, though, minus a powerful news peg, it would probably not rise to the level of nationally relevant news on the crowded and hyper-competitive opinion pages of America's newspapers of national record. Ultimately, the author wisely decided to target a limited number of geodemographically-selected locations for their worthwhile and well-written op-ed: Wyoming, the state in which the bells then resided and therefore an American locus for the controversy, as well as the American cities with the largest Filipino populations: Los Angeles and San Francisco. Since the writer lived in greater Chicagoland, and Chicago is perennially in the top five in Filipino population, the *Chicago Tribune* and *Chicago Sun-Times* constituted promising venues, too.

In general, pitching venues in smaller markets increases the chance that our public opinion writing will be accepted for publication, since the largest metro newspapers find themselves bombarded with submissions not just from thoughtful unaffiliated and freelance writers wanting to speak out but also from paid representatives and professional writers and publicists working for interest groups and think-tanks. Acceptance rates at newspapers such as the *Dallas Morning News*, *New York Times*, and *USA Today* hover around one percent, and standing out in that kind of a crowd is a statistically difficult prospect. Conversely, some smaller city and county newspapers experience a shortage of well-conceived, well-written opinion pieces on topics of relevance to their readers.

For those wishing to test the waters of the top one hundred online and print publications in the US, online directories such as the Op-ed Project are great places to start. Keep in mind that all but a few of the national newspapers of record (*New York Times, Washington Post, Wall Street Journal, USA Today* and their ilk) will be looking for local or regional relevance. You, as the public writer seeking to place your opinion piece, needn't reside in the cities or states where you submit your work, but the subject matter of your piece should have resonance there. Most newspapers will require the writer to include their physical address and daytime phone number as a condition of submission. While such information is not typically published with the op-ed, it does establish at a glance the writer's geographic proximity to an issue and serves as a way for newspapers to verify that you are who you say you are, and that, in many cases, you belong, directly or indirectly, to the core communities in which the newspaper is most widely read and circulated. For this reason and others, many outlets will publish the guest columnist's email address, so that readers have a way to talk back, correct, or continue the conversation.

Often the most competitive op-ed venues offer the most helpful counsel for those seeking publication. For example, the *Dallas Morning News* provides a wealth of practical advice for public writers contemplating a potential viewpoints submission. The opinion editors at the *News* advise writers to:

1. Select a topic you feel passionate about. If you're not excited by it, you'll never get your readers interested.

2. Have an opinion. That's what makes an op-ed column different from a news story or a feature article: It expresses the view of the writer.

3. Make sure your topic is appropriate for a short, 600-word column, rather than a master's thesis. To help you focus, try writing your main point in one sentence.

4. Express your opinion in the first paragraph or two. Let your readers know where you're headed; don't leave them guessing.

5. Provide concrete support for the points you make. Statistics, expert testimony and research are ways to persuade others that you're being reasonable.

6. But don't get carried away with numbers or quotes. While they can help make your argument, they're only the backup singers. You're the star.

7. Draw on your own personal experience, too, if it's relevant and helps to illustrate your viewpoint. That can be very persuasive.

8. Avoid sounding too preachy. You'll be more likely to persuade others if you don't lecture them; just talk to them.

9. Give your writing some personality. People should have some sense of you after reading your words.

10. Have a good last line. It's your final chance to drive home your point. End with a bang, not a whimper.[1]

BRACE YOURSELF FOR BLOWBACK

Embracing the power of the op-ed means accepting the fact that you will become a lightning rod for the arguments you make. Sometimes the storm will pass, and the thunderbolts will spare you; other times you will take a direct hit.

For many years, the pain of going public with my views kept me from tackling opinion writing for national and international audiences. Looking back, I wish I had confronted my fears sooner. Still, on the days when I know one of my op-eds is about to go live online or hit the newsstands across the country or the world, I can't help but lay low, expecting hailstones. Thankfully, the response we as public writers receive when we put ourselves out there is more likely to be positive than negative. Old friends and colleagues we haven't heard from in years will email to say, "Nice work." Family members who typically let our declarations and protestations pass without comment will step up to say, "I'm glad you wrote that."

Inevitably, though the "public" in "public writer" involves bracing ourselves for blowback from those who don't like what we have to say or object to our right to say it. Often our op-eds, if well-calibrated, generate a mixed response indicating that we have touched a nerve. Not long ago, I wrote a piece exposing ageism in academe. For a few days all was quiet, and I worried the piece had flopped, since silence or indifference is the worst result an op-ed writer hoping to begin a necessary conversation can expect. Shortly thereafter, I received a supportive email from a US military veteran, in which he thanked me for

---

1. *Dallas Morning News* Editorial Staff, "Tips for letters to the editor and op-ed submissions," December 2, 2018, https://www.dallasnews.com/opinion/2018/12/02/tips-for-letters-to-the-editor-and-op-ed-submissions/.

my column and asked for my advice on the ageism he was experiencing on the campus where he taught as a PhD candidate. Not long after that a less welcome email arrived in my inbox from a higher-up where I teach, who seemed troubled by my penchant for speaking out in national outlets. For several months after my scolding I kept my views on higher education to myself, until I summoned the courage to write once more and buck the growing trend against the quiet suppression of free speech at colleges and universities.

Sometimes going public with your views can even be life- or livelihood-threatening. I think of my colleague Stephen Bloom at the University of Iowa, who, as a decorated author and public writer, once wrote an exposé of the state in the lead-up to the Iowa Caucuses in early 2012. I've known Bloom for years, and once edited his thoughtful work for an anthology I published. And while I knew him to be a stranger in a strange land in the landlocked Midwest (Bloom is originally from New York), I was saddened to learn that he had received death threats when his piece ran in the online version of *The Atlantic*. While he had lodged some fair arguments (for example his well-substantiated points about rural suicide), what most incensed residents of my home state was the "waste-oids and meth addicts" comment he makes in the passage that follows—a pernicious generalization that the editors at *The Atlantic* should have caught:

> Many have simply packed up and left the state (which helps keep the unemployment rate statewide low). Those who stay in rural Iowa are often the elderly waiting to die, those too timid (or lacking in education) to peer around the bend for better opportunities, an assortment of waste-toids and meth addicts with pale skin and rotted teeth, or those who quixotically believe, like Little Orphan Annie, that "The sun'll come out tomorrow."
>
> It's no surprise then, really, that the most popular place for suicide in America isn't New York or Los Angeles, but the rural Middle, where guns, unemployment, alcoholism and machismo reign. Suicides in Iowa's rural counties are 13.55 per 100,000 residents; New York's suicide rate is 5.4 residents per 100,000.[2]

2. Stephen G. Bloom, "Observations from 20 Years of Iowa Life," *The Atlantic*, December 9, 2011, https://www.theatlantic.com/politics/archive/2011/12/observations-from-20-years-of-iowa-life/249401/.

Bloom may have assumed his opinion piece, published in the online version of a magazine headquartered in New England, would not be widely read by his neighbors in Middle America—an all too common mistake made by writers who presume that thinking-person's magazines such as *Harper's*, *The Atlantic*, and the *New Yorker* are only read by highly educated people, or, put another way, that highly educated people do not live in great number in states like Iowa. That may be generally true, as the Census Bureau numbers at the time showed that just over seventeen percent of Iowans held a Bachelor's degree and only eight percent held a graduate or professional degree. However, in Johnson County, Iowa, where Bloom lives and teaches at the flagship state university, the percentage with bachelor's degrees countywide topped fifty-one percent, and reached sixty percent within the city limits of the author's adopted hometown. Readers in Iowa City, Iowa, do in fact read *The Atlantic* in significant numbers, and their overall level of educational attainment tracks closely with the magazine's highly educated readership overall. As of 2015, when Christina Davia undertook an analysis of the magazine, approximately seventy-seven percent of *The Atlantic* readers held a college degree, while nearly forty-one percent of readers possessed a postgraduate degree.[3] At the time the magazine called its readers "affluent and accomplished" and characterized them as "representing a vital audience of the country's most influential thought leaders."

The takeaway? Assume your op-eds, columns, and other opinion pieces will be read by your neighbors, family members, and work supervisors, and steel yourself for the inevitable push back. The response to Bloom's piece from native Iowans was swift and merciless. Then University of Iowa President Sally Mason responded with a lengthy rebuttal-cum-letter to the editor, the beginning paragraphs of which read:

> The recent article at *The Atlantic* by Stephen Bloom, a professor at the University of Iowa, has generated considerable statewide and national reactions about Iowa. I disagree strongly with and was offended by Professor Bloom's portrayal of Iowa and Iowans. Please know that he does not speak for the University of Iowa. As president of the University, I have the

3. Cristina Davia, "Magazine Analysis, *The Atlantic*," February 10, 2015, https://cristinadavia.wordpress.com/2015/02/10/magazine-analysis-the-atlantic/.

246 Zachary Michael Jack

opportunity to travel far and wide across this great state frequently, and the Iowa I see is one of strong, hard-working and
creative people. In this cynical world that can harden even the
greatest optimist, the citizens of Iowa continue to believe.[4]

Angry detractors called for Bloom to be fired for the views he expressed. Fortunately for Stephen, the Iowa Caucuses came and went,
and the immediate threat passed, though had he not had tenure, he
very likely might have found himself looking for a new job.

WRAPPING UP

The op-ed is a uniquely powerful genre for any public writer courageous enough to attempt it, as it epitomizes the civic promise inherent
in reaching the widest possible audience with passion and purpose.
Public writers unafraid to treat past personal and professional experiences as gifts to be given rather than as experiences to be withheld for
shame or fear of judgment will find the satisfactions of the form many
and varied.

The op-ed has the power to advance public discourse as few other
public writing genres can. Almost exactly one year after my piece "We
Live and Die by Chemical Agriculture" appeared in the opinion pages
of the *Des Moines Register*, for example, the issue of pesticide drift was
raised at the Iowa statehouse. Yet, none of the bills attempting to regu-
late pesticide use were allowed to make it to a floor vote. Meanwhile,
the *Register* reported that about nine out of ten, or 89.6 percent, of
pre-kindergarten-through-twelfth grade school buildings in my home
state were within two thousand feet of cropland, a distance within
which a 2006 National Institutes of Health study found an increased
risk of potentially harmful pesticide spray drift from nearby croplands.

A timely op-ed can begin a wider discussion or spearhead a larger
grassroots campaign, but it cannot in and of itself overcome powerful commercial or corporate interests and deeply entrenched legislative
lobbies. Coming to terms with the limits of the op-ed's power alongside its sizable potential for doing good should make us respect the
genre all the more. As the public writer well knows, there are no guarantees in life or in art, only earnest effort toward a better, fairer end.

---

4. Sally Mason, "Stephen Bloom 'Does Not Speak for the University,'" *The
Atlantic*, December 15, 2011, https://www.theatlantic.com/politics/ar-
chive/2011/12/stephen-bloom-does-not-speak-for-the-university/250073/.

15 Blogging for Bigger Audiences

Many of us have started a blog at some point in our lives, though too few of us have kept at it. Many thousands of new blogs are pressed daily all over the world, making for a tower of Babel at worst and a uniquely bustling marketplace at best. Indeed, the website *Hosting Tribunal* estimates 500 million blogs worldwide accounting for over two million blogs posts daily.[1] Clearly we as a species feel a powerful urge to communicate with others in a way that transcends workplace presentations, water cooler gossip, and kitchen-table talk. Blogs offer us the space to develop our thoughts in a way that pushes back on a social media-driven culture that increasingly dictates how many characters we can use to express our feelings. Even Instagram's generous max puts the kibosh on the blog posts of four hundred, five hundred, and six hundred words that thoughtful writers post as a matter of course.

Even traditional print editors have learned to appreciate the form. In his book *Developmental Editing: A Handbook for Freelancers, Authors, and Publishers*, university press editor Scott Norton writes that blogging now demands respect as "its own art form," pointing out that for authors who invest in it, a blog "can become their number-one marketing tool for books or other projects that put money in their pocket."[2] Norton is right; no matter how steep the competition for eyeballs, the blog remains the best way for public writers to put their work before large audiences without the help of an intermediary. Blogs provide an ideal venue to build a following, to develop a partnership or collaboration, or simply to make serendipitous connections with like-minded people around the globe. When I assign blogs to my workshop students, it's not uncommon for them to receive replies from readers halfway across the world.

---

1. "How Many Blogs Are There?" *Hosting Tribunal*, accessed October 15, 2019, https://hostingtribunal.com/blog/how-many-blogs/.
2. Scott Norton, *Developmental Editing: A Handbook for Freelancers, Authors, and Publishers* (Chicago: University of Chicago Press), 19.

It might seem that two-way communication—true communion with the reader—would be the primary driver of the long hours writers spend blogging, but recent studies suggest that the blogger's individual passion for their field justifies the outlay of time and energy. In their study of the most popular science bloggers, British researchers Mathieu Ranger and Karen Bultitude find that the most commonly reported motivations are primarily intrinsic, born of personal interests and enjoyment. In their study, blogging is related to a love of science and a love of writing, and writers who enjoy both are drawn to the platform as a way to express that pleasure.[3] Put simply, avid bloggers do what they do to follow their bliss.

Here are some of the other key findings about science blogs as summarized by another popular science blogsite, *From the Lab Bench*:

- Popular science blogs were updated less frequently (less posts per day) than popular non-science blogs.

- Popular science blogs had significantly fewer blog posts containing at least one non-text element (image, video, audio, etc.) than popular non-science blogs, but science blogs used more graphics and tables.

- 7 out of the 10 science blogs focused 90 percent or more of their content on science.

- Posts from the most popular science blogs were longer on average than posts from the most popular non-science blogs.

The study also finds that most popular science bloggers are not academics. In the study's parlance they function as "transmitters" who, as Ranger and Bultitude put it, "seek satisfaction through sharing their passion with other like-minded individuals." Put simply, science bloggers share the public writer's passion for disseminating information to a wider public. Public intellectuals accustomed to submitting their work to print outlets increasingly turn to blogs to diversify their practice and expand their audience. While the readership of a personal blog is likely to be smaller at first than it might be for the same work published in established print venues, the most successful bloggers can earn article and book contracts as fruits of their labors, promising larger audiences in the end.

---

3. Mathieu Ranger and Karen Bultitude, "'The kind of mildly curious science interested person like me': Science bloggers' practices relating to audience recruitment," *Public Understanding of Science* 25, no. 3 (2016): 361–378.

A compelling example is the popular, long-running science blog *Not Exactly Rocket Science*, begun in 2006 by blogger Ed Yong. In closing the site in 2019 after a successful thirteen-year run, Yong explained that he had begun his blog on "little more than a whim." He recalls:

> It was my first proper foray into science writing. I told my friends that I wanted to get regular practice, and to build up a portfolio of work that I could then show editors. But mainly: I really wanted to write. I had an urge to explain, to describe, to tell stories—an itch that my day job at a cancer charity wasn't scratching.[4]

Over more than a decade, Yong wrote, by his own account, over eighteen hundred pieces under the banner he created, articles he initially made available at no-cost to an audience that numbered mere dozens. As *Not Exactly Rocket Science* became more popular, Yong moved the site to a succession of paying communities: the ScienceBlogs network (then run by the now-defunct *SEED* magazine), the *Discover* blogs network, and finally to the *National Geographic* blog *Phenomena*. Yong's story makes a wonderful prima facie case for the public writer as blogger. Based on Yong's energy, cogency, and clarity as a transmitter of scientific information, editors offered him freelance work, and conference organizers invited him to speak about his successful entrepreneurial start-up. Social scientists queued up to study the success of his blog. What began with the intellectual itch Yong couldn't quite scratch while working a day job at a nonprofit, spurred a career as a public science writer. Yong puts it his way: "This blog changed my life. It gave me a career. It cemented my desire to write. It connected me with communities that opened my eyes to the art of journalism and the realities of social justice. It led to friendship and love."

Yong would go on to write for *National Geographic* and to accept a position as the first staff science writer for *The Atlantic*. In that capacity he quickly learned the differences between public writing for an established print periodical and the homegrown process of writing and editing a blog of his own making. The differences Yong outlines aren't themselves rocket science, but they do bear repeating—blogs are shorter and more informal; they take more tonal liberties, and they are

---

4. Ed Yong, "An Elegy for Not Exactly Rocket Science," *Not Exactly Rocket Science*, accessed October 15, 2019, https://www.nationalgeographic.com/news/2017/01/not-exactly-rocket-science-blog-ends/.

less likely to feature the author's original reporting or breaking news, and more likely to synthesize and analyze the work of others.

The coverage of the science blogging study as reported in the blog *From the Lab Bench* offers a prime example of the ways in which blogs do not often break news but instead transmit, translate, and explicate it. The study's authors—Ranger and Bultitude—both work as academics, and their study originally appeared in the academic journal *Public Understanding of Science*, where it occupied seventeen pages of text and two full pages of mostly scholarly references. When *From the Lab Bench* blogger Paige Brown Jarreau read the study in the scholarly journal, she took on the task of distilling its findings in a succinct post of well under one thousand words. In another excellent example of the serendipitous boon of blogging as a public intellectual, one of the study's original authors, Karen Bultitude, posted a lengthy response in the comments section of Jarreau's post on *From the Lab Bench*.

While Jarreau is perhaps best known as a blogger, by day she works as a science communication specialist for a state university. Like Yong, she created *From the Lab Bench* not as a means of making a living, but on top of the demands of a hectic nine-to-five salaried job. She happened upon Ranger's and Bultitude's study not by accident, but because it paralleled her own research on the science of science writing. Jarreau had completed postdoctoral research on science communication at the time she featured Bultitude's research on her blog, and before that she had pursued a doctoral degree in biomedical engineering. She was pursuing her doctorate, in fact, when she experienced an epiphany. As she explains to her readers, "I realized that I loved writing and communicating about my research just as much (or more) than working at the lab bench."[5] Now that epiphanic moment finds itself inscribed in her blog's tagline: "Science is my interest, writing is my passion." Jarreau's *From the Lab Bench* reminds us that our avocations—the fields of study that, metaphorically speaking, we may have minored rather than majored in, make perfect fodder for public intellectuals looking to reach a wider audience. Changes in major, false career starts, mid-career 180s, all these bear unexpected fruit for the blogger open-minded enough to query what unscratched itch compelled their life change in the first place. At heart, many public writers are Renaissance men and women whose talents might have led them to any number of

---

5. Paige Brown Jarreau, "My Story," *From the Lab Bench*, accessed October 15, 2019, http://www.fromthelabbench.com/about.

successful careers. That same virtuosity compels them to explore the exciting borderlands between disciplines and professions.

In the real world, successful blogs don't always arise from formal credentials in the field. For example, I was never a professional athlete, though I have blogged successfully about sports for years. I was, however, a former failed Division One walk-on, a one-time sports editor, and a faculty member in a Masters in Sports Leadership program, so I was adjacent in ways that well-qualified me to comment on pro sports. In some ways, such field-adjacency represents the blogger's best chance at magnetizing a sizable audience beyond their home discipline.

GUEST BLOGGING

While the ease and accessibility of blogging platforms make it easy for us to follow Yong's and Jarreau's leads as blogger-entrepreneurs, the fraught, time-hungry, often lonely nature of a start-up venture causes many otherwise promising bloggers to lose faith before they've pressed their first dozen postings. Too often blogs fall into what Norton calls "low traffic and high engagement sites." In other words, relatively few people may discover the piece due to its abysmally low ranking in search results, but those who do read the piece are engaged by it.

One sensible way to avoid blogging's boom-and-bust cycles is to guest blog for another established site prior to striking out on one's own. Serving as a guest blogger introduces our work to the blogosphere and expands our platform as we learn the ins and outs of an industry far more nuanced than it might seem at first blush. More and more, blogs function like magazines, and many successful magazines, including *National Geographic* and *Discover*, host blogs. And just as most of us would submit our work to an established magazine before creating a magazine of our own, it makes sense to treat blogs and blogging similarly.

I ramped up my own blog practice years ago with the release of my popular history *March of the Suffragettes: Rosalie Gardiner Jones and the March to Voting Rights*. The publicist for the Bay-area publisher was keen to have me submit a series of guest posts. Initially, I was skeptical. I was a busy writer-academic with lots of scholarly deadlines, and, to be honest, I had yet to fully appreciate the ways in which popular bloggers serve as industry influencers. One of my first tasks was to figure out, organically, how to go about writing a guest blog for a blogsite run by a self-described thirty-something dreamer with a love of words and "a book geek and word nerd with a passion for YA and MG fiction." As an academic and a serious historian, I knew that simply regurgitating the research I had done on the votes-for-women marches of the early twentieth century would be yawn-inducing and wholly out of keeping with the site, which was designed with the sort of happy primary colors often associated with young readers. But while I wanted my guest blog to avoid sounding too serious or stuffy, I didn't want to pander or dumb it down either, as neither choice would honor the reader. I decided on a combination of the personal and the semi-scholarly. My guest blog post would share stories of where and how I had first discovered the book's title character, a question asked frequently of me on book tours. I'd talk, too, about how I developed my love of history in Mrs. Bidlack's fifth-grade classroom. Neither of these topics had been included in the preface to my book, though I had considered both when writing it, so I felt certain my guest post would do more than rewarm old material. As a professor, I also wanted to make my contribution educational, figuring that many of the few thousand people that followed the blog were also teachers, librarians, and others who worked with young adult readers. I wanted my post to be something that young historians and their teachers might find useful, not just anecdotal. I knew from experience on book tours that many who buy and recommend books are also writers in their own right and read as much to hone and advance their craft as for the enlightenment of digesting another's findings. In my blog post's final paragraph I tried to bring the disparate strands of the post into a single coherent paragraph:

> As a writer and researcher, I believe in walking through the looking glass with both your notepad and your mind open, moving laterally, joyously, from one research find to another—something the Internet (the smart-as-a-whip "Aunt Google," as I sometimes call her in classes) makes not only enlightening but enjoyable. While my otherwise fine fifth grade history class failed to introduce me to the proud, fightin' spirit of my suffrage foremothers, it did, in my epic research paper on Maine, at least show me the vertigo-inducing, chutes-and-ladders feeling of historical research at its finest and most life-giving. That's the breathless feeling I hope I've at least partly bottled in *March of the Suffragettes: Rosalie Gardiner Jones and*

the March for Voting Rights. May it march on to the most un-expected places.

In the end, I found myself impressed by the caliber of a highly in-tentional blog community I had initially dismissed. The site owner's decision to host a giveaway of my book generated considerable online buzz, and the lucky winners came away happy, with one of the site's followers writing: "This is such an important book, especially at this time of year. An excellent teaching tool and important person to know about in our history." A happy publicist, a happy blogsite owner, and a happy reader made for a happy public writer.

ANGIE'S LISTS

Angie enrolled in my workshop on locating markets for professional writers, hoping to find ways to leverage her existing interests and ex-pertise into publication credits. Early on I cautioned that going from interest inventories to cover letters and query letters to polished sub-missions in ten weeks would constitute a tall order for any writer, but Angie got right to it, and I could tell she wouldn't be thwarted. Work-ing on deadline was nothing new to her, as she held a position in a grant writing office. In that sense she could already call herself a public writer in practice.

I invited Angie to begin her ideation process with a list of certifica-tions, licensures, and professions she's held in her lifetime. I'm always amazed by the full and varied lives my workshop participants live, and Angie is no exception. Though she was still in her twenties, she gen-erated a list that included everything from a Mental Health First Aid Certificate to a Green Dot Certification to a license as a writing tutor. She had also interned at an impressive list of local nonprofit agen-cies ranging from the National Alliance of Mental Health to the Hu-manitarian Service Project. Early in our workshop Angie volunteered publicly that as a teen she had sought treatment for an eating disorder (ED), something she hoped to write about to an audience beyond her friends, family, and coworkers.

After a week or two of market research, Angie found two blogs that seemed a good fit for a guest piece. The first was the Butterfly Founda-tion for Eating Disorders, whose blog invites guest writers to contrib-ute their recovery narratives. Through a partnership with Dove, the organization sponsors workshops designed to help teachers help their students cultivate positive self-esteem and body image. In particular, Angie appreciated the organization's emphasis on family therapy as part of a strong support system. Ultimately, she determined that another eating disorder site called Project Heal, a grant-giving agency in the United States for individuals who can't afford treatment, would be a more appropriate online venue for her work. Project Heal's blog was interested in help-giving stories from individuals suffering from eating disorders, or loved ones helping sufferers heal from an eating disorder.

THE BLOG TRAP

In her first draft, Angie fell into what I sometimes call the Blog Trap, wherein a skilled writer, writing on in topic about which they feel strongly, drafts a piece that is far too lengthy to be blog-sized. The blog's informal ethos effectively primes the pump, opening the floodgates to the more personal, less guarded voice we're happy to hear emerging in our draft. When we find our authentic voice, we feel liberated, and write volumes from the same pleasure-principle Ranger and Bultitude posit as the chief motivating factor for successful bloggers. Often the issues we blog about have been simmering for years if not decades, such that our thoughts, once formed, rush onto the page in a torrent. By the time we've stemmed the flow, what began as a discrete, manageable post is now essay-length. And since everything on the page comes from an integral and essential place, it feels impossible to cut.

As Angie was crafting "Thank You Mom," she found that she kept digressing from her intended topic: an elaboration of seven support-giving methods her mom had used to aid in Angie's recovery. Under each bullet point Angie had proposed to describe the context of the support she had been given, and why it proved life-giving for her. The piece as conceived offered a strong organizational principle and a formal, seven-point architecture, but it quickly turned into a two-thousand-word opus in which she recounted her recovery process in full. Angie was a seasoned enough writer not to blame herself for the spontaneous overflow. Instead she treated the first draft as a generative exercise, overwriting to find the scope of her idea. Once she had opened the floodgates, it felt more productive and authentic to write her whole recovery story because she could then delve more fully into all of the significant incidents that helped her develop a healthy attitude.

In the drafts that followed, Angie called on existing grant writing skills to limit the coverage of the guest blog she intended to produce, isolating two main components that helped most in her recovery: journaling and a family support system. Focusing on those two ideas helped reduce her draft's length to better conform to Project Heal's pieces, which typically ran 600–1200 words.

Enthusiastic bloggers with overlong first drafts should take heart, recalling that a two-thousand-word first draft of the kind that Angie first penned breaks into three right-sized six-hundred- to seven-hundred-word posts. When my own posts begin to outgrow their confines, I look for the fine fracture points within them to tell me where a new piece or post may be breaking off. Like peanut brittle, it's natural to let smaller pieces of thought or inquiry snap off into more manageable chunks.

THE FINE ART OF PITCH-MATCHING

Nearing submission now, Angie made one final deep dive into Project Heal's blogsite, looking more closely for the nuances of tone, topic, angle, and approach that distinguish any well-curated collection of freelance work. In workshop we call this next-to-final phase "pitch-matching" to suggest the process of fine-tuning one's work to better match the pitch of work previously appearing on the target site. It's meant to be an honorific process, as organic as hearing a snippet of a lovely tune on the wind and whistling it back in homage, the way songbirds answer one another's calls not with the same exact tune, but in pleasing variations. Edits made to match pitch may be major or minor, but the end result should be a submission that suits the length, technique, style, tone, subject matter, and interests of the intended outlet. We're not looking to be imitative or derivative at this stage— our work has an integrity and power all its own—but to use the sample piece or pieces featured on our target blog as templates for success: pieces that have come before ours that made muster and therefore give us confidence that our piece can be published there, too, if we follow their lead.

Many emerging public writers overlook the pitch-match because they have not yet achieved sufficient distance from their work to be able to name the tune they are playing or the one they are trying to match, or because they want to rush their work into publication.

Often, I find that writers most resistant to pitch-matching are those overly enamored of their own originality. They forget that they're pitching as a guest, not calling the shots as a blog owner or host. For the public writer the pitch-match process should be outward-looking and analytic; it's an occasion to step aside for a moment from the private battle with one's own work and its potential and to redirect one's efforts at analyzing not only what the blog says it's looking for in its submission policies, but also what, reading between the lines, it truly is looking for.

Angie invested fully in the pitch-match prior to her guest submission, and her efforts yielded newfound awareness. Post-pitch-match analysis, she noticed that her piece focused on past experiences whereas most of Project Heal's freelance contributions seemed to be set in the present. Additionally, she worried that her piece would represent too big a departure from the site's preferred messaging. For example, one of the bloggers pitch-matched argued that ED sufferers should assimilate the voice of the eating disorder into their own, while Angie's piece argued exactly the opposite. In fact, Angie had pitch-matched her target blog so thoroughly, she told us, she briefly succeeded in "psyching herself out." In other words, she had analyzed the outlet's other successful guest posts so completely that she had become fully cognizant of the smallest deviations her piece made from the norm those other works established. In workshop we reassured her that the comparisons such a deep dive inevitably beget temporarily cause paralysis-by-analysis. While she briefly considered throwing in the towel, we knew her fleeting yet intense moment of self-doubt was actually a sign of increased writerly awareness. She had sufficiently distanced herself now to be able to put her work in a larger context, one that considered the outlet and its preferences, precedents, and past published pieces alongside her own ready-to-pitch piece.

Weeks after our workshop ended, I opened my email to find an enthusiastic email from Angie. She was elated to report that her guest blog, "Saying No to ED" had been accepted for publication. She was full to overflowing with gratitude for her fellow workshoppers, without whom she insisted her publication would not have been possible. Emails like Angie's are my absolute favorite to receive, full as they are of well-deserved joy at a major life breakthrough. It's a reminder that no matter how much a writer has published there's always joy to be experienced when one's work goes out into the world and joins the larger conversation.

New Blogs, Old Dogs

My own career has been blessed with many books, but that fact didn't lessen the joy I felt when several years ago I became a regular blog contributor to a popular sports site. I was an old dog, but I was learning new tricks, and it felt great. For public writers like me, learning to blog effectively is less about chronological age and more about the willingness to invest in what an evolving platform has to teach us. When I first started blogging professionally, I felt as if I was back in school again, only this time the instructors—my bosses—were a generation younger than me. Now those same young lions edit my blog posts before they go live to thousands.

Before each post I dutifully check off a list of items proven to help individual blogs reach the largest possible audience. Here's a short list of the difference-makers that have had the greatest positive effect on my own blog post analytics:

1. Use keyphrases. If you blog professionally, the site for which you blog likely contains a plug-in to help you optimize your post for your chosen focus keyphrase and, via a Suggest tool, helps you locate the first ten keywords in your post. The terms found using the Suggest (both Yoast and Google offer their own competing tool) amount to combinations of words that are logical and used by actual people to search for work like yours on the web.

2. Use a focus keyword. The focus keyword—or keyphrase—is the search term that you want your page to rank highly on in a Google search. Ideally, when Web users search for your chosen keyphrase they will find your post. Yoast SEO has its own input field for this and evaluates your blog post's content to provide feedback on how to improve the content for that focus keyword or keyphrase. If in doubt Google your suggested keyword and keyphrases and examine the first two results pages. If articles and posts you find there are similar to your own post, it means your keywords and keyphrases are playing nicely with the search engine's algorithm.

3. Include internal links. When I first began blogging professionally, I found this piece of advice counter-intuitive. Why would a blogsite that pays its expert contributors for their views want to give readers an easy way to click out of their post to the blogsite or website of a competitor? The truth is, blog readers are drawn to interactivity, and embedded links allow them greater agency and self-direction. Links also offer an easy visual way to attribute intellectual property (a cyber approach to citing one's sources) as well as generate valuable user data for advertisers. For example, back in the days when he independently owned and operated *Not Exactly Rocket Science*, Edward Yong might have easily linked his readers to analogous content on, for example, *National Geographic*. If a large enough number of readers clicked over from Yong's posts to the *National Geographic*, it would suggest a powerful synergy between the two sites, an overlap of interest and demographics that could be monetized. Surely *National Geographic* noticed such a synergy (and the potential for increased site traffic and ad revenues it promised) when it offered to host Yong's site.

4. Use images. Most of our posts can benefit from photos, video, audio, tables, charts, graphs, and the like. Photos and other visuals can help attract visual learners and casual Internet surfers as well as those conducting Google Images searches. They can also help illustrate concepts, experiences, and places that are otherwise difficult to capture in text. If a picture is indeed worth a thousand words, images, pull quotes, sidebars, and other supporting graphics can also help shorten your blog posts to more readable and digestible lengths. Take care, however, that if you insert an image or graphic in your post that you have obtained proper permission. If you're lucky, the blogsite for whom you're writing maintains a paid subscription to a royalty-free image library such as Getty Images or iStock. For example, Angie's blog post was published with a stock photograph of a hand holding up a post-it note on which is written "You are beautiful"—an attractive graphic with an affirmation that resonates perfectly with the takeaway of her piece. However, if you or your publisher don't have access to a stock photo library, consider taking your own screen-resolu-

tion images or using a copyright-free or public domain image from, for example, Wikimedia Commons or the Library of Congress. Even so, you'll need to attribute the source of the photo and sometimes the specific individual or entity who created the content or holds its copyright. Always read the fine print when selecting stock images or historic photographs for publication, as individual images may have their own unique copyright restrictions and some historical and archival material made available to the public may require express written consent to use in your blog post.

5. Keep your posts short, but not so short as to feel slight. In an era when social media platforms like Instagram can double as blogging services, it's important to find the sweet spot between feature length (often 1500 words or more) and the ubiquitous social media posts of fifty words or fewer. While three-hundred-word blog posts are around average, most sites find something closer to four hundred words or more to be ideal for news- or current events-driven content. And even four hundred words may feel slight on topics of depth and sensitivity, including the content covered by a blogsite like Project Heal. At about nine hundred words, Angie's "Saying No to Eating Disorders" guest post would be too long for many news-driven sites, but when the topic is how a sufferer recovered, over time, from a serious condition, four hundred words would surely feel inadequate.

WRAPPING UP

Blogging remains an evolving genre, and as such its parameters and best practices are ever-changing. Boundary-pushing public writers might be tempted to float two-thousand-word blog posts without focus words, keyphrases, and illustrative images or graphics, but such significant stylistic departures are far less likely to succeed when sophisticated algorithms help determine search results. Established public writers willing to learn the tricks of the blogging trade are certain to grow their audience and leverage their influence in ways that feed their serious and scholarly work.

16 Writing to Change the World

Editorials, open letters, empathy and immersion journalism, calls to action, and public statements can all help change the world in times of cultural turmoil. The sheer length and diversity of the list of social change outlets can cause us to wonder if writing for social justice is best regarded as a single genre, a series of related genres, or something else entirely—perhaps an aspiration, an inspiration, an impetus, or an intention?

When students arrive in my writing for social change workshops, we wonder aloud why such an influential strain of writing lacks its own dedicated section at the bookstore. Maybe it's because social change is as social change does, which is to say a writer whose primary goal is to affect positive transformation is a writer for social justice by practice, regardless of the genre in which they write.

Synthesizing a number of scholarly definitions, MissionBox Global Network suggests the following working definition for this sometimes mercurial genre: "Social change is a significant, lasting alteration in a society's culture, values, norms or behavior, especially as it relates to the goal of making the world a more equitable . . . place."[1] For the University of Wisconsin, Madison, which recently inaugurated a Writing for Social Change workshop series, social justice writing evinces "a commitment to diversity, inclusion, and change." In effect, social change writers are activists who use text as a tool to persuade and to raise awareness. At Walden University, where all graduate theses, dissertations, and projects must address social change, dissertation editor Lydia Lunning writes this to her students:

> You may feel overwhelmed by being asked to explain how what you've been doing at your desk, alone in the library, or on your computer in your precious free moments could

---

1. Kendra Shaw, "An Introduction to Social Change," *Mission Box Global Network*, July 2, 2019, https://www.missionbox.com/article/390/an-introduction-to-social-change.

amount to something that could change the course of other people's lives—but that is exactly what you are meant to do. [2]

Lunning recommends that writers "start with the *tangible* impact this new knowledge will bring and with the one individual or group of individuals you know will specifically benefit, and then see how far the wave crashes."

Public writing for social change is intended to change the public's mind, and, consequently, its practice. That's a conspicuously high bar, for while many readers can point to books that inspired them, many struggle to name a title that actually changed the way they live their daily lives. A respected professor of mine once claimed that any piece of writing must decide what it wants its readers to think, know, or believe, but for me social justice writing goes one step further, challenging readers to change what they do.

Public writers with a citizen's heart, an instinct for equity, and a desire to beget systemic change are well-served by answering the question Walden University poses to its degree candidates: how might our findings make the world a better place? How might we use our writing skills to become change agents? As Lunning notes, it's difficult to know where to begin when one decides to enlist their writing skills in service to social causes. An important first step for all public writers eager to craft life-altering, status-quo changing, equity-engendering work is to locate the bedrock issues that animate us.

WRITING TO CHANGE THE WORLD

When I lead writing for social change workshops, I take care to avoid the too-easy "What (or whom) makes us angry?" prompt so often used to incite strong feelings among passionate, highly spirited writers. For me, "What makes you angry?" usually elicits topics of hermetic concern or personal annoyance, as in: "Drivers who cut me off in traffic make me angry." Instead, I like to frame the question as, "What makes you indignant?" Unlike anger, which is an emotion we tend to over-personalize, indignation often entails thinking about others. In *To Kill a Mockingbird* Atticus Finch declares, "The one place where

2. Lydia Lunning, "How to Write for Positive Social Change," *Walden University Writing Center*, October 1, 2013, http://waldenwritingcenter.blogspot.com/2013/10/how-to-write-for-positive-social-change.html.

262   *Zachary Michael Jack*

a man ought to get a square deal is in a courtroom, be he any color of the rainbow, but people have a way of carrying their resentments right into a jury box." It's Atticus's sense of indignation, rather than his raw anger, that prompts him to defend the falsely accused Tom Robinson in Harper Lee's classic novel of social justice. Finding what we're indignant about is an important first step in determining which causes most call to us and, by extension, which are most worthy of our words. Once we as public writers for social change find our most resonant topics, the pieces we write come more naturally, motivated both by our emotional connection to the subject matter and to a body of supporting knowledge and scholarship we've assembled. When writer and cause join, however, passion can easily run amok. For these reasons I recommend that writers for social change begin with 500- to 750-word drafts of shorter, more manageable pieces, letting the length restriction guard against passion removed of reason.

Atticus Finch insists that "The courts are the great levelers," and though Atticus couldn't possibly have known it at the time, the Internet may be the greatest leveler of the twenty-first century. In a digital age, social justice writing that leverages its brevity is more likely to reach readers. In previous centuries, book-length treatments such as *Uncle Tom's Cabin* or Upton Sinclair's *The Jungle* served as the preferred vehicles for change messages, as they reached audiences with the time, money, and literacy to put the novel's social justice-minded lessons into practice. In the era of Harriet Beecher Stowe, individuals who could afford to read a novel were often also those best-positioned to work for social uplift. Since then the locus of ameliorative writing has migrated, like so many other aspects of popular culture, to shorter work that translates well into multiple platforms accessible to a wider cross section of the reading and viewing public. The open letter represents one such highly adaptable, appealingly succinct written artifact of social change.

THE OPEN LETTER

Once the public writer decides they really do want to change the world, or at least one small corner of it, the open letter serves as an ideal gateway. The idea of tackling a letter feels more natural and organic to many activists than penning a formal public policy analysis, a white paper, or a researched essay, since many of us have been composing letters since elementary school. The real difficulty of the open letter lies in the ideation and pre-writing it requires—whom will be addressed and what will be the topic? Once those preliminaries are decided and the writing has begun, the letter often generates its own forward momentum.

In her book *Dear Madam President: An Open Letter*, Jennifer Palmieri takes what would have been a traditional campaign memoir read almost exclusively by political junkies and widens the audience. Addressing a series of open letters to "Madam President," Palmieri, a former Hillary Clinton communications director, establishes an epistolary intimacy with her reader that proves convincing. Here is an excerpt of one of her early missives:

> I wasn't sure how to address you in this letter. Doesn't *madam* suggest you are married? Are we still going to define women— the first woman president, no less—by relation to a man? I could go with the gender-neutral salutation, "Dear President." It doesn't matter if you are a man or a woman so long as you can do the job.
> Bullshit.
> It matters.
> And you are going to bring an entirely new perspective to the office. You will expand our nation's comprehension of what it means to be a leader. In its best moments your presidency will bring us a more fully realized sense of leadership— one that combines the best qualities of women and men.
> There will be many challenges. World and congressional leaders will test you. America will judge you differently than it did your predecessors. People will scrutinize you, your ambitions, your clothes. You are a unique individual yet you are expected to represent all women. Be conscious of it, but keep a positive attitude. It doesn't mean everyone who doubts you is sexist. We inherited this world with all its flaws. We didn't create it. All of us are attempting to adapt and grow.
> Given all the gains women have made in the past one hundred years, having a woman president may not seem like that big of deal. It is.[3]

---

3. Jennifer Palmieri, *Dear Madam President: An Open Letter to the Women Who Will Run the World* (New York: Grand Central Publishing, 2018).

Beyond the salutation "Dear Madam President," six specific rhetorical strategies lend Palmieri's piece the distinct appeal offered by an open letter:

1. The writer keeps her sentences short. At less than ten words on average the sentences are shorter than most deadline news copy.

2. The writer personalizes the method of address, using the second person "you" twelve times—more than any other single word in the piece. In fact, for Palmieri the second-person accounts for nearly fifty percent of her total pronoun usage, suggesting that hers will be a letter more about the letter-receiver than about the letter-writer. As a result, the letter looks outward at a larger injustice.

3. The writer keeps the punctuation unobtrusive and unpretentious. No semi-colons need apply here, presumably because not many us think, or speak, in semi-colons when we're burning with a sense of indignation.

4. The writer stays focused. Palmieri's letter functions like a short essay in its unwavering fixation on a single desired outcome: the election of our first female president. Its laser focus mimics the dogged obsessiveness of the activist determined to beget change.

5. The writer minds her tone. Most notably, Palmieri's open letter transcends the "whininess" critics wrongly use to marginalize activist voices. Later Palmieri will suggest that the election of 2016 was stolen from Clinton, but in the preceding excerpt there's no off-putting self-pity or finger-pointing accusations, just frank, declarative, forward-moving sentences. The author's decorum is indicated by the complete absence of informal contractions such as "it's," "we're," "we'd" and "I'd" that lend ammunition to those who want to discredit the author as overly naive.

6. The writer records in stereo. Though her literal addressee is clear—Madam President—the actual audience, to extend the metaphor, is multi-track. Ostensibly, Palmieri addresses her letter to Clinton, the woman who would have been president.

But she's simultaneously writing to the unnamed woman president of the future destined to shatter America's highest glass ceiling once and for all. Meanwhile, she's also talking to herself, aiming to rekindle her hope for a better future while summoning her courage to fight for deserving candidates she's determined shouldn't be disadvantaged by their chosen gender.

As a genre, the open letter stands the test of time, as MLK's "Letter from a Birmingham Jail" attests. King wrote his epistle on scraps of newsprint available to him in the city jail, and allies smuggled his words out to the wider world, bit by bit, until eventually the fragments were assembled and published in the *New York Post* Sunday magazine. MLK's epistle is a powerful example of the think globally, act locally mantra. In it he addresses the local clergy of Birmingham, Alabama, though in fact he writes to all people of faith and moral purpose who believe in St. Thomas Aquinas's notion that, as the reverend puts it, "An unjust law is a human law that is not rooted in eternal law and natural law. Any law that uplifts human personality is just. Any law that degrades human personality is unjust." Later in his epistle, MLK puts a finer point on it, writing in his letter's most quoted passage:

> Moreover, I am cognizant of the interrelatedness of all communities and states. I cannot sit idly by in Atlanta and not be concerned about what happens in Birmingham. Injustice anywhere is a threat to justice everywhere. We are caught in an inescapable network of mutuality, tied in a single garment of destiny. Whatever affects one directly, affects all indirectly.[4]

The indirectness of King's approach is part and parcel of the genius of the open letter as a public writing genre. He might have addressed his letter to Bull Connor, the Birmingham commissioner of public safety whose often brutal policing brought King to Birmingham in the first place. Yet, true to his name, Bull Connor would have been far too stubborn to read the words of a black man he regarded as an outside agitator and radical. Nor did King address his letter "Dear White Southerner" or "Dear White America"; neither demographic was prepared in April 1963 to confront its own institutional racism. Nor did he

4. Martin Luther King Jr. "Letter from a Birmingham Jail," *The Atlantic Monthly*, August 1963; "The Negro Is Your Brother," 212, No. 2: 78–88, http://web.cn.edu/kwheeler/documents/letter_birmingham_jail.pdf.

formally name his piece by the alternate title that it would later appear under in *The Atlantic Monthly*, "The Negro Is Your Brother." Instead, Reverend King ostensibly addresses a very narrow audience consisting of colleagues in his field, fellow educated clergy who concede the racial injustice of segregation but oppose his public demonstrations against it. MLK makes a logical yet impassioned appeal to those who share his faith and his profession, allowing the rest of the nation to read, at safe remove and over-the-shoulder, an inside or internal debate among learned pastors, preachers, and bishops. His letter begins:

> 16 April 1963
>
> My Dear Fellow Clergymen:
>
> While confined here in the Birmingham city jail, I came across your recent statement calling my present activities "unwise and untimely." Seldom do I pause to answer criticism of my work and ideas. If I sought to answer all the criticisms that cross my desk, my secretaries would have little time for anything other than such correspondence in the course of the day, and I would have no time for constructive work. But since I feel that you are men of genuine good will and that your criticisms are sincerely set forth, I want to try to answer your statement in what I hope will be patient and reasonable terms.

While the open letter gestures at familiarity, it's clear from context that MLK knew his letter would be read by an audience much wider than the eight clergymen who penned the "Call to Unity," and to whom he was responding. Dr. King belies his intentions for a wider readership throughout the first paragraph, which includes context the clergy would have already known (the fact that he was incarcerated in the city jail, for example) but that he hoped to highlight to readers far removed from Birmingham, Alabama. King, like Palmieri, records as if in two-track stereo with the surface track reserved for a highly specific addressee (his fellow clergy) about a particular topic, while the second track plays to a wider public eager to listen in on a national question staged as an internal debate.

PUBLIC STATEMENTS

In times of enduring cultural turmoil or controversy, thoughtful citizens across the land feel compelled to take a stand on the issues of the day, for fear of having their silence mistaken for complicity or tacit approval of unjust actions. For everyday citizens and prominent figures alike, such public statements are often articulated in the pages of newspapers, published on personal blogs or websites, or issued via social media. In the aftermath of the police killing of George Floyd and the national protests that followed, ex-president George W. Bush and former first lady Laura Bush joined many other politicians, including former presidents Barack Obama and Jimmy Carter, in issuing public statements supporting the protestors and decrying America's history of racist acts.

Statements like the one written by the Bushes are exceedingly difficult to write, with potential for misstep, misunderstanding, or misinterpretation at every turn. Unlike the open letter, whose down-to-earth ethos is enhanced by its familiar form and directed at a known recipient (for example, MLK's clergymen), the public statement often comes packaged with greater gravitas or formality—evincing an "on high" tone that feels more official. For example, Bush's statement arrived at the nation's newspapers and magazines as a press release dramatically marked "For Immediate Release," and, in big bold caps "STATEMENT BY PRESIDENT GEORGE W. BUSH." While such formalities do convey an Oz-like authority, they can be problematic when what readers need is someone they admire and trust to get off their high horse and get real. Because public statements, like editorials, are often written by two or more writers collectively, or are penned to represent the views of an entire organization, it can be difficult for them to convey intimacy or to make the desired human connection.

Writers of such sensitive pieces as these do well to invite friends and colleagues to read drafts prior to publication, as, when writing to heal an injustice, it's easy to become preachy, pedantic, or partisan in a way that damages ethos and turns even sympathetic readers away. In the first two paragraphs of their public statement below, notice how expertly George and Laura Bush manage to avoid those pitfalls, crafting a timely communique that reads more like an open letter to the nation than a political or polemical statement:

> Laura and I are anguished by the brutal suffocation of George Floyd and disturbed by the injustice and fear that suffocate our country. Yet we have resisted the urge to speak out, because this is not the time for us to lecture. It is time for us

to listen. It is time for America to examine our tragic failures—and as we do, we will also see some of our redeem-
ing strengths.

It remains a shocking failure that many African Americans, especially young African American men, are harassed
and threatened in their own country. It is a strength when
protesters, protected by responsible law enforcement, march
for a better future. This tragedy—in a long series of similar
tragedies—raises a long overdue question: How do we end
systemic racism in our society? The only way to see ourselves
in a true light is to listen to the voices of so many who are
hurting and grieving. Those who set out to silence those voices do not understand the meaning of America—or how it becomes a better place.[5]

The public statement isn't perfect, certainly. Some might fault a voice
that at times feels removed, distant, and a little too willing to settle
for abstraction over gritty truth. But in its willingness to ask difficult
questions ("How do we end systemic racism in our society?") and to
name abuses both particular ("brutal suffocation of George Floyd")
and pervasive ("injustice," "tragic failures," "harassment") it demonstrates the courage of its convictions. Even resistant readers are likely
to appreciate the statement's summoning, as Lincoln put it, of the an-
gels of our better natures, and its hopeful vision that we can indeed
become a better and more equitable place.

EDITORIALS

If they are fortunate, public writers experience the happy accident of
a piece that goes viral, enacting social change by virtue of its wide
circulation. Such is the case with the most read editorial of all-time,
one that decries a different kind of violence against a cherished ideal.

In 1897, eight-year-old Virginia O'Hanlon wrote a letter to the editor of the *New York Sun*, where veteran reporter Francis Pharcellus
Church was tasked with responding to it in his unsigned editorial of

5. George W. Bush, "Statement of George W. Bush," George W. Bush Presidential Library, June 2, 2020, https://www.bushcenter.org/about-the-center/
newsroom/press-releases/2020/06/statement-by-president-george-w-bush.
html.

September 21, 1897. The piece has since become history's most re-
printed newspaper editorial, appearing in part or in whole in dozens
of languages in songs, movies, posters, and even stamps. Totaling less
than forty words from start to finish, the question O'Hanlon poses in
her letter to the editor allows no equivocation in reply:

> DEAR EDITOR: I am 8 years old.
>
> Some of my little friends say there is no Santa Claus.
>
> Papa says, 'If you see it in THE SUN it's so.'
>
> Please tell me the truth; is there a Santa Claus?

Within days Church had issued his equally forthright, though considerably longer, response:

> Virginia, your little friends are wrong. They have been af-
> fected by the skepticism of a skeptical age. They do not be-
> lieve except they see. They think that nothing can be which
> is not comprehensible by their little minds. All minds, Vir-
> ginia, whether they be men's or children's, are little. In this
> great universe of ours man is a mere insect, an ant, in his in-
> tellect, as compared with the boundless world about him, as
> measured by the intelligence capable of grasping the whole of
> truth and knowledge.
>
> Yes, Virginia, there is a Santa Claus. He exists as certain-
> ly as love and generosity and devotion exist, and you know
> that they abound and give to your life its highest beauty and
> joy. Alas! how dreary would be the world if there were no
> Santa Claus. It would be as dreary as if there were no Virgi-
> nias. There would be no childlike faith then, no poetry, no
> romance to make tolerable this existence. We should have no
> enjoyment, except in sense and sight. The eternal light with
> which childhood fills the world would be extinguished.
>
> Not believe in Santa Claus! You might as well not be-
> lieve in fairies! You might get your papa to hire men to watch
> in all the chimneys on Christmas Eve to catch Santa Claus,
> but even if they did not see Santa Claus coming down, what
> would that prove? Nobody sees Santa Claus, but that is no
> sign that there is no Santa Claus. The most real things in the
> world are those that neither children nor men can see. Did
> you ever see fairies dancing on the lawn? Of course not, but

that's no proof that they are not there. Nobody can conceive or imagine all the wonders there are unseen and unseeable in the world.

You may tear apart the baby's rattle and see what makes the noise inside, but there is a veil covering the unseen world which not the strongest man, nor even the united strength of all the strongest men that ever lived, could tear apart. Only faith, fancy, poetry, love, romance, can push aside that curtain and view and picture the supernal beauty and glory beyond. Is it all real? Ah, Virginia, in all this world there is nothing else real and abiding.

No Santa Claus! Thank God! he lives, and he lives forever. A thousand years from now, Virginia, nay, ten times ten thousand years from now, he will continue to make glad the heart of childhood.[6]

If the persuasive power of an editorial is measured in part by its circulation, then surely Church's long-ago social change epistle possesses an abiding power. Note how well "Yes, Virginia, there is a Santa Claus" has aged. Though it was penned in a late Victorian era known for purple prose and long-winded, high-minded, highly ornate sentences, its language, syntax, and sentiment seem to belong as much to our own plainspoken day as they do to the Victorian age.

In today's crowded marketplace editorials may lack some of the persuasive power they enjoyed in Church's day, but when well-timed and well-written, they continue to shape public opinion. Unlike the personal commentaries and op-eds discussed in prior chapters, which are pieces contributed by guest columnists and readers, editorials are most often written by individuals appearing on the publication's masthead.

In 2019, the *Orlando Sentinel* published an editorial of bracing honesty. In June of that year the editorial board shattered newspaper convention not just by announcing its endorsement before the two major party candidates were known, but by declaring that it would endorse anyone *but* sitting president Donald J. Trump. In an editorial that energized many social change activists, the editors sent this shot across the president's bow:

---

6. Francis Pharcellus Church, "Is There a Santa Claus?" New York *Sun*, September 21, 1897, accessed October 15, 2019, https://www.newseum.org/exhibits/online/yes-virginia/.

We're here to announce our endorsement for president in 2020, or, at least, who we're not endorsing: Donald Trump.

Some readers will wonder how we could possibly eliminate a candidate so far before an election, and before knowing the identity of his opponent.

Because there's no point pretending we would ever recommend that readers vote for Trump.

After 2½ years we've seen enough.

Enough of the chaos, the division, the schoolyard insults, the self-aggrandizement, the corruption, and especially the lies.

So many lies—from white lies to whoppers—told out of ignorance, laziness, recklessness, expediency or opportunity . . . .

There was a time when even a single lie—a phony college degree, a bogus work history—would doom a politician's career.

Not so for Trump, who claimed in 2017 that he lost the popular vote because millions of people voted illegally (they didn't). In 2018 he said North Korea was no longer a nuclear threat (it is). And in 2019 he said windmills cause cancer (they don't). Just last week he claimed the media fabricated unfavorable results from his campaign's internal polling (it didn't).

According to a *Washington Post* database, the president has tallied more than 10,000 lies since he took office.

Trump's successful assault on truth is the great casualty of this presidency, followed closely by his war on decency.

Trump insults political opponents and national heroes alike with middle-school taunts. He demonstrates no capacity for empathy or remorse . . .[7]

Writing as a collective, the editorial board functions like the board of any organization or institution, speaking when possible with one voice in an attempt to shape the views of its many constituencies and to guide future action in a manner consistent with institutional values. As curators and keepers of information they hope to reach the wider

7. *Sentinel* Editorial Board, "Our Orlando Sentinel endorsement for president in 2020: Not Donald Trump," June 18, 2019, https://www.orlandosentinel.com/opinion/editorials/os-op-sentinel-not-endorsing-donald-trump-2020-20190618-63ya7cyb5ngf3irllodwxnznui-story.html.

public to inform and to persuade. Working together, they endeavor to make sense of a difficult and nuanced political picture, to sort out a mess, and to replace confusion with clarity. Are the arbiters fair and open-minded? In this case the evidence suggests yes, as except for Lyndon Johnson in 1964, the *Sentinel* backed Republican presidential nominees from 1952 through 2004, when they endorsed John Kerry over a second term of George W. Bush.

Editorials Take a Village, or at Least a Staff

To mark a somber Memorial Day on May 24, 2020, a team of writers and editors at the *New York Times* combined efforts in a remarkable if not historic collaboration. Their project in this case wasn't to pen a standard group editorial, but to construct an entire Page One from a sampling of the names and snippet obituaries of Americans who had died from COVID-19. Simone Landon, an assistant editor at the graphics desk, spearheaded the effort to turn page one into a "rich tapestry."[8] Staff members from the national desk, digital news design, software engineers, graphics editors, art directors, researchers, and interns compiled and formatted a list of nearly one thousand names culled from hundreds of newspapers as representative of a larger death toll, which was then nearing 100,000. The sheer drama of the page-one display is impossible to recreate on a small scale, though even a sample conveys its power:

> Alan Lund, 81, Washington, **conductor with "the most amazing ear"** Theresa Elloie, 63, New Orleans, **renowned for her business making detailed pins and corsages**, Florencio Almazo Morán, 65, New York City, **one-man army**, Coby Adolph, 44, Chicago, **entrepreneur and adventurer**

While it's true that open letters and editorials often address events and issues pertinent to the humanities, public writers with deep expertise in, and passion for, the sciences should find these social change genres every bit as relevant to their practice. In recent years more than a thousand of the world's experts on artificial intelligence (AI), including Stephen Hawking, served as signatories for open letters advocating

---

8. John Grippe, "The Project Behind a Front Page Full of Names," *The New York Times*, May 23, 2020, https://www.nytimes.com/2020/05/23/reader-center/coronavirus-new-york-times-front-page.html.

a ban on "offensive autonomous weapons" and "killer robots," speculating that they would end humanity if a strict prohibition were not put in place. Meanwhile, the editorial board at the nation's newspaper of record, the *New York Times*, collectively called for future scientific exploration of Mars, arguing that "whether it's practical or not, humans will continue to explore the heavens so long as the moon, Mars, and the myriad celestial bodies beyond fire our imagination and curiosity."[9]

PARTICIPATORY WRITING

Even public writers who earned their chops as reporters and editors are sometimes reluctant to practice the social justice genre known as participatory writing and also sometimes by analogous terms such as *advocacy journalism*, *civic journalism*, and *empathy journalism*. Traditionally, the writer-reporter isn't supposed to play favorites or advance pet causes, as both are seen as supplanting objectivity with unwanted advocacy. Similarly, public intellectuals who teach at universities, work at labs, and sit on boards of directors sometimes fear coming out too publicly, or too strongly, on issues in ways that might jeopardize their position or complicate or compromise their institutional mission. For a growing number of devotees, however, participatory writing offers a perfect middle ground between the eye-witness advocacy of the activist and the objectivity-by-distance of the well-trained public scholar or intellectual. As its name implies, it calls for the writer to enter the fray, not with bias or with preconceived notions, but with a mind made open by firsthand experience in arenas from which the writer endeavors to report firsthand experience. While conventional journalists argue that participating in, or with, one's subject spoils any pretense of objectivity, participatory writers argue just the opposite: that only through doing can a public writer fairly understand and competently characterize their subject.

In the social sciences participatory writing is better known as participant observation and refers to a type of qualitative data collection widely used in cultural anthropology, sociology, communication, human geography, and social psychology. A kind of participant obser-

9. *New York Times* Editorial Board, "Mars Beckons," *New York Times*, November 27, 2018, https://www.nytimes.com/2018/11/27/opinion/mars-exploration-nasa-insight-space.html.

vation powers the *New York Times* best-seller *Gang Leader for a Day: A Rogue Sociologist Takes to the Streets.* Rather than study urban poverty from the comforts of his University of Chicago ivory tower, then sociology graduate student, later turned sociology professor, Sudhir Vankatesh joins a Southside gang to observe its hierarchical structure from the inside out. Vankatesh endeavors to explore and problematize his newfound belonging, emerging with an insider's perspective that would have been impossible had his work been purely theoretical.

Other participatory writers have risked domestic and personal comfort for the sake of their immersive investigations. Journalist-Academic Ted Conover has traveled across the country in *Rolling Nowhere: Riding the Rails with America's Hoboes*; smuggled himself across the US-Mexico Border in the company of undocumented immigrants in *Coyotes: A Journey Across Borders with America's Illegal Migrants*, and worked for a year inside a notorious correctional facility in *New Jack: Guarding Sing Sing.* Like Vankatesh, Conover is an academician determined to bring a scholar's acumen to his immersions into various social groups and subcultures and to document their otherwise hidden dynamics. Conover won the National Book Critics Circle Award for nonfiction, in part for his willingness to experience the issues about which he writes firsthand, emerging from that unmediated access with exceptional insight and compassion. His "Author's Note" in *New Jack: Guarding Sing Sing* speaks to the care with which he deploys participant methodology to educate the public on conditions within one of America's most notorious prisons, as Conover reminds his readers: "This is a work of nonfiction, describing events that I witnessed and participated in. No scenes are imaginary or made up . . . . Like all officers, I kept a small spiral notebook in my breast pocket for note-taking; unlike most of them I took many notes."[10]

For emerging and apprenticing public writers, participatory writing can feel intimidating, appearing to require the kind of financial or physical hardship that writers with jobs and families find difficult to justify. Yet, many immersive investigations are more doable than one might assume. A case in point is Barbara Ehrenreich's now classic *Harper's* magazine article (and later a book of the same name) "Nickel-and-Dimed: On (Not) Getting By in America" in which the public

---

10. Ted Conover, "Author's Note," *Newjack: Guarding Sing Sing* (New York: Vintage 2001), https://archive.nytimes.com/www.nytimes.com/books/first/c/conover-newjack.html?scp=29&sq=perk%2520street&st=cse.

writer dips into the world of minimum wage-earners for one month. Ehrenreich needn't give up her name or earthly possessions to engage in her shorter-term experiment, though her equity-minded immersion nevertheless yields significant insight into personal and occupational identity. She writes:

> I became another, occupationally much diminished, "Barbara Ehrenreich"—depicted on job-application forms as a divorced homemaker whose sole work experience consists of housekeeping in a few private homes. I am terrified, at the beginning, of being unmasked for what I am: a middle-class journalist setting out to explore the world that welfare mothers are entering, at the rate of approximately 50,000 a month .... Happily, though, my fears turn out to be entirely unwarranted: during a month of poverty and toil, my name goes unnoticed and for the most part unuttered. In this parallel universe where my father never got out of the mines and I never got through college, I am "baby," "honey," "blondie," and, most commonly, "girl."[11]

An even more approachable model for participatory methodology comes from writer Alice Walker in her now classic piece first published in *Ms.* magazine "In Search of Zora Neale Hurston." Posing as kin to the undervalued African American writer and folklorist, Walker learns what became of the literary luminary who inspired much of her own writing. She sets the scene in first-person:

> Eatonville has lived for such a long time in my imagination that I can hardly believe it will be found existing in its own right. But after 20 minutes on the expressway Charlotte turns off and I see a small settlement of houses and stores set with no particular pattern in the sandy soil off the road. We stop in front of a neat gray building that has two fascinating signs: Eatonville Post Office and Eatonville City Hall.
>
> Inside the Eatonville City Hall half of the building, a slender, dark-brown-skin woman sits looking through letters on a desk. When she hears we are searching for anyone who might have known Zora Neale Hurston, she leans back in

---

11. Barbara Ehrenreich, "Nickel-and-Dimed: On (not) getting by in America," *Harper's*, January 1999, 37.

thought. Because I don't wish to inspire foot-dragging in people who might know something about Zora they're not sure
they should tell, I have decided on a profoundly simple, but
profoundly *useful* lie.

"I am Miss Hurston's niece," I prompt the young woman,
who brings her head down with a smile.[12]

Determined to direct the attention of *Ms.* magazine's most social justice-minded readers to one of America's most neglected writers of col-
or, Walker eventually goes in search of Hurston's grave. Unable to find
it, and suspecting that the author's burial site is, in fact, unmarked, she
pays for a commemorative headstone out of pocket. Readers remember
"In Search of Zora" for many reasons, but it's the participatory element—the discoveries Walker makes on-site in Hurston's hometown
among the people who knew her best—surely account for the piece's
inclusion in *The Best American Essays of the Century.*

Public writers determined to hear all sides practice the empathy
writing popularized by Conover, Ehrenreich, and Walker, in still more
logistically manageable, financially sustainable ways. Whether the information gleaned as part of the firsthand immersion experience appears in a work verbatim or merely informs the piece on background,
participations bring the public intellectual's work down to earth, con-
ferring on it a special kind of experiential knowledge highly valued by
readers and by the marketplace. Suppose, for example, that an urban
writer wants to research the industrial agricultural food chain and the
costs and benefits of a corn-centered diet powered by cheap petroleum.
They might begin by attending their local farmers' market, where they
might interview independent food producers. Or they might follow
the participatory method of author and public intellectual Michael
Pollan, who in the final section of his best-selling book *The Omnivore's Dilemma*, prepares a meal using only ingredients he has hunted,
gathered, or grown himself. Expanding the depth of his immersion, he
recruits local foodies to help him hunt feral pigs, gather wild mush-
rooms, and search for abalone. He makes salads of greens from his
own garden, bakes sourdough breads using wild yeast, and prepares
desserts from cherries picked in his neighborhood.

Participatory writing promises to take the already engaged and engaging work of the public writer to a new level. Yet, it also brings

12. Alice Walker, "In Search of Zora Neale Hurston," *Ms.*, March 1975, 75.

added risks and responsibilities of which the public writer must be mindful. For instance, social scientists can choose to be either "covert" or "overt" when employing participant observation, with many arguing that the covert method yields the best data. However, while going undercover may promise the greatest potential for what sociologist Jun Li calls the "emancipatory paradigm," it also can lead to the deception, and lack of informed consent of those studied, as well charges of tokenism and appropriation. Li won a prestigious one-year fellowship to study problem gambling among women in Canada, and quickly learned that participant observation was the only field method that allowed her to observe what gamblers did in real-life contexts. While her chosen method yielded "detailed, authentic information unattainable by any other research method"—information that stood to help women overcome their addiction—the covert nature of her method ultimately troubled her conscience. She recalls of the experience:

> I was emotionally disturbed by these unexpected awkward situations that occurred in the field. I felt that my disguised interaction with these female gamblers had unintentionally infringed their right to privacy, and also subjected myself to psychological pressure and inner conflicts. I also felt that in order to carry out an ethical research, I should not use the end to justify the means, even though the potential research benefits would outweigh psychological risks. To avoid ethical dilemmas inherent in research concealment, in the subsequent field trip I was determined to make my research overt. It was out of question for me to unveil my research inside casinos, but nevertheless I decided to try it on the bus. After obtaining permission from the driver, I announced that I was doing research on women's gambling experiences and I would appreciate their information and participation. Female gamblers generally took my flyers, but they rarely offered to participate in research. A woman expressed her concerns, "I don't want to talk to you about gambling because you work for the government."
>
> Another woman explained further, "You know why I don't want to come to your study? I would feel guilty if I come to your interviews because I know I would lie to you. I don't want to talk because I don't want my private life going public. Believe me, the gamblers who come to you will lie to you. You

won't get the truth." From this woman's honest remarks on the discrepancy between the public accounts and private lives of female gamblers, I started to understand why it was difficult for women to tell their gambling stories. Regardless of my efforts, the overt approach I attempted was unsuccessful because my research disclosure immediately changed social relationships and silenced voices. Once female gamblers were made known of my research role, they started to view me differently, treating me as a suspicious outsider who should not be entrusted because I did not share their experiences. This perception and suspicion immediately created a more awkward social space between me and them, the researcher and the researched.[13]

Li isn't alone in her emotional reaction to the sometimes intense realizations brought on by immersive practice. Ehrenreich faced a similar discomfort when writing about her fellow minimum-wage workers in *Nickel and Dimed*. Though her book achieved best-seller status, critics pointed out that the author, an upper-middle-class white well-paid to write the story of low-wage workers in America, failed to transcend the privilege that afforded her social experiment in the first place.

Wrapping Up

Public writers needn't be avowed social justice warriors to write effectively and movingly about the causes they believe in. Professional writers not afforded the privilege of advocacy in their day-to-day work may instead choose to channel their earnest hopes for social change into open letters, editorials, public statements, participatory writing, and empathy journalism, generating a multitude of social justice-minded pieces written with heart. Though it comes with its own set of built-in liabilities and ethical dilemmas, participatory and immersive nonfiction writing enjoy a new vogue among readers weary (and wary) of armchair, low-risk treatments written by drive-by journalists and risk-adverse or exploitative academics.

---

13. Jun Li, "Ethical Challenges in Participant Observation: A Reflection on Ethnographic Fieldwork," *The Qualitative Report* (2008) 13 no. 1. 100–115, https://nsuworks.nova.edu/cgi/viewcontent.cgi?article=1608&context=tqr.

Afterword: On Becoming a Public Writer

At our next professional gathering we're unlikely to have a business card thrust into our hand that reads "Jane Doe, Public Writer." To paraphrase Forrest Gump, a public writer is as a public writer does. And like a poet's, our calling card is earned less by formal credential than by devoted practice. If a poet is one who writes poetry, a public writer is one who writes for and serves the general public. Being a public writer is as much a civic practice and a habit of mind as it is a formal job title.

How do we know when we've crossed the invisible threshold from exclusive devotion to our professional colleagues to a place where we give equal time and care to readers outside our field? The answer varies. Many trained journalists occupy the role of public writer early in their careers, though few have the professional opportunity to write with the length, depth, and substance afforded the public intellectual. Perhaps the transformation truly happens when we begin to worry as much about how our work will be received by our next-door neighbors as by the gatekeepers and powerbrokers in the corner office. It's then that we begin to feel the full responsibility of communicating with readers beyond our hall, floor, or office suite. As we publish more of the quintessential public writing genres discussed in this book—popular scholarship, popular science, business, or history writing, public statements, institutional or government messaging, grant narratives, evidence-based news analysis, explanatory reporting, blog posts, editorials and op-eds, open letters, first-person journalism, narrative nonfiction, and more—we feel with each piece published a newfound degree of freedom. Not so much freedom that we feel adrift or unanchored from our profession, but floating free of its stifling protocols, self-serving conventions, and specialized, coded language. Finally liberated, we observe, analyze, and explore in ways we've never been free to before.

Others, too, will let us know when we have crossed over to become true public writers. As we embrace our new identity, we'll no doubt grow frustrated with those who think only of the insular concerns of their profession while neglecting the needs of those who exist outside that bubble. We'll follow national and international news more closely, eager to add our voice to the growing public discourse. Eventually, our worlds will collide, and we will inevitably disappoint our most hide-bound colleagues. *What happened to you,* their reaction will seem to say, *I thought you were one of us.*

That's the perfect time to remind ourselves that we have joined a new *us*—one that leaves plenty of room for being ourselves while respecting our chosen professions. We've joined a fellowship of public writers past and present who long to be heard, to be understood, and, most of all, to make a difference with our words in a world we're determined to care for and call home.

About the Author

Zachary Michael Jack teaches courses in public and professional writing in the Masters in Professional and Creative Writing program at North Central College in Naperville, Illinois, where he serves as a faculty member in the Writing, Leadership, Ethics, and Values (LEV), and Chicago Area Studies (CAS) programs. Jack's columns, commentaries, and analyses have appeared in many of the nation's best-circulated publications, from *USA Today* and the *Los Angeles Times* to the *San Francisco Chronicle*. The author of more than twenty books on subjects ranging from history, to sport, to the environment, to leadership and social change, Jack leads public writing workshops nationwide, drawing on publishing experience in multiple academic disciplines and previous careers as a newspaper section editor, assistant public radio producer, and outreach librarian.

CPSIA information can be obtained
at www.ICGtesting.com
Printed in the USA
BVHW070402010223
657531BV00008B/465